# THE VISUAL ENCYCLOPEDIA OF
# AMERICAN
# LANDMARKS

# THE VISUAL ENCYCLOPEDIA OF
# AMERICAN LANDMARKS

150 OF THE MOST SIGNIFICANT AND NOTEWORTHY HISTORIC, CULTURAL AND ARCHITECTURAL SITES IN AMERICA, SHOWN IN MORE THAN 500 PHOTOGRAPHS

THOMAS W. PARADIS

HERMES HOUSE

# CONTENTS

# INTRODUCTION

The 150 National Historic Landmarks included here collectively illustrate the United States' cultural landscape, and provide a narrative of the country's social, economic and political history. The cultural landscape refers to everything that humans have built for themselves upon the earth. What we build and how we build it provides a visual biography through which our cultural values, preferences and challenges are interpreted.

## WHAT IS AN HISTORIC LANDMARK?

In the United States the term National Historic Landmark is an official status that is recognized by the federal government. Landmarks are typically 50 years old or older when designated. Officially begun in 1960, the National Historic Landmarks program is under the jurisdiction of the National Park Service (NPS), which in turn is overseen by the US Secretary of the Interior. According to the NPS website, National Historic Landmarks are "nationally significant historic places designated by the Secretary of the

Interior because they have exceptional value or quality in illustrating or interpreting the heritage of the United States". They comprise an elite subset of properties already listed on the National Register of Historic Places. Out of 80,000 properties on the National Register, only 2,500 have been designated as National Historic Landmarks.

The National Register was the product of a major piece of Congressional legislation passed in 1966: The National Historic Preservation Act. To this day, the Act is considered America's most significant preservation-related legislation ever passed by the government. Prior to its passage, the federal government's traditional view of preservation had been limited primarily to sites of national historical significance. The Act broadened this concept, establishing a process to formally recognize state and local historic entities as well.

The Secretary of the Interior was directed by the Act to establish an ongoing list of historic sites and properties worth saving. Dubbed the National Register of Historic Places, as it remains today, the list was expected to

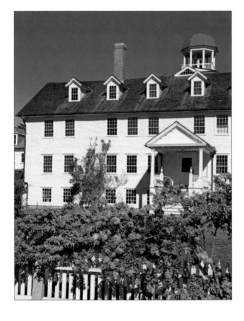

*Above: Entire districts may have landmark status. No longer occupied by a religious sect, Canterbury Shaker Village documents the lifestyle of a significant community.*

include "sites, buildings, objects, districts and structures significant in American history, architecture, archaeology and culture" regardless of whether they were significant at local, state or national levels. Additionally, this was the first time Congress invoked the term "district" to include whole areas worthy of historic preservation. The National Register would thereafter allow and encourage the inclusion of entire neighbourhoods, expanding the previously limited focus on individual sites or properties. Consequently, National Historic Landmarks, as a collective subset of the Register, includes a mix of historic districts as well as individual properties.

## THE IMPETUS TO LEGISLATE

Americans increasingly witnessed the destruction of older neighbourhoods, downtown business districts, and other-

*Left: The Santa Fe Plaza celebrates a regional identity. It also represents the era of the Santa Fe Trail.*

wise historically meaningful places. Following the Great Depression and World War II, the boom years were underway, and modern living had an impact upon American planning, architecture and urban development with the demand for new in place of old, and for functional over aesthetic considerations. By the 1950s the United States' historic resources were generally interpreted as irrelevant, obsolete and often derelict by those envisioning grand redevelopment plans. Modernism looked to the future rather than the past. During the middle of the 20th century, Victorian mansions and working-class neighbourhoods alike were erased from the urban scene. Only after the 1970s did America's collective culture recognize what was being lost and attempt to save much of what was left.

## NOMINATIONS

The National Register and, by association, the National Historic Landmarks program require a rigorous application process. Extensive guidance is freely available. The nomination form for the Register is not burdensome but can be intimidating to individuals not familiar with conducting historic research or writing descriptively about places. Technically, anybody can submit

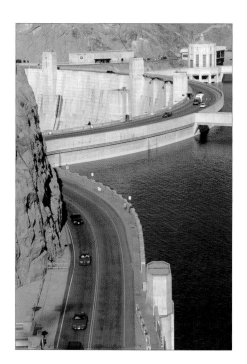

a nomination, though the typical approach is for local or state historic preservation officers or specialists to assist with the required research and writing. However, despite a credible, standardized process for accepting properties to the National Register, this is still largely a subjective enterprise replete with contradictions. Neither the Register nor the inventory of Landmarks should be considered as a comprehensive listing of the nation's significant historic resources. More nominations for both are submitted every year, gradually adding to the total. If nobody submits an application for a particular site, there is no chance of its inclusion on either the Register or the more elite set of Landmarks.

Further, numerous factors contribute to either the success or failure of a particular application – anything from the writing style of the application form to the individual sentiments of the reviewers in any given place and time. It is still curious, for instance, as to why such prominent historic sites as the Golden

*Left: The Hoover Dam represents a major feat of engineering, and was once the world's largest concrete structure.*

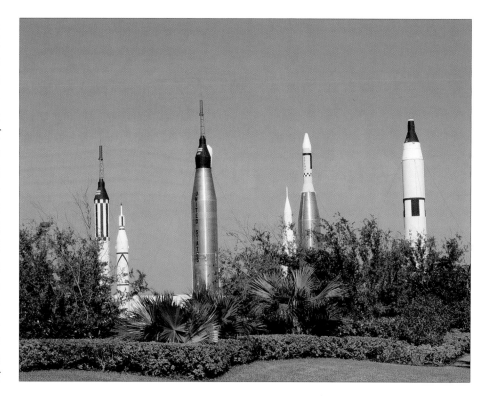

*Above: The rocket garden at Cape Canaveral, Florida, is a landmark familiar around the globe.*

Gate Bridge in the West or the Gettysburg Battlefield in the East, which clearly are landmarks, are not yet listed as National Historic Landmarks.

It is necessary to keep in mind, therefore, that the list remains incomplete. Given the subjectivity of the National Register and Landmarks nomination process, we should not believe that one particular site or place is somehow more "historic" than another. Elevating something to the status of "historic" implies that everything else is not historic. Americans are conditioned to seek out the "historic" sites and museums, and to pay special attention to the displays or landscapes located within the boundaries of a museum or historic district. We are conditioned to believe that whatever is outside the "velvet rope" is not worth learning about. Still, it is admittedly impossible to save each and every historic resource as time marches onward. We must pick and choose. The National Register helps us to do that, and provides an ever-increasing inventory of places worth protecting.

## CHOOSING THE LANDMARKS

The task of narrowing down the number of national landmarks to the 150 privileged for inclusion here was not easy. The most important criterion for selection was this: which landmarks most effectively provide an understanding of the American cultural and material landscape, its people, origins, values and aesthetics? Some of those not chosen were more relevant to, say, maritime activities (for example, ships, boats and submarines), or to important, national figures such as past American presidents.

Many of the landmarks consisted of individual properties located within larger landmark districts. In Savannah, Georgia and neighbouring Charleston, South Carolina, for instance, multiple individually designated landmarks are found within the boundaries of their respective historic districts. Though all such individual properties within each district are not discussed in detail, this book actually includes far more than 150 landmarks, due to this strategy of inclusion.

*Below: The Visitor Center at the Wright Brothers Memorial celebrates the achievements of Wilbur and Orville Wright, and has achieved landmark status in its own right.*

*Above: The Peavey-Haglin Experimental Concrete Grain Elevator's innovative design helped it achieve landmark status.*

## RESEARCH METHODS AND SOURCES

Every one of America's National Landmarks could easily deserve its own chapter rather than the page or two allowed here. The place for beginning this research was the nomination forms. These already required extensive historical research for their respective applications to the National Register. I then consulted numerous books and research articles, reputable online sources

*Above: Some landmarks, such as those at Nicodemus, may appear to be relatively unremarkable but represent significant cultural developments.*

and additional local materials to better contextualize the landmarks within the broader American landscape.

## THE SCOPE OF THE BOOK

This is not a tourist guide to the United States. Although those landmarks most accessible to the public were favoured, these places do not necessarily function as tourist attractions. Readers intent on visiting various landmarks are, therefore, encouraged to conduct further research. A quick internet search for any landmark will yield a wealth of information. A few are privately owned, although visually accessible from public thoroughfares. Alternatively, some landmarks have been converted into house museums or, more intensively, into bustling retail districts oriented primarily to tourists. Places such as the historic districts of St Augustine, Florida, or Silverton, Colorado, come to mind with respect to this latter trait.

The landmarks included here tell their own story, and each and every one is significant in the history of the United States of America. All provide a snapshot in time of the lives of ordinary people, as well as some notable personalities who have added to the country's rich cultural heritage. The Wounded Knee Battlefield in South Dakota and the Rohwer Relocation Center Memorial Cemetery in Arkansas are particularly representative of this type of landmark.

Other landmarks are peaceful, such as Mount Auburn Cemetery, built as a landscaped pleasure ground as well as a burial site before the notions of public parks and recreation space were dreamed up. Plenty of sites point to the nation's industrial heritage. The extraction of precious metals, for instance, generated population booms in specific areas, as people moved en masse to find employment. With them moved all the essential services necessary to set up communities. For industries that quickly went bust when the precious metals were depleted, ghost towns remain to retell the story. Still others include little physical infrastructure at all. The Beginning Point of the First Public Land Survey in Ohio, for instance, represents one of the most transformative processes the American landscape has ever undergone. Yet, the landmark site itself consists of little more than a modest historical marker. At another extreme are landmarks such as the Peavey-Haglin Experimental Concrete Grain Elevator

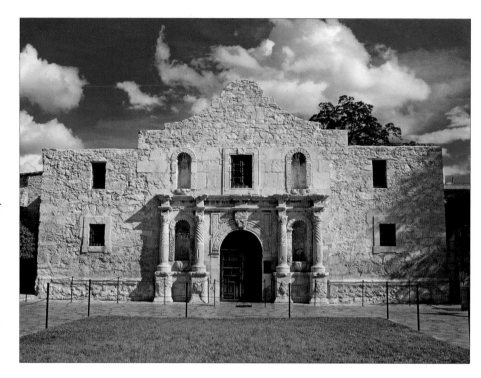

*Above: The Alamo, a reminder of an era of Spanish expansion and the site of a significant battle.*

in Minnesota. Not exactly designed as a tourist attraction, the grain elevator consists of a slender, round cement cylinder. Yet, this place played a key role in transforming the American agricultural scene.

At the other end of the spectrum are landmarks that beautify the landscape and enrich the environment with cohesive architectural plans that appeal to grandiose visions, huge skyscrapers that have fostered ambition and engineering feats, or sporting arenas that create entertainment and recreation. Finally, the country's history can be better understood through its choice of landmarks. These are the buildings or districts valued.

*Below: The Ohio Theatre was the most lavish of its time when it was built. It paid homage to the people's fascination with the world of Hollywood.*

# THE GEOGRAPHICAL REGIONS

The 150 landmarks are organized into ten chapters, each covering distinct geographical regions. The states that make up the regions have a collective identity. First, they may have a similar climate and geography or geology in which specific industries allied to the land or coastline have thrived, and upon which certain industrial landmarks have developed. They may have a common history in response to conflict, and include populations with a shared cultural heritage.

## NEW ENGLAND

The United States' most northeasterly region is typically defined as six states – Maine, Rhode Island, Vermont, Massachusetts, New Hampshire and Connecticut. The urban hub of cultural and economic activity during English colonial times was the city of Boston. As numerous landmarks indicate within this chapter, the characteristic New England patterns of housing, worship, architecture and agricultural approaches diffused west and north of Boston as the population grew. For some time New England contended with its own frontier to the west, attempting to establish an English stronghold in previously indigenous territories. Initially a home for persecuted Puritans from England, their aim was not really to create a new world, but to establish a familiar version of their old one. From town and street names and the medieval pattern of metes and bounds surveying, to late medieval and English Georgian architecture, New England appeared and functioned much like home.

By the early 1800s, trends in national architecture, housing and transport meant the region was being integrated into the mainstream. The region eagerly adopted Greek Revival and later Victorian architectural styles, canal and rail networks,

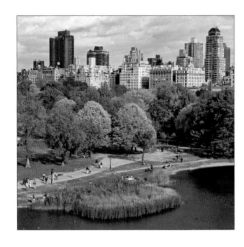

*Above: The chapter on New England features parks, gardens, historic houses and buildings, and early industry.*

*Below: The United States is split into ten geographical regions for the purposes of this book, with each region including several states within its boundary. Each chapter represents one region, with some states appearing in more than one.*

and became one of America's first cradles of industrial production. Later, as New England farmers bolted for better agricultural lands in the Midwest, much of New England returned to lush forests of oak and maple by the 20th century, providing a veritable carpet of green across the rolling hills. Numerous New England traditions moved west and with them the New England village was transplanted throughout upstate New York and into the northern Midwest. Today, Boston remains the urban hub of New England, a region dominated by tourism, education, technology and service industries.

### MID-ATLANTIC

The Mid-Atlantic area comprises English colonies that were settled between their neighbours to the north in New England and to the south in the Upland South. Later to become states, they were New York, New Jersey, Pennsylvania, Delaware and Maryland. Much more culturally diverse than Puritan New England, it was here that numerous disenfranchised populations from Europe sought freedom to live as they wished. What became America's premier mercantile city of New York began as the late medieval walled town of New Amsterdam in the early colony of New Netherlands. A population of Quakers, mostly German and led by William Penn, established Philadelphia in 1681 as the hub of their own colony in Pennsylvania. William Penn mounted an advertising campaign back in Europe, selling the colony as a tolerant place

*Above: The Chesapeake is synonymous with government. The White House is situated there.*

where immigrants could live and worship as they pleased. Thus, an array of Europeans flooded into the Philadelphia port after 1700.

As a cluster of mercantile cities, the Mid-Atlantic region has the highest population density of all the regions.

### CHESAPEAKE

Although often grouped within the larger Mid-Atlantic category, the Chesapeake is interpreted as a distinct region in this book. It encompasses parts of six states as well as the District of Columbia. It includes 17 million people. The region's geographic focus is Chesapeake Bay and, along with all the tributaries that feed into it, there are more than 17,700km/11,000 miles of coastline and waterways within its scope, which provided access for trade far inland. Maryland and its domain became an integrated part of this Tidewater South, with its own competitive mercantile city of Baltimore.

Long before the American Civil War, these colonies found themselves in the cultural "middle", a transition zone between Northern and Southern interests. As a compromise, the permanent

*Left: The Mid-Atlantic region is particularly rich in historic landmarks, with many internationally significant sites, such as the Chrysler Building.*

federal government was wisely placed here, as an effort to appease both Northern and Southern loyalists. Chosen by George Washington, the nation's capital and its ambitious Baroque-style street plan emerged near the otherwise quiet inland settlement of Georgetown. Today the Chesapeake region is home to America's centre of political power and part of the nation's core manufacturing and high-tech region of the greater northeast.

### DEEP SOUTH

Still one of the most culturally distinct regions of the United States, this broad swath of lowlands extends from the Carolinas through Mississippi and Alabama and into eastern Texas. It includes the Florida peninsula. The four dominant English colonies along the eastern seaboard were Virginia, North Carolina, South Carolina and Georgia, along with their respective coastal trade cities. Beyond the English coast were additional New World empires that vied for regional control, notably those of France and Spain. Both gained strong footholds in the South, providing for a diverse array of settlement patterns and cultural practices that still influence the southern landscape today.

Most influential in shaping the region's human geography was the plantation system of agriculture, which had spread from Barbados around 1640.

*Below: The Deep South has a history of cultural diversity. New Orleans has a strong French, Spanish and British flavour.*

*Above: The Midwest is the home of the Gateway Arch.*

*Above: The Great Plains was referred to in the 19th century as the Great American Desert.*

1700s, methodically divided up the continent west of Pennsylvania into orderly square-mile grids. As railroads allowed settlement away from the rivers, hundreds of new railroad towns were settled along the tracks. With these new towns came Main Street, another American innovation, with orderly rows of brick commercial buildings lining the primary business street.

Many of the original farmsteads and small towns have disappeared and today large farms of agribusiness dominate the vast scale production of crops.

The so-called plantation revolution expanded the system deeper into North and South America, where favourable sub-tropical climates allowed for the production of cash crops such as tobacco and cotton, which were in high demand throughout Europe. Although distinctive Southern building ways and farming patterns remain, global corporations, urban growth and expansive modern suburbs are now replacing a long-depressed agricultural economy that never truly recovered from the Civil War.

## MIDWEST

Considered part of America's interior heartland, the Midwest consists of the tall-grass prairie states surrounding the Great Lakes, broadening out to the states along the Mississippi River. Again, America's interior waterways, namely the Ohio and the Mississippi, expedited settlement of this region. With the opening of the Midwest to settlers during the 19th century, the nation's size had instantly doubled in area. First canals, and later railroads, linked booming eastern cities to the Trans-Appalachian West. Chicago became the new gateway to the West. The industrial revolution focused on the northern Midwest around the Great Lake's region.

The human landscape of this region was further defined by an American innovation, that of the Township-Range survey system that, begun in the late

## UPLAND SOUTH

Perhaps more ambiguous than other American regions, the Upland South is considered, for purposes here, a transition zone between the Midwest and Chesapeake regions and the cultural core of the Deep South. Still, this east-west stretch of land is imbued with its own distinct cultural and political characteristics that don't quite allow its easy "annexation" into its neighbouring Midwestern or Southern regions. The Upland South, as described here, contains portions of Kentucky, West Virginia, Alabama, Missouri, Illinois and Georgia that are aligned closely with the rolling hills and modest uplands of the southern Appalachian and Ozark mountains – generally a rural area without any dominating urban economies. The cultural characteristics of the region

*Below: The Upland South is a relatively small geographical region, home to Churchill Downs racecourse.*

were generally a product of migration streams from Pennsylvania, Virginia and surrounding middle states, as western lands were opened to settlement during the early 19th century.

## GREAT PLAINS

Once the realm of nomadic indigenous tribes, the American government and military focused their efforts after the Civil War on removing Native Americans. As the so-called Indian Wars subsided by the 1880s, homesteading Americans populated this short-grass region with new railroad lines, farm towns and rural farmsteads. This north-south swath of land rises in elevation 1,500m/5,000ft between the Mississippi River and the Rocky Mountains. Sitting on the western side of the Plains, Denver is well known as the "mile-high city" for good reason.

For more than a century Americans have cultivated these marginal lands, despite the increasing aridity toward the west. The Dust Bowl of the 1930s was not caused by drought so much as overuse of an otherwise fragile and arid ecosystem. Since then, farming on the Plains has increased in scale, with mechanized agribusinesses and extensive, fenced cattle ranches. Most of the water required for this intensive land use comes from underground and is predicted to run out one day.

## MOUNTAIN WEST

As transcontinental railroads were connecting the populated East with the West Coast, access to valuable ores became a reality. The rugged Rocky Mountains dominate the eastern part of this region. Fortunes were to be made here, however, as prospectors discovered untold quantities of silver, gold, copper and other extractive resources. Most of it was shipped east to fuel America's Industrial Revolution and manufacturing boom. In typical colonial fashion, raw materials moved eastward while manufactured goods moved west. Many of the towns settled throughout the Mountain West hold a legacy in extractive mining activities.

Urban populations and their commercial districts swelled quickly during the boom years, only to be devastated just as quickly when the nearby resource was exhausted. It is no surprise that the concentration of so-called ghost towns is the highest within this region. Although some mining continues, this area now thrives instead on tourism and resort development. Certain towns, railroads and scenic routes now depend on summer residents and travellers. Staged gunfights and renovated main-street buildings combine with jeep tours to offer visitors a taste of an imagined "Wild West". The Mountain West consequently attracts people seeking amenities and second homes rather than valuable ores.

*Below: The Mountain West will be forever associated with the Gold Rush, and towns that boomed and went bust, such as Bodie.*

*Above: The states that make up the Desert Southwest have a strong Spanish, Mexican and Pueblan heritage.*

## DESERT SOUTHWEST

Although considered the Southwest with respect to the United States, this region was perceived as the north by Mexicans and former Spanish colonists. Arizona and New Mexico were latecomers to statehood, both retaining their "territorial" status until upgrading to states in 1912. Strong legacies of Native American Pueblo and Hispanic cultures survive throughout the Southwest, variably blended with contemporary American lifestyles. In New Mexico there are thriving communities whose backgrounds are Spanish, Pueblan and Anglo cultures. In Utah one finds the hub of the Mormon culture at Salt Lake City. Mormon influence diffused into other parts of the Southwest, notably Colorado and Arizona.

Extractive mining activities and railroad settlements provided further diversity as Arizona became one of the nation's premier sources of copper. Government and technological development have influenced the region's economy more recently, where one finds the home of the first nuclear weapon at Los Alamos, and sizeable military contracts fuelling the growth of cities including Tucson, Phoenix and Albuquerque. Securing a sustainable water supply and promoting conservation among Southwestern residents now constitute the region's biggest challenge.

## PACIFIC

Part of the broader Pacific Rim, this strip of territory bordering the world's largest ocean presented an aspirational challenge for a century of Americans. The goal was to access lucrative Asian markets, but first they had to find a route west. A first step was taken with Jefferson's Louisiana Purchase of 1803 and the subsequent Louis and Clark expedition to find a northwest passage. In 1869 America's first transcontinental railroad was complete. By the 1870s eastern American culture was dominating western cities from Seattle and Portland to San Francisco and fledgling Los Angeles.

The region first thrived on extractive economies involving timber and mining. Much of the Northwest was settled by transplanted New Englanders and Midwesterners, who brought their architectural and farming practices with them. Southern California developed later, and not until the world's largest artificial harbour was reamed out of the Los Angeles coastline. American influence was felt in faraway places such as Alaska and Hawaii, both of which became intertwined with America's military, mining and agricultural complexes. The region is now tied more than ever into the global economy of the Pacific Rim. Los Angeles, San Francisco and Seattle provide 21st-century hubs for global trade and finance.

*Below: The Pacific region has an abundance of preserved historic sites, such as the Santa Barbara Courthouse.*

# CHAPTER ONE

# NEW ENGLAND

AMERICA'S MOST NORTHEASTERLY REGION IS
TYPICALLY DEFINED AS SIX NEW ENGLAND STATES:
MAINE, NEW HAMPSHIRE, VERMONT,
MASSACHUSETTS, RHODE ISLAND AND
CONNECTICUT. THIS AREA WAS ONE OF THE
EARLIEST TO BE SETTLED IN THE UNITED STATES.
THE LANDMARKS CHOSEN FOR INCLUSION
REPRESENT DIVERSE ELEMENTS OF THE
LANDSCAPE. THERE ARE PARKS AND CEMETERIES
WITH VISIONARY DESIGNS THAT SET TRENDS
ACROSS THE NATION, HISTORIC INDUSTRIAL
DISTRICTS FOCUSING ON THE TEXTILE HERITAGE
AND WHALING INTERESTS OF THESE STATES, AS
WELL AS RESIDENTIAL DISTRICTS CATERING FOR
RELIGIOUS COMMUNITIES AND WEALTHY
INDIVIDUALS.

*Left: Old Deerfield has an architecturally cohesive style.*
*This peaceful historic district was once a frontier settlement and the*
*scene of clashes with Native Americans.*

# BOSTON COMMON
## BOSTON, MASSACHUSETTS

Considered the oldest public park in the United States, the rural Boston Common grew innocently and largely unplanned. Its innovators were thinking practically when they set aside 20ha/50 acres of land in 1634, only four years following the founding of Boston. Borrowing from their familiar English roots, the "common" was set aside on the west edge of town as a communal pasture land primarily for raising cattle and grazing animals, to be shared by surrounding farm families.

### HOME FROM HOME

The common became a distinctive component of New England town plans. It was an English land-use tradition transposed on to the emerging New England landscape. One resident Englishman wrote of the Boston Common in the 1660s, "On the South there is a small, but pleasant Common where the Gallants a little before Sunset walk with their Marmalet-Madams, as we do in Morefields, etc. till the nine a clock Bell rings them home to their respective habitations, when presently the Constables walk their rounds to see

*Right: Young children cool off at the Frog Pond, Boston Common, on a hot day one summer in the early 20th century.*

good orders kept, and to take up loose people." The Common must have felt familiar in a largely unfamiliar land.

Since the early 1700s, the Common increasingly acquired more public-park amenities and became the growing city's focus for landscape design. The tree-lined Tremont Mall was installed as early as 1722, and the Frog Pond, originally intended as a watering hole for cattle, was lined with stones in 1824. The 19th century saw similar pleasant thorough-fares outlining the edges, and cutting through, the Common. The Oneida Club, the first organized football club in the nation, used the space as a playing field after 1862. Following the Civil War, Boston's citizens added another quality to the Common in the form of sculptures, paths and monuments. Larger-scale commemorative works include the soldiers and sailors monument and the Parkman Bandstand. Livestock continued to graze for two centuries at Boston Common.

### A TIMELESS SPACE

Boston Common played an important local role in the American Revolution and the Civil War, serving as a gathering and mustering-out point for the militias of both conflicts. The central burying ground was established in 1756 on the Boylston Street side of the Common, in which veterans of the Battle of Bunker Hill and the ensuing British occupation were interred.

The Common has remained surprisingly undisturbed for four centuries as the metropolis has expanded around it. The open space is enhanced by what frames its edges, including numerous historic buildings and neighbourhoods of Boston. Easily accessible by foot in one of America's prominent "walking cities" are the Back Bay district of elegant 19th-century townhomes, the colonial Georgian row houses of Bunker Hill, the Federal-style Massachusetts State House and the entrances for the Tremont Street subway – the first of its kind in the nation. Certain original topographic features survive, including Flagstaff Hill and Frog Pond.

*Left: Boston Common is one of America's quintessential public spaces, shaped by numerous earlier generations and their cultural traditions and values. Today the space is still in common usage, though for recreation rather than grazing animals.*

# MOUNT AUBURN CEMETERY
## CAMBRIDGE, MASSACHUSETTS

Few might imagine the potential influence of a cemetery on the landscape of a nation. Such is the case with Mount Auburn. With its unanticipated dual role as burial ground and recreational site, this 44.5ha/110-acre plot inspired America's distinctive rural cemetery pattern in addition to the public parks movement.

### A RURAL LANDSCAPE
In the face of stifling urban growth, Harvard professor Jacob Bigelow (1787–1879) promoted the concept of a rural cemetery in 1825. Bigelow's ideal plan embodied the Picturesque tenets of English Romanticism then gaining attention in America. This innovative, rural burial ground would at once serve the living and the dead, providing a pastoral natural design for solace and inspiration. In 1831 this dream became a reality 6km/4 miles west of Boston. Its promoters looked directly to Europe for additional inspiration, specifically to the picturesque French cemetery of Pere Lachaise, outside Paris. Mount Auburn's plan incorporated the natural features and contours of the land, taking advantage of existing topography and opportunities for

*Right: Mount Auburn Cemetery inspired many of America's public gardens.*

panoramic views and valleys. On opening, the Picturesque grounds were visited by increasing throngs keen to escape the congested, industrialized city. An array of guidebooks provided walking tour routes and encouraged the Cemetery's blossoming recreational use.

### A MODEL FOR THE FUTURE
Nine major American cemeteries used Mount Auburn as their model by the 1840s, as well as numerous smaller ones throughout New England. Andrew Jackson Downing, America's first landscape designer, cited Mount Auburn as an example when lobbying President Millard Fillmore for a Picturesque design for the emerging Mall grounds in Washington, DC. To Fillmore he wrote, "A national park like this …would exercise as much influence on public taste as Mount Auburn in Boston

has done." America still had no public parks, but was fortunate to have the finest rural cemeteries in the world. Downing's work directly influenced Frederick Law Olmsted, the father of American landscape architecture, as well as his contemporaries in the development of New York's Central Park, itself the role model for public parks nationwide. As for Mount Auburn, this model American cemetery and recreational retreat remains today as it did originally – a sacred site and pleasure ground.

*Below: The first burial was in 1832. Since then the Cemetery has become the final resting place of many distinguished people.*

*Below: The architecture of Bigelow Chapel reflects 19th-century America's romantic notions of the Middle Ages.*

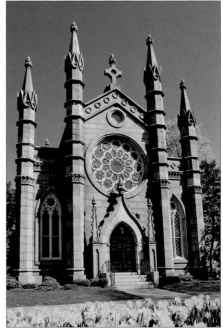

# OLD SHIP MEETING HOUSE
## HINGHAM, MASSACHUSETTS

*Above: Old Ship represents the earliest form of Puritan meeting house in New England, a wood-framed structure with Georgian-style details.*

The only surviving example of a 17th-century Puritan meeting house is found at Hingham. Construction began in 1681 and made use of late Medieval-era building practices still common in Europe at that time.

The Old Ship Meeting House was so named because the curved timber trusses in its roof look like the inverted framing of a ship's hull. Such curved timbers were common in late medieval Europe, though no precedent for the plan of Old Ship Meeting House has been verified. The original church was widened on the northeast side in 1729, with a second addition of equal scale on the opposite side in 1755. The effect was to create a wider church, on which a hipped roof was superimposed over the original, steeply pitched one. A new pulpit and a gallery around three sides were also added in the 1755 makeover, and the old Medieval, leaded-glass windows were replaced with wooden sliding sashes. Two new porches featuring Georgian-style decorative detailing were also added. The actual curved roof framing was concealed in 1731 when a flat ceiling was hung under the tie beams. An early preservation effort in 1930 attempted to restore the structure to reveal its earlier appearance and many 19th-century alterations were removed, as was the 1731 ceiling.

**MEETING HOUSE EVOLUTION**

With successive generations of English colonists and the early Americans came an identifiable evolution of the meeting house form. Architectural historians have recognized four periods of meeting house evolution, moving from the earliest and crudest structures to more church-like buildings with Greek Revival-style gable fronts and steeples. The Old Ship Meeting House represents the first period of 17th-century wood-frame structures with some Georgian detailing. This simple and regionally distinctive building form, known as the New England meeting house, was developed by the Puritans. Their plans were typically rectangular with two or more storeys and a gallery placed beneath a hipped roof and central cupola. The earliest Puritan meeting houses were crude frame buildings typically 6 x 9m/20 x 30ft and without the embellishments of towers, spires or crosses. The congregation had to tolerate uncomfortable benches with narrow seats and a single timber for back support. Men and women were segregated, each gender sitting on opposite sides of the building. Unlike traditional churches, meeting houses were designed with the entrance on the side rather than the front, with the pulpit on the opposite side. Benches were arranged facing the pulpit with the entrance behind them. This "four-square" New England meeting house plan remained popular throughout New England settlements well into the 18th century.

*Below: The original plan demonstrates formal, Renaissance-era architecture.*

# NEWPORT

## HISTORIC DISTRICT, NEWPORT, RHODE ISLAND

Founded in 1639, Newport became a thriving seaport town by the 1680s. Its trade network extended throughout the middle and southern colonies, across the Atlantic Ocean to Europe and south to the West Indies. Newport's extensive mercantile activities further led to its status in the early 1700s as the principal slave-trading centre for New England. Approximately 50–60 ships from Newport were engaged in trafficking slaves, and their owners became some of the city's leading merchants. The town's prosperity was evident in its growing built environment, which included 900 dwellings and more than 400 warehouses and stores by 1761. Its prosperity peaked between 1740 and 1775.

### AMERICAN REVOLUTION

Newport's opportune geographic situation on the prosperous New England coast was also its undoing. As the Revolution ramped up, the British Army occupied the city on 8 December 1776 and retained control there for

*Below: A range of 19th-century architectural styles reveals the progression of Newport's growth over time.*

*Above: Newport's prosperity funded the construction of Georgian buildings.*

nearly three years. Newport's population declined dramatically from around 9,000 to 4,000 people between 1774 and 1784. Ironically, many of the city's houses were dismantled by the British for firewood during the stifling American blockade, accounting for the destruction of 480 structures. The Americans finally re-occupied Newport on 26 October 1779, followed by the supportive French Army in July 1780. Although peace had finally returned – Newport's former prosperity as a trade centre did not recover.

### RESORT TOWN

By the early 19th century Newport was discovering a new opportunity – that of a summer resort. In 1950 Newport still had more than 400 houses built before 1840. Further economic change and urban development continued to take its toll, however, specifically through an urban renewal project during the 1960s. America's urban renewal program was a federally funded approach to removing older urban areas considered to be a slum or blighted.

Fortunately for Newport, an impressive collection of historic architecture remains. Included in today's district are a rare variety of smaller, modest structures integrated within more prestigious historic homes of the wealthy merchant class. Such diversity provides a level of historic authenticity not often found.

The district has an impressive collection of noteworthy high-style Georgian architecture. Some of New England's most distinguished and advanced Georgian-style public buildings and homes are found within the district.

*Below: Newport slowly transformed from a mercantile city to an oceanside resort.*

# OLD DEERFIELD VILLAGE
## HISTORIC DISTRICT, DEERFIELD, MASSACHUSETTS

Springfield was the first town settled along the fertile Connecticut River Valley in western Massachusetts in 1636. After the 1650s, settlement moved north from Springfield along the valley, resulting in a series of towns on the edge of unknown wilderness and the long-time homes of indigenous tribes. Deerfield, an outlying community, remained on the edge of the western English frontier for half a century. The English cultural system instructed that the natural wilderness was placed there by God to be "improved", thus legitimizing the settlers own "legal" acquisition of Native American lands. The original purchase of 3,250ha/8,000 acres for the Deerfield settlement was completed by 1667, with the village formally laid out in 1671.

### A NEW TOWN PLAN

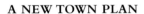

Like many emerging New England settlements, the English colonists made use of town planning strategies familiar from their homeland, but with some creative twists. English settlers were determined to eradicate the medieval land tenure system of feudalism from their homeland, enabling settlers to finally own outright individual plots of

land. Still, they retained a town plan similar to medieval English villages that allowed for both protection from outside invaders and internal social control and vigilance. This hybrid town plan, part Medieval and part early American, materialized in Deerfield, where landowners lined up their Colonial homes along what is simply called The Street.

Closer to tradition, however, farm land around the village was assigned in

*Above: This Georgian-style home with a gambrel roof is typical of the 18th-century Colonial buildings carefully restored in today's village. In New England fashion, the homes sit on their own lots and are set back from the street.*

common, with agriculture remaining a shared enterprise among the farmers. Both labour and farm implements were shared, especially given the scarcity of both during the early decades. By the 1660s the English frontier settlements had abandoned the traditional brick row houses with shared walls familiar in their homeland, in favour of free-standing, wood-frame homes placed on adjacent, individually owned lots. In Deerfield, land for the common or training ground – serving as the focus of the meeting house and town well – was reserved on the west side of The Street at its midpoint. All landowners were required to maintain a portion of the common field fence, which grew to 22.5km/14 miles long by the early 1700s.

*Left: The broad Connecticut River Valley, home to Old Deerfield.*

## KING PHILIP'S WAR

Connecticut River Valley towns suffered a heavy loss of life and property as disputes with Native Americans occasionally escalated into armed conflict. The most notable early conflict is referred to as King Philip's War of 1675–76. King Philip was the nickname given by the English colonists to Metacom, the leader of the Pokanoket tribe. It had been 55 years since the first settlement of the Massachusetts Bay Colony, and the Native American peoples found themselves in slow decline and losing their land. King Philip became an inspirational leader who was determined to make a stand against the English. Although only one part of a much wider regional conflict, the village of Deerfield was attacked by a coalition of Native Americans who concentrated their efforts for their cause. The village was quickly abandoned after the attack and the ensuing Bloody Brook Massacre. The Massacre occurred as a contingent of soldiers was returning from Deerfield, having retrieved any grain left behind following the attack. At a point where their path crossed a stream, they were ambushed and 71 soldiers were killed within minutes. The brook was said to have run red with blood.

*Below: In 1704 Native Americans, with the support of French troops, attacked Deerfield.*

## PROSPEROUS TIMES

Deerfield became an important regional agricultural centre that supplied impressive amounts of wheat and beef to English forces during the French and Indian Wars of the 1740s and 1750s. It was during this time that the population stabilized. Collective prosperity increased, enabling the construction of fine Georgian-style homes with furnishings imported from England and, increasingly, produced by skilled craftspeople along the Connecticut River Valley. Stall-fed oxen were raised for trade with faraway cities, including Boston and New York. In 1799 Deerfield Academy, a co-educational boarding school, was established in the town, providing an education centre.

## A RENAISSANCE OUTPOST

It is much of this late Colonial and early Federal period of Deerfield's landscape that survives today. The original street pattern remains largely unchanged, the original survey of village lots still exists, and the north and south meadows beyond the village remain in agricultural use. The 53 buildings in the village provide excellent examples of late Georgian, Federal and Greek Revival architecture characteristic of Revolution-era New England towns. According to *Memorial Hall* author Susan McGowan, the village of Deerfield was "first, a ring of governance that was small, tight and rarely extended beyond Deerfield itself; second, a ring of economics that was slightly wider and included the nearby towns with barter and trade; third, a ring of kinship and religion that stretched further down the Valley; and fourth, a ring of military involvement which included the larger world of Springfield, Hartford, Boston, and even Europe and England".

Deerfield may have started as a frontier outpost, but it has never been completely isolated from the outside world. On a larger scale, Europeans were expanding into lands well beyond their homelands, causing conflict between fellow European nations and Native American populations, all competing for land and survival. With its own town plan borrowed in part from Medieval practices, its architecture for housing and public buildings signalled the arrival of Classical Renaissance ideas into the vast wilderness of western New England. Today, Deerfield participates in the most recent globalization trends through its presence on the internet and visits from history enthusiasts.

*Below: Architecture of Renaissance Classicism appeared in Deerfield by the mid-18th century.*

# NEW BEDFORD
## HISTORIC DISTRICT, NEW BEDFORD, MASSACHUSETTS

New Bedford specialized in the whaling industry soon after initial settlement in the 1760s. In the days before petroleum and electricity, the demand on both sides of the Atlantic for whale oil, sperm oil and whale bone increased, providing the impetus for New Bedford's whaling industry and its supportive infrastructure. The town prospered as America's leading whaling port by taking advantage of its deep, natural harbour. The first locally constructed whaling vessel departed for London in 1767 loaded with whale oil. The New Bedford fleet grew to include 50 whaling sloops only eight years later.

The port's continued and growing prosperity in this trade was temporarily and violently suspended during the American Revolution. Following British raids up and down the coast when the town was abandoned, fires destroyed 11 houses, 76 shops, 26 storehouses, two rope-walks, and 34 ships. Stability and growth returned after the war. New Bedford reached the height

*Below: The US Custom House at New Bedford, where ship captains registered their crews and declared their cargoes.*

*Above: A whaling ship under repair in the 1880s. Towns like New Bedford prospered from the whaling industry.*

of whaling activities in the decades prior to the Civil War. In 1841, 10,000 men were employed in whaling, with US $12 million invested in ships and equipment. By 1857 the fleet comprised half of the nation's whaling ships.

### DEMISE OF AN INDUSTRY
In the 1850s kerosene was discovered, ushering in the world's ultimate dependence on fossil fuels. The ensuing discovery of petroleum in Pennsylvania accelerated the availability of kerosene for artificial lighting, because petroleum could be distilled and cracked to produce kerosene. The availability of petroleum quickly dealt a fatal blow to the whaling industry in America. The last whaling voyage from New Bedford ended on 20 August 1925.

### THE DISTRICT TODAY
The section of the city that comprises the current historic district features 20 buildings constructed between 1810 and 1855. Both Federal and Greek Revival architectural styles are well represented in the district. An outstanding example of the Greek Revival style is found in the United States Custom House, constructed in 1834–36. The 1853 New Bedford Institution for Savings is a Renaissance Revival edifice. Seamen's Bethel, a two-storey frame church, was rebuilt in 1867 following a fire. Its front facade was redesigned and the present tower was added at this time. Herman Melville featured a description of the church in *Moby Dick*. In all, the district still represents the essence and landscape of a bustling commercial district of a New England seaport.

# OLD NORTH CHURCH
## (CHRIST CHURCH), BOSTON, MASSACHUSETTS

*Above: A hurricane devastated the second tower in the mid-20th century. Similar weather damaged the first tower.*

Old North Church (officially Christ Church) is the oldest surviving church in Boston. It was constructed between 1723 and 1740, and in 1745 received eight bells brought to America from England. Prior to the building of Old North, puritan colonists had employed variations of the simple foursquare meeting house with side-entrance plan and no steeple or tower for their places of worship. Foursquare is a simple cube-shape building, typically two storeys high, with a low hipped roof and possibly four spacious rooms. Boston book and print dealer William Price played a significant role in New England's shift away from the meeting house plan in favour of a more elaborate English church design. Price, born in England, was familiar with the new Georgian-style churches in London designed by Christopher Wren following the Great Fire of London of 1666.

Built on the highest hill in Boston's North End, the exterior of Old North is a clear adaptation of Wren's London churches. The interior is strikingly similar to that of Wren's St James, Piccadilly. As such, Old North is credited as the first building of any kind in the English colonies to be developed in the Wren or Georgian style.

With a prominent front entrance and slender tower, the building is oblong with longitudinal aisles separating sets of box pews. The original Georgian tower and spire were added to the front (west) end of the main building between 1724 and 1737. The 30m/100ft tall, square brick tower was topped by a spire (steeple) that added another 58m/191ft to the height. The original tower included three setback stages, reminiscent of Wren's churches.

Although the church has survived the centuries, its trademark spires have not been so fortunate. The original spire blew off in 1804 and was replaced by another. A hurricane toppled this second tower in 1954.

*Left: The current Old North Church spire is a replica of the original.*

### THE LANDSCAPE TODAY

A visit to the area surrounding Old North Church remains similar to the densely settled urban landscape of Medieval London. This part of Boston was constructed in the haphazard and concentrated manner that reflected Medieval English town building. The church's otherwise dominating facade and tower are hemmed in on three sides by brick row houses interrupted only by narrow streets and alleys.

### PAUL REVERE

The bells of Old North Church attracted a legendary figure in American history. Fifteen-year-old Paul Revere gained permission with six friends to form a guild of bell ringers. The group practised their skills once a week at the church. Old North was employed as a signal tower when two lanterns were hung in the spire on the night of 18 April 1775 to notify patriots across the Charles River that British forces were moving out of Boston by water and were en route to Lexington and Concord.

*Below: Old North Church can be seen in the distance as Paul Revere made his journey, in 1775, to warn of the impending arrival of the British.*

# PARSON CAPEN HOUSE
## SALEM, MASSACHUSETTS

Considered one of the most significant remaining examples of Colonial building traditions in New England, the Parson Capen House is built around a framework of heavy oak timbers that are morticed and tenoned together and held in place by wooden pins. Its second storey overhangs the first storey in the front, typical of cantilevered

*Above: Architectural students are often introduced to post-Medieval English architecture in America with the image of Parson Capen House, built in 1683.*

Medieval architecture. The third storey also projects slightly outward at both gable ends, and the overhangs are supported by wooden brackets.

Its interior floor plan is typical of a 17th-century colonial house, with its characteristic hall and parlour design. The hall, placed on one side of the massive brick chimney, doubled as the kitchen and living room. Opposite the hall on the other side of the chimney is the parlour.

That the house has survived with such a degree of integrity is remarkable. Still, one can imagine that several centuries of maintenance and alterations have whittled away the original structure. A major restoration attempt in 1913 brought significant changes: one being a new chimney. The windows were altered too, replacing horizontal strips of casements with paired vertical frames. Although the timbers are original, the interior woodwork and exterior finishing have been replaced over time. However, the house still enjoys its prominent location on the town common near the meeting house, indicating the central role of its earlier occupant, the reverend Joseph Capen.

# QUINCY MARKET
## BOSTON, MASSACHUSETTS

Following decades of economic decline in many cities after the 1950s, city councils and urban planners searched for new reasons to attract people to their ailing downtown cores as newly constructed freeways whisked shoppers out to new suburban developments. By the end of the 20th century most cities had found new niches in the booming tourism industry, focusing their downtowns around themed shopping ventures, large-scale entertainment venues and professional sports arenas.

Following its inclusion as a national historic landmark, Quincy Market provided a stage set for a risky new venture

which ultimately proved so successful that cities from Seattle and San Francisco to Baltimore and St Louis have replicated it. Quincy Market became the nation's first so-called festival marketplace in the 1970s, the result of blending a public historic preservation project with a specialty retailing and entertainment development. Nowadays, the bustling Quincy Market is one of Boston's most popular urban tourist attractions.

*Right: Quincy Market and Faneuil Hall (foreground) provided the setting for a grand experiment in urban revitalization during the 1970s.*

## EARLY HISTORY

Long before its tourist appeal, Boston was maturing by the early 19th century into a dominant seaport and commercial centre. The city emerged as a hub of local and regional trade and soon outgrew its original market constructed in 1742 in Faneuil Hall. It was Josiah Quincy who was ultimately responsible for building the expansion to Faneuil Hall (Quincy) Market.

In 1823, Josiah Quincy was elected mayor in the town, and is credited with initiating plans for building a new and expanded marketplace immediately east of Faneuil Hall. Given the waterfront's location directly east of the Hall, the new site required artificial infill to push the waterfront a distance away. On the filled site, Quincy proposed the construction of a fairly typical market house consisting of a lengthy, one-storey structure with a gable roof supported by brick piers. However, noted Boston architect Alexander Parris, 1780–1852, had grander ideas. Parris' design produced a more monumental collection of buildings designed with stylish combinations of granite and brick, and ornamented in the popular Greek Revival style of architecture. The resulting central marketplace and its flanking rows of stores became one of the most impressive, early 19th-century markets in the United States.

*Above: Today, Quincy Market, at the heart of the city for 250 years, retains its festival marketplace image and is one of Boston's primary visitor attractions.*

## THE MARKET TODAY

Little altered today, Faneuil Hall Market is known as Quincy Market for the city leader that conceived it. The Market consists of an elongated, two-storey structure of granite, including two long, gable-roofed wings extending outward from a higher centre section capped with a large saucer dome. On each side of the centre isles of each wing are 128 separate retail stalls.

Reflecting the ever-growing need for land, the waterfront east of the Market has since retreated even further east. In the 1950s the Market's physical connection with the waterfront was broken with the construction of the elevated Fitzgerald Expressway (Interstate 93), which nearly adjoined to the eastern end of the Market. Once considered a modern transportation saviour, however, this particular freeway proved temporary. The so-called "big dig" project, a US $14.6 billion reconstruction of Boston's roads around the downtown area, relocated the freeway underground in a massive tunnelling project that presented its own challenges prior to its celebrated completion in 2007. One result was the removal of the aboveground expressway, providing a new, open landscape for the public at the east end of the Market.

*Below: With its Federal-style architecture, Faneuil Hall served as Boston's original hub for local trade and now anchors one end of the Quincy Market retail scene.*

# CANTERBURY SHAKER VILLAGE
## CANTERBURY, NEW HAMPSHIRE

*Above: The Shakers used traditional New England architectural styles, although they adapted them to suit their communitarian lifestyle and principles.*

The nation's early decades were characterized by a substantial amount of social and religious experimentation. For its part, the communitarian movement emerged and gained followers, especially in the northeastern states during the late 18th and early 19th centuries. Largely socialist and devoutly religious, variations of communitarian settlements materialized for groups such as the Oneida perfectionists, the Shakers, and followers of French social theorist Charles Fourier. All communitarian groups of the time sought to provide their own versions of the model town plan that would hopefully be replicated as the American frontier moved west.

Fourier recommended settlements of 1,600 people that could combine both agricultural and industrial pursuits as they worked toward a communal form of harmony. His theory of "association" constituted a form of social evolution that would ideally improve society while reducing class conflict through gradual stages of voluntary co-operation.

One particular group invoking the social goals of the communitarian movement was the Shakers, which ultimately established 21 villages scattered throughout New England, New York and the Midwest.

### A MODEL FOR THE FUTURE

The communal village model played a significant role in shaping influential Americans who would become leaders in the later design of suburban communities. Frederick Law Olmsted and Llewellyn Haskell among them, were responsible for the plan and design of the nation's first notable, comprehensively planned suburban communities. The lasting legacy of these experimental socialist communities, therefore, can be seen today through the designs and plans of suburban neighbourhoods.

One of the most intact Shaker villages can still be experienced in Canterbury, New Hampshire, now a National Historic Landmark due to the continued integrity of its built environment. Located 19km/12 miles northeast of Concord, the Canterbury Shaker Village consists of a complex of religious, residential and workshop facilities placed high on a hillside. The village includes 24 contributing buildings placed on approximately 5ha/13 acres of land. All of the buildings were constructed between 1792 and 1923, with the bulk of them constructed prior to the American Civil War. This particular village is considered among the most intact and authentic of the surviving Shaker villages. In the context of America's early 19th-century communal organizations, the Shakers comprised the largest and most successful group that is still well known.

### SHAKER IDEOLOGY

The village's spatial layout and architecture comprised a blending of familiar New England building traditions and creative local planning strategies. Standard Georgian-style floor plans and exterior facades were adopted for all residential buildings and some of the workshops. Typical of 18th-century New England, the village's Georgian buildings employed variations of the centre hall plan with two rooms up and two rooms down on each side of the centre entrances.

*Below: This typical 19th-century Federal-style church reflected the cultural ties of the Shakers to their larger New England region.*

Beyond employing the English Georgian building tradition, however, the Shakers planned their village layout and building forms according to their own communal values and family structures. Shaker society was defined by celibate, communal living, with the genders considered separate but equal.

Adopting the basic Georgian-style plan for residential buildings, the Shakers added separate entrances, staircases, and sleeping quarters for men and women. Given that Shakers did not believe in procreation, village populations grew only through the adoption of orphan children into one of the all-male or all-female "families", or by allowing individuals to convert.

The workshops were also designed with separate work places for men and women. Because hard work was considered to be sacred to the Shakers, the workshops occupied a special place in the village, as did the meeting house. Only through hard work and communal dedication could the Shakers hope to achieve self-sufficiency and separate themselves from the "world's people". Their motto of "hands to work and hearts to God" underscored this ideology. Unlike the Amish, however, the Shakers readily accepted new technologies and conveniences, including the advent of electricity, indoor plumbing,

*Below: Brothers and sisters of a Shaker family lived, worked and worshipped together, necessitating the construction of spacious residential buildings.*

telephones, televisions and automobiles. Still, "odd or fanciful styles of architecture" were frowned upon.

### THE SHAKERS

The Shakers, or more officially The United Society of Believers in Christ's Second Appearing, numbered 6,000 members at its peak in the 1850s. The Protestant religion began in 1747 as a breakaway sect from the Society of Friends (Quakers) in England. Known early on as "shaking Quakers," or Shakers, their reputation grew from the fervour of their worship services. The Shakers sat in silent meditation as they waited to be "moved by the spirit", at which time they would start to tremble violently, spin around and dance — hence the term Shaker.

*Above: An early map of the Canterbury Shaker Village reveals their adoption of Georgian-style architecture on separate building lots.*

The sect's total population declined to 2,400 by 1874. No new members were accepted after 1964, and few remained by the 1980s. The Village had been designed and inhabited for two centuries. Of the surviving 20th-century Shaker villages, the one at Canterbury served prominently as the home of the central ministry after 1947 and a progressive hub of Shaker ideology. The Shakers are now celebrated for their success with communal self-sufficiency, their belief in pacifism, equality of the sexes and for their superb workmanship on furniture and handicrafts.

# KINGSCOTE
## NEWPORT, RHODE ISLAND

The first of Newport's elaborate summer "cottages", the Kingscote house was one of the earliest successful attempts to demonstrate a radical new approach to house and landscape design during the early 19th century. America's premier Gothic-Revival-style architect, Richard Upjohn (1802–78), designed the home for George Noble Jones in 1839. It served as his summer retreat and a permanent residence for his mother and sister. Jones was a wealthy planter and land speculator from Savannah, Georgia. He was one of the first to build a summer residence in Newport, in an out-of-town setting. The exterior design and floor plan of Kingscote were one of the first American residential examples of what would become known as the Gothic Revival style of architecture. The asymmetrical, unpredictable floor plan provided a bold demonstration of the Picturesque design philosophy.

### THE PICTURESQUE

Prior to Kingscote, Americans had favoured formal, geometric Renaissance-era design schemes dominated by formality and symmetry for architecture, street layouts and landscaping.

Thomas Jefferson had introduced and promoted the idea of a national grid system for town planning, which was eventually referred to as "township and range". By the 1830s a distinct alternative to Renaissance formality emerged from Europe, referred to as the Picturesque style. Coupled closely with the emerging Romantic movement, the origins of Picturesque design are traceable to English aristocratic estate owners

*Above: Kingscote provided one of America's earliest models for the budding Romantic movement.*

of the 18th century. The Picturesque mode, which emphasized rugged wilderness in the landscape reflected a fundamental shift in European and American attitudes toward nature and landscaping. The ideal of "all nature is a garden" gained momentum on both sides of the Atlantic, reversing the prior commitment to formal architecture and landscaping dating to the Renaissance modes of the 16th century.

If credit can be given to one individual for promoting the Picturesque landscaping mode in America, it is undoubtedly Andrew Jackson Downing. Well acquainted with the English landscape movement, by the 1830s Downing sought to adapt its ideals to North America and to answer increasingly louder calls to improve American home life. Downing promoted a strong

*Left: Interior collections of the Kingscote property include those from five generations of the King family.*

distinction between his own definitions of the beautiful and the picturesque. Any landscape design should purposely integrate any existing visual qualities inherent in a site. Natural land forms and topography, native vegetation and flowing water should, therefore, be incorporated into any construction site.

Kingscote served as one of America's first influential Picturesque projects that would set the trends for the following six decades of the Victorian era. Given that Alexander Davis' influential book *Rural Residences* was published only a year prior to the construction of Kingscote, it is likely that the book served as the direct inspiration for Upjohn's Gothic Revival design. *Rural Residences* became one of America's first-ever pattern books for house plans, and it laid the groundwork for a fundamental shift in the design of American homes. Not only did Kingscote solidify Upjohn's architectural career, but it established the primary philosophies of the budding Romantic Movement in the United States.

### THE GOTHIC REVIVAL

Kingscote included all of the trappings of the early Gothic Revival style. The house is constructed with wood and was originally painted beige. The paint had actually been mixed with sand to

*Above: The ceiling panelling and built-in sideboard in the dining room reflected Colonial American design.*

provide the appearance of a sandstone facade. The highly irregular, Picturesque floor plan required an equally intricate roofline composed of multiple gables, chimneys and Gothic detailing that included Romantic hood mouldings over the doors and windows, and lancet

*Below: The Picturesque, irregular floor plan of Kingscote provided unique opportunities for room shapes and interior designs.*

(pointed arch) windows that helped to define the style.

The exterior landscaping also encapsulates the Picturesque ideals promoted with its curved drive and walkways, and a circular mound in front of the house.

### KINGSCOTE

The house changed ownership less than 30 years later, in 1863, when it was purchased by William Henry Hunter King. William's nephew, David King Jr, in turn leased the home in 1876 and expanded and remodelled portions of it. A red slate roof was added, and the home's interior was redecorated by the New York firm of Leon Marcotte. On 1 June 1880 the house was formally christened Kingscote, given its stewardship through the King family up to that time. Other monumental changes occurred during the King years, including a new and larger dining room designed by Stanford White, partner in the prestigious architectural firm of McKim, Mead & White. The prominent architect further designed and constructed two master bedrooms and nursery rooms. Although much larger in scale than the original Kingscote home, the additions maintained the irregular, Picturesque design mode, allowing them to fit in well with the original house.

# MORSE-LIBBY HOUSE
## (VICTORIA MANSION), PORTLAND, MAINE

By the middle of the 19th century, two architectural styles had been popularized as representing the heart of the Romantic Movement in America, including Gothic Revival and Italianate. Like the Gothic Revival, Italianate style diffused to America from England as an appropriate Picturesque mode of architecture. Both Italianate and its cousin, the Italian-villa style, were inspired initially by the original villas and manors of northern Italy. Although the Gothic Revival remained popular up to the American Civil War, it was Italianate designs that dominated American residential and commercial architecture between 1850 and 1880.

American versions of Italian villas appeared in the forms of country and suburban homes as well as urban town houses and main-street retail buildings. Early Italianate-style homes were adapted directly from Andrew Jackson Downing's influential pattern books through the 1850s and 1860s. By 1873 Italianate had become America's style of choice, surpassing the earlier level of interest in the Gothic Revival. In tune with the Romantic, Picturesque ideals of the time, Italianate and Italian villa

*Above: The Morse-Libby House was designed to replicate an Italian villa.*

designs incorporated irregular, flowing floor plans that took advantage of the new "balloon frame" construction method to allow for greater experimentation and interior openness. Consequently, authentic reproductions of Italian villas rarely occurred in the USA, favouring instead the drive for creative expression. The result was the creation of a distinctly American version of the Italianate style.

An earlier variation of this style, the Italian villa's Picturesque floor plan and dominant campanile were best suited to country or suburban settings.

*Left: An Italian villa in Liguria, Italy, was a typical house prototype promoted in America during the mid-19th century.*

### ITALIAN INFLUENCE

The Morse-Libby House, or Victoria Mansion, exemplifies the American villa style in grand fashion and is considered America's finest remaining example. The two-and-a-half-storey mansion includes a central four-stage entrance tower, or campanile, a feature that distinguishes this elaborate villa style from more common Italianate forms. The walls of the house are brick, but were covered in stucco to resemble brownstone ashlar construction. The building's corners are marked by rusticated quoins, and the original roof was metal.

The house, designed by architect Henry Austin (1804–91), from New Haven, Connecticut, was completed in 1863, following delays caused by the Civil War. The elaborate and well-preserved interiors are credited to artistdecorator Giovanni Guidirini, who imported 11 Italian artists to complete his designs. Frescos comprising painted medallions decorate the walls and ceilings, revealing images of Italian peasant society.

### NAMING THE HOUSE

The house was built as a summer residence for Ruggles Sylvester Morse, a hotel owner from New Orleans. Morse died in 1893 and the house was purchased in 1895 by J. R. Libby, a local merchant from Portland – hence the identifying name, Morse-Libby House. The Libby family moved out in the late 1920s. The name Victoria Mansion is also used, reflecting the donation of the little-altered house to the Victoria Society of Maine Women in 1943, with the intention that it should be opened to the public as a museum.

### RESTORATION CHALLENGES

Numerous conservation issues have, not surprisingly, necessitated a variety of historic restoration attempts. The property was designed with the latest innovations, and appeared grand and elaborate when complete. The writers of the national

*Below: The mansion's interior design features intricate Venetian, Gothic and Rococo elements.*

register nomination form in 1970 noted "a very serious condition" that would "cause irremediable damage to the rich interiors unless quickly corrected". The metal roofs were leaking, allowing considerable amounts of water to sneak into the home. Some plaster on the third floor had already been damaged. By the early 1980s the exterior facade was in need of repair, especially the sand-

*Below: The interior decor was designed by Giovanni Guidirini.*

*Above: The elaborate walls and ceilings are decorated with painted medallions and frescoes.*

painted wooden cornices and porches. Paint with embedded sand had been used to replicate the appearance of sandstone, much of which needed to be replaced altogether. Portions of the stone facade and porches required replacement. The variety of brownstone used for the house was in later years determined to be an insufficient building material. Quarried from Portland, Connecticut, the brownstone under the front porch had fared especially poorly due to roof leakage. The stone had undergone repeated "soakings", which led to frequent freeze-thaw stresses, further exacerbating its already weak qualities. Following impressive efforts to find a suitable replacement material, it was decided to replace the stonework with sand-painted wood, which had already been used elsewhere on the original structure.

In 1982 Morgan Phillips, who has supervised numerous restoration projects on the house, said that the house's "interior painted decorations, completely intact, are a remarkable survival".

# MARBLE HOUSE
## NEWPORT, RHODE ISLAND

Marble House provides one of America's most symbolic reminders of the wealth generated and fortunes made during the booming late 19th-century Industrial Revolution. Under the direction of Richard Morris Hunt (1827–95), America's premier architect of the time, the Marble House was built as a summer resort for Mr and Mrs William K. Vanderbilt. William was the brother of Cornelius Vanderbilt II, who was head of the New York Central Railroad. The New York Central was constructed to connect the great and growing metropolises of New York and Chicago with the industrial Midwest. When Cornelius II died, however, William became the president and chairman of the company. Through the family's control of the railroad, the Vanderbilts embodied the apparently limitless possibilities afforded by American industrial growth during what became known as the "gilded age". Only through the accumulation of amazing wealth could such summer "cottages" be constructed.

*Below: The exquisite and opulent decor of the interior rooms mirrored the grandeur of the exterior.*

*Above: Marble House was one of the earliest and grandest examples of Beaux-Arts classical architecture to appear in early 20th-century America.*

### BEAUX ARTS STYLE
The Marble House design was inspired by the Greek Parthenon, The White House and the Petit Trianon (1760–64), which served as a garden retreat on the grounds of Versailles in France. These European icons served to inspire a revival of formal, classical architecture that dominated American civic architecture from the 1880s through the 1920s. The classical French influence was provided by the Ecole des Beaux-Arts and the American architects who studied there.

The principles espoused by the Ecole des Beaux-Arts, in France, where Hunt trained, were rooted in the design of earlier royal architecture coupled with the favoured architectural styles of the Italian Renaissance. What came to be known as the Beaux-Arts style in America ultimately dominated the design of monumental civic and residential architecture by the late 19th and early 20th centuries, including railroad stations, city halls, libraries and wealthy town homes.

### RICHARD MORRIS HUNT
Hunt initially struggled with reconciling American tastes and fashions with the design philosophies of the Ecole, though he actively engaged with the Ecole's philosophies and concepts and manifested them within each of his commissions. His more prominent influential projects included the

*Above: The Marble House interior provides a showcase for French interior design.*

Metropolitan Museum of Art (1894–5), the base for the Statue of Liberty (1881–5) and the Chicago Columbian Exposition Administration building (1891–3). Such high-profile projects provided inspiration for advances in civic architecture and urban planning that ultimately lasted for decades into the 20th century.

One of Hunt's opportunities to express Beaux-Arts classicism came when he earned the contract to design the Marble House, which became one of the earliest and most prominent Beaux-Arts houses in the United States. Its completion in 1892 overlapped with his internationally acclaimed work at the Chicago Columbian Exposition, which opened in 1893, dubbed the "white city" based on the eye-popping, white-faced classical architecture.

### ALVA VANDERBILT

The house was the result of Hunt's collaboration specifically with William's wife, Alva Vanderbilt. Alva envisioned the house as a "temple to the arts" for private use by the Vanderbilt family, also conscious of the family's public

influence on aesthetic tastes. She already knew what she wanted with the construction of Marble House. She wrote, "…the gem of the Marble House idea was born at the foot of the Acropolis. I doubt not this place has been a manger cradle for many a divine idea which later grew into immortal beauty." The home's interior became a virtual showcase of French styles, a combination of Hunt's training at the Ecole and Alva's earlier experiences in Paris. The house was instrumental in elevating the social status of the area.

The name "Marble House" is well founded, given its construction with around 46,000sq m/500,000sq ft of the appealing stone within its 50 rooms. The exterior is faced with white marble from Tuckahoe, New York. The total amount of marble throughout the house accounted for US $7 million of the total US $11 million price tag for construction, making it the most expensive of all of Newport's so-called summer "cottages". The exterior's exquisite Beaux-Arts classical style is expressed dramatically with the house's two-storey entrance portico supported with massive Corinthian-style columns. Similar Corinthian pilasters are built into the front elevation on both sides of the symmetrical structure. The building itself is U-shaped and constructed with load-bearing brick, faced in the omnipresent white marble. Soon after its completion, Alva divorced William in 1895. Alva became a leader in the women's suffrage movement too, opening the house to the public in 1909 to raise awareness of the movement. Suffragettes Julia Howe and Anna Howard Shaw spoke at the event.

*Below: The white marble, after which the house is named, is revealed brilliantly on the exterior of the home's back elevation.*

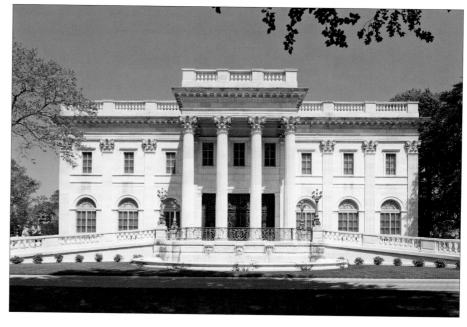

# THE BREAKERS
## NEWPORT, RHODE ISLAND

Following the Civil War, America entered into a long period of relative peace that enabled the growth of industrial production. The years between 1865 and 1900 were characterized either by America's most embarrassing era of political corruption, corporate greed and sinking national morals, or consisted of the nation's most innovative and progressive periods ever seen, depending on your viewpoint. This was the time when America became the world's leader in industrial mass production and corporate growth, accompanying immense social and technological advances and the

*Below: The exquisite mansion, The Breakers, represents the extent to which the accumulation of wealth was possible. The 70-room house, which was modelled on the palaces of Italy, stands on the site of a former wood-framed house.*

flowering of public education. Some historians have described this era as the American Renaissance.

**THE GILDED AGE**

Published in 1873, *The Gilded Age,* by Mark Twain (Samuel Clemens) and Charles Dudley Warner, emphasized and poked fun at the seemingly endless greed, immoral business practices and political corruption that defined the times. It was the era of great optimism and scientific advancement, especially for those who could benefit from the expanding opportunities of industrial enterprise. As the gap between the rich and poor widened, waves of rural farm families migrated to the booming cities to find industrial work. Increasingly successful capitalists sought new ways to spend their fortunes.

At the extreme top of the income ladder was the Vanderbilt family. The

family earned prominence during these decades in the world of finance, as patrons of the arts and as taste makers for international society. According to Thomas Gannon (1982) in his *Newport Mansions: The Gilded Age,* "if the Gilded Age were to be summed up by a single house, that house would have to be The Breakers". In concert with its neighbouring summer resort mansions, today The Breakers serves as a powerful monument to the great family fortunes that were accumulated during the booming years of American commerce and industrial production, concentrated in New England and the Midwest.

In the midst of this industrial core region, Newport emerged during the 19th century as the luxury summer playground of America's rich and famous. The ensuing collection of summer "cottages" served as the material manifestations of that elite social class.

*Above: Interior spaces were designed for entertaining and showcased the Italian Renaissance style.*

## THE VANDERBILTS

How did the Vanderbilts ascend to the top of the socio-economic ladder? The story of Cornelius "Commodore" Vanderbilt is one of the classic success stories of the American Industrial Revolution. Cornelius first employed his business savvy to amass incredible profits from the steamship industry. His ships commanded the coastal trade along the Atlantic seaboard and to the West Coast via Nicaragua. Eventually, he concluded that the route to future profits was with the railroads, which he envisioned as the future of American overland transportation. His interest moved away from the steamship industry to invest in the railroads.

Realizing that the budding rail network in the Northeast remained highly inefficient with a complex array of smaller companies, the Commodore sought to improve the network through consolidation. The result was the immensely prosperous New York Central Railroad, essentially providing a high-speed overland connection between New York City and Chicago and the greater Midwest. The railroad allowed Cornelius to become America's wealth-iest man, who passed on the legacy and wealth to his son William. The inheritance of US $90 million was the largest estate ever bequeathed in American history and proved the apparently limitless wealth that could be accumulated from the Industrial Revolution. Not to be outdone, William more than doubled the family fortune in the following years, in turn providing US $200 million to his own heirs. William's son, Cornelius, was provided with one quarter of that sum, providing the funds that would later build The Breakers. The project was fitting for the period referred to as the American Renaissance.

## ITALIAN-RENAISSANCE STYLE

Completed in 1895, this house was considered the most opulent within the resort, which was to become the social capital of America. The Breakers was the product of a collaborative effort between the Vanderbilt family and Richard Morris Hunt, America's premier architect of the time. The house constitutes the fullest expression of Beaux-Arts Classicism in America, and survives as one of only a few of Hunt's projects not demolished. With 70 rooms and interior spaces designed for entertaining, The Breakers is one of America's most elaborate properties in the Italian Renaissance, or Renaissance Revival, architectural style.

By the 1920s simpler versions of the Italian Renaissance style had spread nationwide for use in the emerging suburban middle-class neighbourhoods and main-street commercial buildings. Grand hotels and civic buildings employed the style throughout the country, though concentrations of this Mediterranean style were understandably found in America's warmer regions of the Southwest, Florida and southern California.

*Below: The sheer scale of The Breakers mansion overshadows otherwise grand houses nearby.*

# ROCKINGHAM MEETING HOUSE
## ROCKINGHAM, VERMONT

"First-period" meeting houses such as the Old Ship example at Hingham were followed by a distinctive "second-period" design during the 18th century. These later colonial structures were typically rectangular in plan with two storeys, gable roofs and double-sash windows. Although still employing a heavy timber frame, the builders of these later buildings were shifting away from their more medieval precedents. A survey in

*Above: This "second-period" meeting house utilized a Renaissance-era design but was still constructed with Medieval heavy timber framing.*

1963 found at least 90 known New England examples of second-period meeting houses retaining a high level of integrity. Rockingham has maintained its characteristics of form, proportion, structure, plan and materials. Such struc-

tures are considered by historians as transitional into the "third-period" type, constructed solely as places of worship instead of combining civic functions such as education or town meetings.

### CONSTRUCTION

The second-period meeting house at Rockingham was begun in 1787 or 1788 and finished in 1799–1801, and was typical of those built in the 18th century. Its late Georgian styling is displayed through its fluted pilasters and a pediment that frames its formal entry. Although revealing its symmetrical, Renaissance-era facade, its interior of massive post-and-beam construction still represented typical Medieval construction techniques. Aside from a light renovation in 1906, this is one of the most intact 18th-century public buildings in Vermont. These Congregational churches are historically significant, however, it is the later "fourth-period" churches that are identified most often today as providing the quintessential image of traditional New England.

# CONNECTICUT STATE CAPITOL
## HARTFORD, CONNECTICUT

The United States Capitol building in Washington, DC, serves as America's premier architectural symbol of democracy and nationalism. It should come as no surprise that the principal architectural features of the US Capitol have been deliberately copied for the designs of numerous state houses (state capitol buildings) around the nation to emulate powerful national symbolism at the state level. The Connecticut State Capitol building, although sporting a Gothic architectural theme rather than a classical Greek one, still includes the signature central dome and cupola

design that makes the US Capitol so distinctive. It represents a Victorian-era variation of the US Capitol idea.

Drivers speeding through Hartford on Interstate 84 are confronted with a dizzyingly detailed castle on a hill, that of the Connecticut State Capitol building. Attracting both admirers and fierce critics since its construction, prominent New York City architect Richard M. Upjohn's (1828–1903) winning design for the new state house competition in 1872 pulled out all the stops on architectural grandeur. A competition was held by a commission of the general

*Above: The central dome and rotunda of the US Capitol were powerful symbols of nationalism, which were ultimately chosen in favour of the original state house plan for a tall tower.*

assembly that attracted 11 architectural entries. The Gothic style prevailed in many of them, even though other Victorian-era styles were becoming popular by the 1870s. Richard M. Upjohn's design featured a revival style referred to as High Victorian Gothic.

Richard M. was the son of Richard Upjohn (1802–78) and became an established architect like his father. Upjohn Sr had become famous for promoting the earlier Gothic Revival movement in the United States through his designs of Gothic Revival churches.

Even today the castle-like structure is considered to be one, if not the finest example of the High Victorian Gothic style adapted to a grand public building in the United States. The interior and exterior retain a high degree of original features, and it is easy to wander through or around the structure and imagine turning the clock back 100 years. More important, the state house's contemporary use is the same as its designers had intended – that is, it is the seat of political power for a densely populated eastern state.

## A LOVE-HATE RELATIONSHIP

The actual state house design is not as originally intended. Upjohn's original design included a tall tower, but the feature was overruled by the commission, which preferred a central dome instead. The initial cost estimate of US $875,000 grew into a US $2.5 million project, and critics of the time debated the pros and cons of Upjohn's elaborate design. One supporter wrote, "The capitol of Connecticut will not only be by far the finest of our state houses, but it will be about the most important and creditable piece of civic architecture in the country." Not everyone agreed. Less than impressed with the plan's grandeur, one critic suggested the architect "had dined on Gothic, with an entrée or two

*Right: Elegant Victorian castle, or embarrassing eyesore? Opinions still vary, depending upon one's perspective.*

*Above: America's High Victorian Gothic style was fairly rare, but fully applied on the State Capitol.*

of French chateaux and a dessert of Renaissance, and had then gone to bed and dreamed this horrible nightmare".

This latter quote does reflect the flexibility afforded to this Victorian-era style. Considered an amalgam of several Gothic forms originating in France, Venice and Tuscany, High Victorian Gothic architecture was unconstrained in its interpretation as opposed to the pre-Civil War Gothic Revival. Rather than attempt correct interpretations of European Gothic forms, Upjohn and others felt free to express a variety of stylistic ideas within their work. As for the Connecticut State Capitol, the final, domed building was completed in 1880, however, it was occupied a year earlier. More than a century later, Connecticut locals and visitors alike generally agree on the magnificence of the state house, regardless of its visual appeal.

# CHAPTER TWO

# THE MID-ATLANTIC REGION

NEW YORK, PENNSYLVANIA, NEW JERSEY, DELAWARE AND MARYLAND ARE THE FIVE STATES THAT MAKE UP THIS DENSELY POPULATED EASTERN SEABOARD REGION, ALTHOUGH ONLY THREE OF THEM FEATURE IN THIS CHAPTER. TODAY THE POPULATION COMPRISES THE CORE AREA OF AN INTEGRATED URBAN REGION KNOWN AS MEGALOPOLIS. ICONIC SKYSCRAPERS, NATIONAL FINANCIAL INSTITUTIONS AND WORLD-RENOWNED MUSEUMS CELEBRATE THE WEALTH BROUGHT TO THE REGION BY EARLY ENTREPRENEURS. INCLUDED TOO ARE STARK REMINDERS OF LIFE FOR THE POOR.

*Left: The skyline of New York City is easy to identify.*

# FORT NIAGARA
## YOUNGSTOWN, NEW YORK

Three flags are flown daily at Fort Niagara, representing the French, British and Americans who sequentially controlled this strategic outpost during the past three centuries. This specific site provides one of colonial America's key lessons in geopolitics. The fort stood on a pivotal piece of land sought after by European nations in their campaigns to control North America. Prior to the completion of the Erie Canal in 1825, this triangle of land at the mouth of the Niagara River was the strategic key for controlling the entire Great Lakes Basin, politically and economically.

Fort Niagara commanded the west end of Lake Ontario at the entry to the Niagara River, which served as the primary trade corridor from the East Coast to the vast interior of North America. Just upstream from the fort is the famous Niagara Falls, where the water

*Below: The map shows the Great Lakes Basin between Canada and the United States, and the strategic forts dependent upon Fort Niagara.*

of the Niagara River dumps dramatically over the Niagara Escarpment. In the context of geopolitics, trade and physical geography, the mouth of the Niagara River is literally the gateway to the upper Great Lakes region. This circumstance led to the fort's development as a supply depot for the entire chain of forts established throughout the upper Great Lakes. It is said that the entire system of Great Lakes' forts would not have been possible without Fort Niagara.

*Above: The Niagara River is a natural fortification at one side of Fort Niagara.*

### FRENCH CONTROL

It was the French explorer La Salle who first recognized the strategic importance of the site. Specific advantages were noted during his expedition, as the river's east side was considered to be naturally fortified. During the 17th century the French, British and Dutch established successful settlements in the region, though the French were the best suited to negotiate the vast interior waterways at the time. They particularly utilized the St Lawrence River to access the Great Lakes region from their settlements in Quebec. The French were consequently the first Europeans to seek control of the Niagara River, recognizing its strategic importance.

A human barrier presented itself, however, in the form of the Five Nations of the Iroquois, arguably the most powerful Native American coalition in North American history. The French had previously alienated the Iroquois because of their alignment with Iroquois enemies. Sporadic warfare ensued off and on between the French and Iroquois throughout the 17th century, providing a continuous challenge to French control of the

*Right: Two uniformed soldiers and two civilians, one a soldier's wife, load cannons at the Battle of Fort Niagara, 1812.*

river. During the 1670s, French relations with the Iroquois improved enough to enable the establishment of Fort Conti, the first French outpost at the site in 1679. La Salle wanted to construct a sailing ship for exploration of the upper Great Lakes, and this first post was designed to support the shipbuilding effort. The final product was La Salle's vessel *Le Griffon* launched during the spring of 1679. Fort Conti and its wooden stockade served as a supply storage facility for operations upstream. Shortly following La Salle's departure on *Le Griffon*, however, the Fort was abandoned after the site accidentally burnt down.

Not until 1687 was a much larger stockade built on the site, named Fort Denonville, under the direction of Governor Denonville. The stockade was overseen by 100 men until a disastrous winter caused most of them to perish.

*Below: This is the largest of the Fort's structures, and is the oldest representative of French colonial power in the United States.*

The third and present Fort Niagara replaced the second, and today no physical evidence remains of the earlier two stockades. By this time the French controlled much of the North American interior, from the northern Great Lakes southward along the Mississippi River Valley to the French city of New Orleans.

## THE BRITISH PERIOD

In 1759 a European-style siege of Fort Niagara led to the defeat of the French at the hands of the British, ending French dominance in the territory now held by the United States and Canada. The British used the fort as the base of operations during the American Revolution for the so-called "Border Wars" with New York and Pennsylvania. Following the Revolutionary War the

British were finally required to relinquish control of the fort, through the Jay Treaty. The last military action involving Fort Niagara came during the War of 1812, when the British recaptured the fort and actually preserved it from destruction – unlike much of the Niagara Frontier that was devastated during the conflict. Peace has prevailed since then. With the completion of the Erie Canal in 1825, the Niagara River ceased to be a major shipping route, thereby diminishing the fort's strategic geopolitical value.

## AMERICAN PERMANENCE

The fort served as a barracks and training station for troops during both World Wars, and the last army units were withdrawn in 1963. The state of New York acquired the property that year for park development.

Fort Niagara contains the most complete collection of 18th-century military architecture in the United States. This includes the 1725 stone chateau, designed and personally supervised by the leading architect of New France, Chaussegros de Lery. The original plans of this building have been preserved in Paris in the Archives of the Colonies.

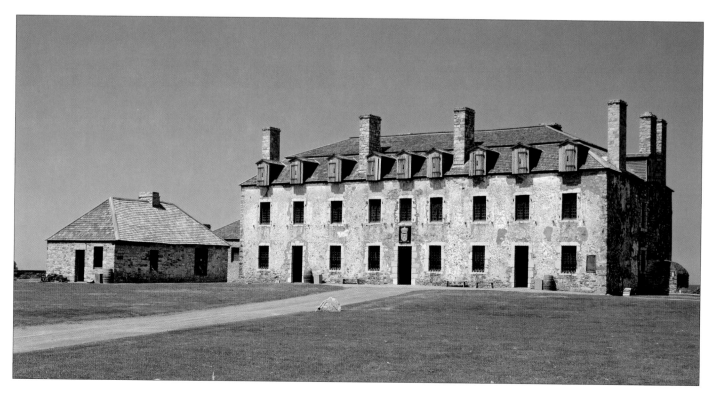

# ELFRETH'S ALLEY
## PHILADELPHIA, PENNSYLVANIA

The two- and three-storey dwellings that front Elfreth's Alley comprise a well-preserved piece of 18th-century Philadelphia. The two oldest surviving dwellings are those at 120 and 122 on the Alley's south side. Dating from the 1720s, they have been continuously occupied for nearly three centuries. The Alley was opened between 1702 and 1704 by mutual agreement between Arthur Wells and John Gilbert, both of whom lived on Front Street. Around 1750 it came to be called Elfreth's Alley after Jeremiah Elfreth, who lived on Second Street, just north of the Alley. Elfreth had acquired title to the properties on both sides of the Alley at its Second Street end. Half of the dwellings still standing were built prior to the American Revolution, while the other half appeared during the federal years.

*Below: A variety of artisans and tradesmen initially occupied the houses of Elfreth's Alley. Historians are certain that Benjamin Franklin frequently visited number 122, given that its tenant in 1728–31 was William Maugridge, a cabinet-maker. Maugridge was an original member of Franklin's Junto.*

**A GEORGIAN LANDSCAPE**

Although the Alley landscape today contrasts sharply with its more modern surroundings, it is this type of residential scene that dominated colonial urban living. The dwellings represent the dominant form of housing in colonial America, that of the Georgian-style, red-brick row house. Their facades are flush with the walkways, predating later innovations of setbacks and front lawns. The door is typically placed on one side of the street facade. This is one room deep, with a fireplace located on the rear or side wall. The stairs are found behind this room in an area called the piazza. This element is often narrower than the back buildings and forms a connecting link between them and the front house. The back buildings are slimmer and therefore provide for a long yard or alley. These are the most typical of Philadelphia row houses, with low ceilings and deep cellars.

Only by the early 19th century did new generations of Americans abandon the traditional row house, favouring instead more expansive lots adorned with free-standing houses set back from the street.

**ROW HOUSES**

The row house concept originated in 17th-century England, prior to its diffusion to the American colonies. By 1700 the British had been increasingly attracted to open space, parks and greenery. New English suburbs were being developed to provide wealthier residents with an escape from the industrial filth of the city. Brick, attached "terrace" houses became the housing of choice within these newer suburban neighbourhoods. Many were decorated with the latest Georgian-style ornamentation, so named for the era of King George III. Combined with newer building codes and regulations following the Great Fire of London of 1666, the Renaissance-inspired terrace house became a distinctly English form. The idea was easily transplanted to America's row houses as its colonial urban populations continued to grow. America's early cities, therefore, took on an appearance that resembled the English motherland.

*Below: Elfreth's Alley was built to look familiar to the English settlers.*

# SANDY HOOK LIGHT
## SANDY HOOK, NEW JERSEY

The lighthouse constitutes a unique building form in the American landscape. It is designed for the specific purpose of guiding maritime traffic along coastal margins. Advances in illuminated aids to navigation were slow to appear during Colonial times. Some of the first lights in Colonial New England consisted of lighted baskets placed atop poles. Colonial lights were generally placed near important trade ports, though rarely near major navigational hazards. Local merchants typically appealed to their own colony for a lighthouse, which the colonial government usually placed in a convenient area requested by local residents. Prior to the Revolution there were at least 11 permanent light stations. The Sandy Hook Light was one of them, still housed today in its original tower, built in 1764.

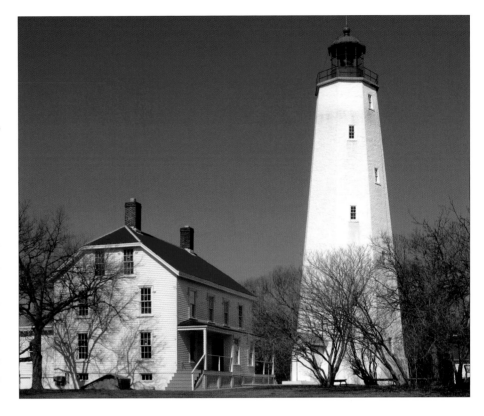

### A FEDERAL PRIORITY

The improvement of navigational aids became an early priority of the new federal government. On 7 August 1789 the government took control of all existing lighthouses and those under construction. The Treasury became responsible for funding all aids to navigation, putting an end to Colonial light

*Below: The lighthouse became a necessity for the safety of global transportation and commerce by the late 18th century.*

taxes. The government's high priority placed on early American lights is highlighted by the fact that presidents George Washington, John Adams and Thomas Jefferson personally approved contracts for lighthouses as well as appointments for lighthouse positions. Still with close government oversight but removed from the presidents, the number of US lighthouses increased to 55 by 1820.

### THE REVOLUTION

Sandy Hook Light is now the oldest surviving example in the United States. The Light is within the Fort Hancock Military Reservation, with New York City located directly north. The tower is octagonal and nine storeys (31m/103ft) tall. The brick structure rests on a masonry foundation, and the base wall is 2m/7ft thick. The Light's original construction was made possible by a lottery financed by New York City merchants in 1761. Their goal was to raise sufficient funds to construct a light

*Above: Early lighthouses were built and maintained by the local population, a fact that discouraged any interest in placing them in the inaccessible wilderness.*

tower on Sandy Hook to better guide ships past the New Jersey shoal into New York Harbour. Ships that benefited from the Light were also required to pay a tax, worth 22 cents per ton of cargo, to assist with the construction costs.

The durability of earlier lighthouses was extremely inconsistent, with some destroyed multiple times by fire or storms. The Sandy Hook Light proved to be extremely durable, and is the only lighthouse still existing that was built before the American Revolution. In March 1776, during the Revolution, the Americans extinguished the light to avoid assisting British movements, even attempting unsuccessfully to blow it up. The British soon repaired the light, however, and the beacon has remained lit continuously since then, except for during the blackouts of World War II.

# ERIE CANAL
## ALBANY TO BUFFALO, NEW YORK

Following the War of 1812, British and American merchants and traders correctly predicted a new era of peace and prosperity. The United States entered what historians term its "take-off" era of economic growth, enabled by a budding transportation revolution. Although blessed with natural interior waterways such as the Ohio and Mississippi rivers, proponents of artificial canals offered wider accessibility to vast interior regions not served by navigable rivers. An effective, overland union between the Eastern Seaboard and the promising agricultural realm of the trans-Appalachian West required a solution to the high costs of inland transportation. The American canal era was about to begin. The Erie became the first major engineering project of its kind in the fledgling nation.

### AN ENGINEERING MARVEL

At this time America's mercantile cities depended upon economic activities surrounding agricultural trade, especially with Europe. The growth of a city such as Philadelphia or New York depended largely upon capturing the inland trade of its hinterland, or regional

*Above: Interior settlements known as "canal towns" grew and prospered as inland trade ports until the railroads took over.*

surroundings. By the early 19th century Americans were eyeing the Appalachian Mountains, which presented a formidable physical barrier to westward migration. The fertile farmland of the trans-Appalachian region beckoned New England farmers tired of remov-

*Below: To move boats inland, the Erie utilized a series of more than 80 locks, allowing boats to float to the next level.*

*Above: The Erie Canal opened in 1825 to much celebration. It was known at the time as the "eighth wonder of the world".*

ing rocks every year from their fields. At a time when overland travel was arduous and costly, the creation of an artificial water route, or canal, was viewed by visionaries of the state of New York as the most viable solution to overcome the Appalachian challenge. Their answer was the monumental Erie Canal, completed in 1825 after eight years of construction.

The canal route took advantage of a natural break through the Appalachian chains, ultimately connecting the navigable Hudson River at Albany with Lake Erie at Buffalo. It consisted of an artificial trench 584km/363 miles long with more than 80 locks to overcome a 169m/555ft elevation difference. The final construction cost was US $7 million. The canal was fully enclosed for the entire route, except for 16km/ 10 miles on its western end. That is, no natural lakes or streams were incorporated into its construction.

The route did take advantage of the Mohawk River Valley, one of the Hudson River's primary east-west tributaries. The project's chief engineer was Judge Benjamin Wright, with a lawyer,

*Above: The peaceful appearance of the canal corridor was deceptive, as the waterway shifted the economic geography of the region.*

James Geddes, serving as assistant chief. The labourers hired to construct the canal consisted primarily of Irish immigrants, assembled by New York City's powerful Tammany Hall.

The canal was known at the time as "Clinton's folly" or "Clinton's ditch" by its detractors. However, its impact on the nation's economic geography and transportation system was nonetheless impressive. The route instantaneously provided an inexpensive and relatively fast trade route that allowed raw natural materials and farm products to be shipped with relative ease to the East Coast. The Erie and its feeders allowed New York to tap into the Great Lakes and upper Midwestern market within a surprisingly short period of time. Once the commanding trade centre of the trans-Appalachian West, New Orleans suffered stiff competition from the Erie's canal boats. By the 1830s that city's dominance over its northern hinterland diminished as ever-more goods made their way to New York instead.

**NEW ENGLAND EXTENDED**
The Erie also provided the impetus for westward migration through upstate New York. New England families settled along the Mohawk River Valley and further west, to present-day northern Ohio, Indiana, Illinois and even southern Wisconsin. Known to geographers as

*Above: The route of the 363-mile canal system that linked the Hudson River in the east with Lake Erie to the west.*

New England Extended, this cultural region exhibits New England qualities today, including Northeastern-style barns, farmsteads, Greek Revival-style homes, and New England village greens.

Following New York's lead, other major cities sought to tap Western markets and attempted their own canal projects. The Chesapeake and Ohio Canal began in 1828 from Washington, DC, ultimately completing 296km/184 miles to Cumberland, Maryland. More successful was Philadelphia's Main Line Canal, including a portage railroad, completed in 1834. By 1840 the nation had already completed 5,353km/3,326 miles of canals, though few became long-term

successes. Other modes of transportation and communication were already competing with the maturing canal network, in the form of the telegraph, railroad and steamship. In 1840 railroads were already in operation throughout the Northeast, but still served primarily as feeders to existing canals. By that year 5,356km/3,328 miles of railroad had been built; two decades later the distance had increased to 14,290km/8,879 miles. The railroad era had arrived, but not before the canals had fundamentally shifted America's migration and trade routes throughout the interior.

*Below: Between 1851 and 1854, the Erie, Baltimore and Ohio, the New York Central, and the Pennsylvania Railroad crossed the Appalachians, rendering the earlier canal system nearly obsolete.*

# LYNDHURST
## TARRYTOWN, NEW YORK

A nostalgia for the European Middle Ages emerged in America during the early stages of industrialism. By the 1830s the Romantic Movement had captured the imagination of Americans who longed for an association with a more agrarian, rural past. Art and architecture quickly became a prominent mode through which to promote American Romanticism, particularly along New York's Hudson River Valley.

### GOTHIC REVIVAL STYLE
Promoted as an early Romantic style, the Gothic Revival harked back to the innovative Gothic cathedrals constructed in England and France between the 12th and 16th centuries. With the Picturesque movement underway in England by the late 1700s, Gothic architecture was recognized as a suitable contribution to the romantic trends of informal, romanticized landscaping.

The revival of Gothic architecture can be dated to England in 1749 with the remodelling of a country house by Sir Horace Walpole. Designed with Medieval elements, Walpole included the prominent Gothic features of battlements (castellated parapets) and multiple pointed-arch (lancet) windows. Picturesque Gothic cottages then appeared throughout England during the 19th century. Queen Victoria spurred an interest in the Gothic as well, with her redecoration of Windsor and Balmoral castles with Gothic-inspired furniture after she assumed the role of monarch in 1837.

By the 1830s, American architects had learned of the British revival and were adopting the more romantic elements of the Gothic style in new American churches and country houses. This was the first generation of suburban living in the United States. The partnership between architect, Alexander Jackson Davis and landscape gardener, Andrew Jackson Downing, soon emerged to promote the new romanticized lifestyle in

*Above: As one of America's most elaborate Gothic-style country homes, Lyndhurst epitomized the flowering of the Romantic Movement in the US.*

the country for middle- and upper-class populations. Highest on their list of preferred architectural styles was Gothic and Italianate, with the Gothic Revival making the earliest inroads.

The first recorded use of the style for a home was the 1832 Glen Ellen Castle in Baltimore County, Maryland, designed by Davis. The house was inspired by earlier models seen by Glen Ellen's owner on a trip to England and Scotland. With Glen Ellen behind him, Davis promoted the Gothic Revival throughout America with his popular house-plan book *Rural Residences*, released in 1837. Likewise, Andrew Jackson Downing, who favoured a return to architecture of the Middle Ages, published *Cottage Residences* in 1842. It was within this cultural context

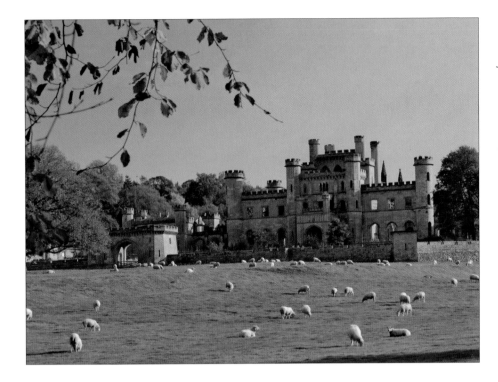

*Left: Lowther Castle in Cumbria, England, provided the inspiration for Lyndhurst.*

of romanticism that Davis designed one of America's most elaborate and exuberant Gothic homes, known as Lyndhurst, in Tarrytown, New York.

## HUDSON RIVER GOTHIC

Built for former mayor of New York, William Paulding, Lyndhurst was one of a series of designs by Davis that came to be known as Hudson River Gothic. Apparently inspired by Lowther Castle in England, the original house comprising the southern end of the building was cruciform in plan, built of brick and faced with white Ossining marble. It was purposely positioned to provide a sweeping view overlooking the Tappan Zee, a local name for the Hudson River, at one of its widest points. The Tappan Native American tribe had inhabited the area in pre-Colonial times, and "zee" was the Dutch word for "sea". The Dutch had settled much of the lower Hudson River Valley, known initially as New Netherlands. The City of New York had initially been New Amsterdam – a walled, medieval Dutch settlement. By the time of Downing and Davis, American culture had come to dominate the Hudson River valley, a centre for early 19th-century Romanticism and the Picturesque movement.

Lyndhurst demonstrated the full potential for applying Gothic Revival styling to country homes. Davis designed the remarkable intricacy of the interior himself, executed by the Irish cabinetmaker Richard Byrnes. While Gothic furniture adorned the inside, Davis was careful to include a variety of Gothic exterior features including turrets, finials, bays, trefoils, buttresses, stone traceries and crenellations. The south and west sides of the home were adorned with wooden porches.

In 1864–5 Davis enlarged the home for its second owner, George Merritt, a New York City merchant. The result was a more Picturesque, asymmetrical design than the original. The roof was raised a storey along the north-south axis, and a wing for a new dining room and pantry was added on the north end. Further additions included a four-storey tower and an elegant *port-cochere* at the porch entrance. This latter feature was converted into a vestibule and library.

Considered the epitome of the Gothic Revival style in America, the Lyndhurst home served for 12 years as the country estate of financier Jay Gould. A shrewd and ruthless operator of unrestrained capitalism, Gould is known not only for his questionable morality, but also for his battle with Cornelius Vanderbilt for control of the Erie Railroad.

Today the mansion is maintained as a museum operated by the National Trust for Historic Preservation.

*Below: The back of Lyndhurst has castellated wooden porches, lancet-arched and trefoil windows, and parapeted dormers.*

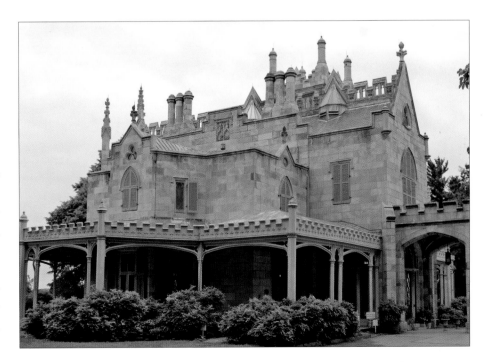

# CENTRAL PARK
## NEW YORK, NEW YORK

Credited as the nation's first consciously planned, large-scale public park, Central Park was conceived as a place where all residents, regardless of social class, could escape the pressures of urban society. The park, in the heart of Manhattan, played a monumental role in establishing the urban park movement in the United States. Designs employed by its creators, Frederick Law Olmsted and Calvert Vaux, were immediately and widely imitated in cities across the country. Not only did Central Park encourage the need for setting aside natural spaces in urban areas, it also influenced the design of America's suburban developments and the budding national park system. A new academic profession was born as well, that of landscape architecture.

### PLEASURE GROUNDS

Prior to the planned design of public parks, residents of congested urban cities enjoyed the grounds of spacious rural cemeteries. Designed as Picturesque landscape gardens, they inadvertently

*Below: Initially, the land for Central Park was on the northern fringe of the city. Since then the city has enveloped the green space.*

*Above: A view of Central Park, revealing its Picturesque, natural qualities purposely designed by Olmsted and Vaux. KEY: 2 Central Park South, 3 Pond, 4 Wollman Memorial Rink, 5 Umpire Rock, 6 The Zoo, 7 Sheep Meadow, 8 The Mall, 9 The Glade, 10 Bethesda Terrace, 11 Conservatory Water, 12 The Ramble, 16 Belvedere Lake, 17 Delacorte Theater, 18 The Great Lawn, 22 The Pool, 23 The Loch, 24 Great Hill, 25 Lasker Pool, 26 Frederick Douglas Circle, 27 Central Park North, 28 Frawley Circle.*

served doubly as public pleasure grounds – an observation not lost on municipal planners. Exploding urban populations during the early 19th century came with a corresponding increase in deaths, necessitating new cemeteries on the urban periphery. Rural cemeteries thus foreshadowed the American public park movement.

Two individuals stood out among the voices calling for social reforms during the 1830s and 1840s. One was the prominent horticulturalist Andrew Jackson Downing, the other was William Cullen Bryant, poet and editor of the *New York Evening Post*. They both shared their direct experiences of England's new royal parks and subsequently urged New Yorkers to set aside land for a similar purpose.

### EARLY PLANS

With growing public support, New York's city leaders successfully encouraged the state legislature to enable the city to acquire land for a public park. The result was the passage of the First Park Act of 1851, which simply allowed the city to purchase a tract of land identified at the time as Jones's Wood – an area promoted by William Bryant. An amendment to the Park Act in 1853 led to the city's acquisition of a much larger tract, including much of the land within today's Central Park. An additional 26ha/65 acres was eventually added as a northward extension in 1863, completing the finalized area for the park.

Described at the time as a Romantic, a trained engineer, an experienced farmer and an accomplished writer, Frederick Law Olmsted was elected by the board of park commissioners as the new park superintendent in 1857. The board announced a competition to determine the park's design, which Olmsted had not initially intended to enter. Calvert Vaux expressed interest in submitting an entry and encouraged

*Above: People strolling through the grounds of Central Park may find it hard to believe they are in the middle of Manhattan.*

Olmsted to join him. Totally unaware of the competitors' names, the board reviewed the submitted plans and awarded first prize to Plan 33 on 28 April 1858. Only then did they discover the names of Olmsted and Vaux attached to the winning entry, simply titled Greensward.

The board required that all entries for the competition meet a set of criteria. Each plan needed to include three large playing fields, a parade ground, a winter skating pond, a major fountain, a flower garden, a lookout tower and a music hall or exhibition building. Many of the entries looked to Downing's earlier work for inspiration.

Olmsted and Vaux ingeniously incorporated the existing natural beauty of the site, its *genius loci*. The city had acquired the land in large part due to its complicated, rocky terrain, which was not suitable for typical urban developments. With Greensward, Olmsted and Vaux turned this into an advantage for the Park's Picturesque design scheme. They exploited natural rock outcrops and converted swampy lowlands into the park's eventually famous lakes. They even included a more geometric, axial design for an elm-lined promenade, or mall, which provided for an element of Classical design amid the otherwise Picturesque, natural setting.

By 1866 most of the work on the park had been completed. Thousands of men were employed to assist with the park's construction, a strategy that would release pressure on the administration to improve the economic woes following the financial panic of 1857.

## CENTRAL PARK AS PROTOTYPE

The legacy of Central Park is far reaching and continuous. Downing had dreamt of creating planned public spaces, providing natural settings for members of every social and economic class to enjoy. This dream came to fruition through the creative and determined work of Olmsted, Vaux and their contemporaries. Even before Central Park was completed, the grandeur of the project had already stimulated a tremendous demand for outdoor recreation. Land values directly adjacent to the park increased measurably.

Other congested cities were quick to borrow the design elements of Central Park, setting the pattern for similar open areas in the great parks of Brooklyn, Boston, Chicago and many other cities and towns as the nation moved west. At the household level, the Picturesque, curvilinear design of Central Park served as a powerful model for purposely landscaping front and back gardens with such romantic features as rolling lawns, diverse arrangements of ornamental plants and trees, and the creative incorporation of topographic features. With the sprawl of American suburban communities following World War II, such Picturesque designs became standard practice throughout from coast to coast. Nineteenth-century romanticism continues to play a significant role shaping the attitudes of Americans to what constitutes attractive communities.

*Below: Central Park and its lakes are one of America's premier public spaces.*

# BROOKLYN BRIDGE
## NEW YORK, NEW YORK

Considered equal in monumental significance to the building of the first transcontinental railroad, the Gothic-styled Brooklyn Bridge was, for 20 years, the largest suspension bridge in the world. The Bridge arches over the East River connecting the New York City boroughs of Manhattan and Brooklyn on Long Island.

### LANDMARK TO COMMUTING
Industrial growth in Manhattan drove an equally impressive residential building boom in Brooklyn, which was considered one of America's first major residential suburbs. Increasing throngs of commuters from Brooklyn were stressing the East River ferry service to its limits, necessitating the construction of an uninterrupted streetcar system linking the two boroughs.

A massive bridge became the ultimate solution, providing an unprecedented challenge of spanning an uninterrupted distance between two masonry piers of 488m/1,600ft. Construction began on the bridge on 3 January 1870 and was completed 13

*Above: The monumental suspension bridge has Gothic towers.*

years later. John A. Roebling designed the bridge, which was completed under the guidance of his son and successor, Colonel Washington A. Roebling. The

*Below: Once the largest suspension bridge in the world, Brooklyn Bridge expedites commuting between Manhattan and Brooklyn.*

Bridge's vertical clearance needed to be high enough to allow commercial sailing vessels to sail underneath. Perhaps the engineering of the bridge's construction is its most remarkable aspect, given the numerous unusual and new construction techniques employed to make it a success, including the use of pneumatic caissons and steel cable instead of iron. The caissons resembled giant boxes at the time of construction, with V-shaped sides and no artificial bottoms. Compressed air filled the caissons to hold back the river water and to prevent the structures from collapsing. Described as two large rooms below the water surface, the caissons enabled workers to remove the mud and stone of the riverbed to prepare the groundwork for the towers. The two massive support towers are built of a combination of limestone, granite, and Rosendale cement. They stand 84m/275ft above the high-water level. The bridge measures 1,825m/5,989ft long. Consistent with popular early Victorian architectural styles, the tower openings consist of giant Gothic pointed arches above the passageways.

### ROEBLING'S LEGACY
Proud of his design, John Roebling described his own vision of the bridge: "The completed work...will not only be the greatest bridge in existence, but will be the greatest engineering work of the continent. ...Its most conspicuous features, the great towers, will serve as landmarks to the adjoining cities and they will... be ranked as national monuments. As a great work of art, and as a successful specimen of advanced bridge engineering, this structure will forever testify to the energy, enterprise and wealth of that community." Today the structure continues to carry traffic across the river, more than a century after its opening on 24 May 1883.

# GENESEO
## HISTORIC DISTRICT, GENESEO, NEW YORK

In the 18th century, as Western lands were acquired from Native Americans, western New York opened up to settlement. Its rich agricultural lands were envied by New England farmers. Promotional publications and maps from land speculators were released around 1800 that encouraged settlement in this so-called "Genesee Country".

The village of Geneseo was founded in 1790 by brothers William and James Wadsworth, during this first wave of migration from New England. By the early 19th century the Wadsworth family had established a prosperous agricultural community focused on the Genesee River Valley. The village of Geneseo became the commercial trade centre that supported its surrounding agricultural activities.

### A EUROPEAN TRANSPLANT

Two of Geneseo's most significant and imposing residential structures consist of the Wadsworth family homes, The Homestead and Hartford House. Built on the south end of main street, The Homestead was the estate of the first generation of Wadsworths, William and James, and reflected their early financial success in the region. It was James' son, however, who became a national figure.

*Below: Hertford Villa in Regent's Park, London, was the model for Hartford House. It was rebuilt in the early 19th century and is no longer in existence.*

Known to history as Union General James S. Wadsworth (1807–64), he built the Hartford House for his bride, Mary Craig Wharton, in 1835. The Greek Revival mansion sits on park-like grounds with a commanding view of the Genesee River Valley.

The design for Hartford House is attributed to a European honeymoon trip taken by newlyweds. The couple were entertained in London by Francis Seymour-Conway, the 3rd Marquis of Hertford. They were so impressed with his villa in Regent's Park that they obtained the architect's plans from Lord Hertford with the intention of creating a replica in Geneseo. The Wadsworth version was given the name of Hartford.

### THE DISTRICT

Geneseo's historic district contains one of the best preserved villages in western New York. The town displays a virtual textbook of architectural styles that date from the 1810s through the 1930s. The full succession of popular American architectural styles can be found here, from earlier Federal and Greek Revival structures to the more Picturesque styles of Gothic Revival, Italianate, Italian Villa, Second Empire, Queen Anne and

*Above: Hartford House was one of two early properties built by the district's founding family for private usage.*

Eastlake. Various Colonial Revival styles are represented as well. Perhaps as impressive as the architecture is the dominance of vernacular housing that still survives intact. Nearly all are wood-framed structures with clapboard siding. Some of the more imposing residences were built with brick. Non-residential properties include two churches, an 1838 schoolhouse and an 1867 library. More than 100 contributing outbuildings provide further historic context within the district, with wood-framed carriage houses, barns and garages being common.

The village provides one of America's clearest expressions of Picturesque architecture and town planning principles. Promoted as an antidote to the dominance of grid street plans and Classical temples, this style promoted the ideals of English Romanticism through the incorporation of informal, natural settings and contexts. The Picturesque, 19th-century Temple Hill Cemetery is also included within the historic district, adding to the romantic qualities of the village.

# BROOKLYN HEIGHTS
## HISTORIC DISTRICT, BROOKLYN, NEW YORK

The process of industrialization in America corresponded with immense urban population growth during the 19th century. In 1820 the new American nation was still fundamentally rural and agrarian, with only 56 towns each containing between 2,500 and 25,000 residents, along with five large cities. By 1870 the number and size of urban areas had exploded to a total of 612 towns, 45 cities and 6 metropolitan areas with more than a quarter of a million residents each.

As American cities industrialized during the decades leading to the Civil War, waves of foreign immigrants and rural Americans were attracted to urban areas in search of work. Cities such as Philadelphia, New York, Boston and Chicago became ever-more congested and polluted, raising fears of disease outbreaks and related ills. Immigrants continued to arrive and were forced to occupy cramped, run-down tenement housing near the city centre. African-Americans competed with foreign immigrants for the poorest urban housing as they continued to migrate to northern industrial cities. Consequently, an anti-urban sentiment rang louder for those who could afford to move away from the city centres. They increasingly

sought more spacious housing on the urban periphery, aided by new transportation such as the horse car, omnibus, steam railroad and ferry.

### THE RISE OF THE SUBURBS
As the wealthy sought refuge from congested urban areas, a vast filtering process ensued. Increasing numbers of middle-class residents purchased the vacated homes of the wealthy, and in turn working-class people moved into the housing vacated by the middle class.

The accumulation of industrial wealth enabled more Americans to escape the "teaming masses" of America's cities, contributing to an increased demand for suburban housing

*Below: The East River was a commercial corridor long before the population began to spill across the river to Brooklyn.*

*Above: Once an early suburb of Manhattan, Brooklyn has since been subsumed into New York City.*

at the urban fringe. At the same time leading proponents of the Romantic movement distributed literature and pattern books advocating the healthier suburban lifestyle. For these reasons the American ideal of suburban living was already well entrenched prior to the Civil War.

### FERRY SUBURB
Brooklyn Heights is considered one of the first and most significant "ferry suburbs" in the United States. After the first established steam ferry in 1814, an

*Below: Brooklyn Heights, in 1924, more than 50 years after the Brooklyn Bridge was completed, was ever expanding.*

*Right: Brooklyn's 19th-century Italianate town houses were set back from the street, in contrast to earlier Georgian practice.*

improved ferry service from Manhattan across the harbour to Brooklyn allowed wealthier, and eventually middle-class, families to easily commute from new homes in Brooklyn to their employment on Manhattan Island. According to historian Kenneth Jackson, by 1860 New York City's population was 813,000 while Brooklyn's had already increased to 266,000. Brooklyn's population doubled 20 years later. Various East River ferries already carried nearly 33 million commuters per year by 1860. Ten years later that number had risen to 50 million per year.

New Yorkers witnessing the population drain from Manhattan were not impressed with the trend, as newspapers, politicians and land developers voiced collective concern over "the desertion of the city by its men of wealth". "Many of the rich and prosperous are removing from the city, while the poor are pressing in", stated the Association for the Improvement of the Condition of the Poor. Although city leaders actually attempted to prevent

*Below: Elaborate entryways are characteristic of Brooklyn's Italian Renaissance style.*

improvements to the ferry service and suggested hefty fare increases, Brooklyn still continued its transformation from suburb into city. By 1890 it became the fourth largest in America.

## ARCHITECTURAL STYLES

Brooklyn's continuous growth after the 1820s enabled a succession of popular architectural styles to emerge. In today's historic district of Brooklyn Heights, private and public buildings display a succession of styles representative of the 19th century. Although punctuated by various modern-era buildings, the

*Below: Urban street scene in Brooklyn's historic commercial core.*

district serves as a textbook example of successive architectural styles between the 1820s and 1900. Most prolific is the Greek Revival style, although the earlier Federal style and later Renaissance Revival style are also well represented.

## BARD LAW

Following an earlier struggle to prevent the Brooklyn-Queens Expressway from bisecting the Heights, the Brooklyn Heights Association began a movement in 1958 to preserve the neighbourhood. The group invoked New York State's new Bard Law, which empowered cities to save "places, buildings, structures, works of art and other objects having a special character or special historical or aesthetic interest or value". As a pioneering effort in America to preserve an entire neighbourhood, success ultimately required a tortuous, nine-year political process. Supported by new local residents, the media and a coalition of preservation interests, the Brooklyn Heights Historic District was finally made official in 1967.

Today the district bubbles with charm. Its tree-lined streets and rows of 19th-century brownstone and brick townhouses are a testament to the influence that individuals and community organizations can exert on politics.

# TENEMENT BUILDING

## 97 ORCHARD STREET, NEW YORK, NEW YORK

The modest, six-storey building at 97 Orchard Street provides a rare glimpse into the challenging living conditions of a 19th-century metropolis. Observers had recognized the increasing problem of overcrowding in New York City as early as the 1830s. The nation was undergoing the greatest wave of immigration in American history, and New York strained severely to accommodate decades of rapid urban growth.

As poor European immigrants and lower-income residents sought work and housing, they clustered within aging New York neighbourhoods not designed for such high densities of humanity. By the Civil War wealthier residents were fleeing to new suburbs such as Brooklyn, while impoverished newcomers gradually took over their former urban housing. To better accommodate the persistent influx of immigrants, the tenement became a common residential solution, beginning

*Below: Orchard Street in 1923, indicating the overcrowded conditions that challenged America's rapidly growing cities.*

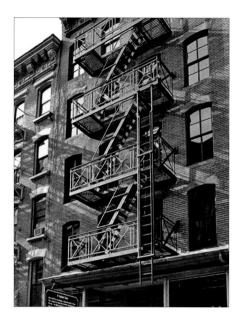

in the 1850s. It was during this time that many of the innovations in multi-unit and multi-family housing occurred in Manhattan.

### OVERCROWDING

The first purpose-built tenement buildings were little more than simple, four- or five-storey "boxes" that provided only the bare minimum of residential necessities. They quickly became overloaded

*Left: The Tenement Museum provides a rare glimpse into the living conditions of Manhattan's poor during the 19th century.*

with people, sometimes covering 90 per cent of the lot with perhaps 18 rooms per floor. Only the front and back of these units might enjoy some access to fresh air and light, unless other tenements were built close by along adjoining alleys. Families were fortunate if they had one or two rooms to themselves. Cellars were typically relegated for cooking and cleaning functions, but remained dark and damp. These filthy spaces soon became incubators for health concerns such as tuberculosis and high infant mortality. By 1865 New York alone had more than 15,000 tenement buildings to house increasing throngs of the urban poor. With the Civil War underway, prominent citizens such as journalist and author Walt Whitman, for one, expressed their outrage at worsening living conditions. Housing reformers made it increasingly clear that overcrowded tenements would continue to serve as breeding grounds for disease, crime and prostitution.

### TENEMENT HOUSE LAWS

Although slow to appear, political pressure eventually forced improvements to urban housing. The landmark Tenement House Act of 1867 mandated certain requirements of builders, including fire escapes and a maximum of 20 people per water closet. Although difficult to enforce, certain builders did attempt to provide improved dwellings, including Alfred White, who envisioned the construction of model tenements with improved lighting and sanitary conditions. His prototype dwelling in Brooklyn was built in 1877, soon followed by other similar projects. Historians have described these early efforts as the first in America to create

*Above: One or two rooms provided residents with their entire living space, in which they ate, slept and socialized.*

decent public housing. A competition in 1878 resulted in the design of the so-called "dumb bell" apartment, resembling a weightlifter's dumb bell when viewed from above. Among other improvements, both sides of the building were indented to allow air and light into the sides of the structure. Although far from perfect, this latest plan was built into the Tenement House Law of 1879. The boom years of the 1880s led to the construction of thousands of dumb bell tenement buildings.

### A TIME MACHINE

The modest tenement at 97 Orchard Street, now housing a Tenement Museum, is a rare surviving example of a Civil-War era dwelling. Erected in 1863–64, it exemplifies the first wave of tenement construction in Manhattan. The scale of the immigration phenomenon in this neighbourhood far outweighed that of other American cities. This tenement, therefore, represents the critical transition stage during which newly-arrived immigrants from Europe who had little choice of accommodation used such tenement housing as a hopeful stepping stone to future

business or home ownership. The tenement's surrounding neighbourhood still retains a high degree of integrity from its peak period of immigration. The building provides a vivid sense of the deplorable living conditions experienced during the mid-to-late 19th century. It is estimated that, during its 72-year tenure as housing, the total number of tenants in this building alone could have been close to 10,000, including 7,000 working-class immigrants. The tenement still exhibits the unhealthy, overcrowded quarters

prevalent throughout the area that ultimately led to the housing reform movement and the successive legislation passed to improve living conditions.

The tenement at 97 Orchard Street is a five-storey, raised-basement structure typical of those erected on the Lower East Side during the 1860s. The facade is faced with red brick and designed in a simple Italianate style. For decades the two lower floors served as commercial space, but the top floors were sealed from the mid-1930s until 1988. At that point the building was discovered by the Lower East Side Tenement Museum with its rooms, wallpaper, plumbing and lighting all preserved as they had been left six decades earlier. In this respect the tenement became a sort of urban time machine. Just as the Lower East Side had witnessed the dreams of thousands of immigrants seeking a better life, this tenement was to enable yet another. Historian and social activist Ruth Abram envisioned a museum that would honour American immigrants. After a search for a suitable tenement, she stumbled across this one in 1988.

*Below: The airshaft of a dumb bell tenement improved living conditions.*

# MEMORIAL HALL
## PHILADELPHIA, PENNSYLVANIA

Memorial Hall in West Fairmount Park is the only surviving large building that remains to remind us of the 1876 Centennial Exhibition. Though recovering emotionally and economically from the Civil War and the assassination of President Lincoln, America turned to optimism, self-pride and confidence for its 100th year. The official national celebration took the form of America's first World's Fair between May and November 1876.

### THE 1876 EXHIBITION
Known as the Philadelphia Centennial Exhibition, the unprecedented event accommodated 10 million people, each paying an entrance fee of 50 cents to experience 182ha/450 acres of exhibits. Its official name was the International Exhibition of Arts, Manufactures and Products of the Soil and Mine. The event was held in Philadelphia's Fairmount Park along the Schuylkill River, recognizing the city where the Declaration of Independence had been signed a century earlier. Every state of the Union enjoyed a building of its own, contributing to a total of 180 exhibition structures disbursed around the grounds. Truly making this a World's Fair were between 25 and 50 exhibits sent by foreign nations. This one set the precedent for numerous fairs to follow.

Other buildings were designed specifically to house advances in machinery, agriculture and science. Apparently the most popular attraction was Machinery Hall, where an array of machines and gadgets essentially ushered in America's age of technology. The hall's most popular attraction, however, consisted of the massive 1,500 horsepower Corliss steam engine, the world's most powerful machine at the time. A new typewriter was displayed nearby, at which its attendant could write a letter home for visitors willing to pay 50 cents. Housewives were introduced in another building to a new flooring

*Below: The Fairmount Park Commission controlled Memorial Hall after 1958. The wings of the building housed a gymnasium and a swimming pool. At one time the structure served as a police station.*

marvel called linoleum, and a telephone on display was one of only 3,000 in existence. Visitors remained frightened by the Otis elevator, not yet convinced its successors would soon be in everyday use in innovative tall buildings never seen before.

### ART MUSEUM
Memorial Hall played its own grand role, housing the exhibition's art collection. Designed by Hermann Schwarzmann in the Beaux-Arts, or Renaissance Revival style, the monumental structure is composed of brick, glass, iron and granite. No wood was used in its construction, to help prevent fire. The main entrance opens into a grand hall. Its most distinctive feature is its iron and glass dome, adorned at the top with a statue of Columbia. Additional figures that symbolize and celebrate industry and commerce are found at the ends of the main facade. The entire hall was America's first Beaux-Arts-style art museum and served as the inspiration for many to follow. The grandiose combination of a symmetrical facade with centre and corner pavilions, triple portals, coupled columns, niches and statues, and sometimes a central dome, all signified "art museum" to Americans for decades following Memorial Hall's construction.

Following the exhibition, Memorial Hall reopened in 1877 as the Pennsylvania Museum of the School of Industrial Art. It also became the home of the Philadelphia Museum of Art, which remained there until 1929. Like many grand, 19th-century buildings deemed obsolete after World War II, it fell into disrepair until the Historic Preservation Movement offered it new life. In 2005 the Please Touch Museum invested US $85 million to renovate the Hall and convert it into the museum's new home.

# ALLEGHENY COUNTY COURTHOUSE
## PITTSBURGH, PENNSYLVANIA

The term "Victorian" is commonly discussed as an architectural style. Technically, the Victorian era comprised the years of Queen Victoria of England's reign between 1837 and 1901. More than a dozen specific styles have been identified as Victorian, typically succeeding and overlapping one another.

One Victorian-era style considered to be truly American, however, is that of the Romanesque Revival. With its typically thick, masonry, round-arch construction, the style is often referred to as Richardsonian Romanesque in honour of its founding Boston architect and promoter, Henry Hobson Richardson (1838–86). His creative, individual interpretation of earlier Roman architecture was considered to be the first indigenous American architectural style to be taken seriously in Europe. Richardson took his cues from the original Romanesque architecture that dominated Catholic Europe prior

*Below: The courthouse served as a model for more modest courthouses and similar civic buildings across the country.*

to AD1200. Richardson's Allegheny County Courthouse and Jail in Pittsburgh was to be his final masterpiece. This and other prominent Richardsonian buildings spawned a national following that produced Romanesque churches, civic buildings, railroad stations and elite residences up to the end of the 19th century.

### A ROMANESQUE SKIN

Construction of the imposing Allegheny County Courthouse and Jail began in 1884 and rose five storeys high, with a large tower that added another five storeys above the main entrance. Massive Syrian arches dominate the two main entrances leading to the interior courtyard, an early Christian form of archway often used by Richardson, rooted to the ground level rather than from supporting pedestals. Much of the style and detail of the attached Courthouse and Jail exhibit southern French and Spanish Romanesque features. The New York State House at Albany provided the model for the structures' general form, which is considered to be early French Renaissance. "It is as if a Romanesque skin had been pulled over the Renaissance body," wrote James Van

*Above: Richardson created his own architectural style, Richardson Romanesque – a quintessentially American style.*

Trump in the mid-20th century. The ensemble involves a combination of Syrian arches, French Gothic dormers, Byzantine capitals and a tower that is Spanish in derivation. The structure has been described as an elongated version of Boston's Trinity Church, which is not surprising given that both shared the same architect.

Richardson agreed with numerous contemporaries who considered the Allegheny Courthouse and Jail and his Marshall Field Wholesale Store in Chicago as the two most prominent works of his rather short, professional career. Suffering from ill health at a relatively young age, Richardson died in 1886 at the height of his own career and his style's popularity throughout the nation. In his last years he wrote, "Let me have time to finish Pittsburgh and I should be content without another day." With the eventual demolition of the store, the Allegheny Courthouse and Jail along with Boston's Trinity Church now remain as the dominant prototype examples of the Richardson style.

# GRAND CENTRAL TERMINAL
## NEW YORK, NEW YORK

The story of this magnificent Beaux-Arts-style railroad terminal embodies the development of New York City. Since the 1830s New York's Manhattan Island had been connected by railroad to the mainland by three separate companies. Typical of the early days of railroad construction, when cities were learning how to accommodate this new transportation mode, the tracks of the various companies literally ran right down the streets to their respective depots. The surface railroads only contributed to the increasing street-level congestion and hazards. Grade-level crossings proved dangerous to pedestrians and horse-drawn traffic, not to mention the noise and filth of steam trains negotiating busy city streets.

Property values generally declined along railroad rights-of-way. For these reasons the city later banned all steam locomotives everywhere south of 42nd Street. For a while the railroad companies detached the trains there and used horses to carry the trains into their terminals. Eventually, the companies retreated and moved their terminals to the north to avoid all of these factors.

### GRAND CENTRAL DEPOT
With peace after the Civil War, prosperity returned and business boomed. Having recently gained financial control of all Manhattan-bound railroad

companies, Cornelius Vanderbilt decided to build a Grand Central Depot to consolidate the railroad termini within one location. Built on the current site of the existing Grand Central Terminal, his station was completed by 1871 and served as the central passenger railroad hub for all Manhattan. This was no small undertaking, as his depot became the largest in the world at the time and featured a large glass and steel train shed 33m/100ft high and 66m/200ft wide. All the same, continued growth in New York City rendered this "little" depot obsolete by the end of the century. Added to that was a devastating accident in 1902 caused by obscured vision from locomotive smoke. The result was a new state law banning all steam engines from Manhattan by 1910. The age of electricity had arrived, and would soon power trains through the city.

Following the accident, the New York Central Railroad proposed a new and larger railroad station. The company's urgency was heightened with the knowledge of new competition from the expanding New York subway system and knowledge of the new Pennsylvania railroad building.

*Left: The Grand Central Terminal, in 1895. It was demolished to make way for the new terminal building.*

*Above: The expansive train shed for Grand Central Terminal, built in the tradition of great European train sheds.*

### A MONUMENTAL CHALLENGE
William K. Vanderbilt II, the son of Cornelius, chose the architects for the new Grand Central facility based on a competition held in 1903. The New York Central station would be magnificent in its own right. Most important, it would be designed to accommodate the new technology of electrified railroads while meeting the growing transportation needs of the nation's largest metropolis.

The plan for Grand Central Terminal included a complete submergence of tracks from 97th Street south, two levels of tracks for commuters and long-distance trains, ramps for passengers instead of stairs, and the development of Park Avenue with easy passenger access to it. As built, the terminal has two submerged levels, with the upper level including 31 tracks and the lower level with 26 tracks.

As a monument to industrialization and corporate power, the terminal above ground is massive, with dimensions 205m/673ft long and 92m/301ft wide and seven storeys high. Three large, arched windows dominate the 42nd Street entrance, flanked by

## PENNSYLVANIA STATION

Designed and built between 1902 and 1911, the Beaux-Arts Pennsylvania Station became the world's largest building since the Egyptian pyramids. However, it succumbed to demolition in 1964. Its destruction led to international outrage, as the *New York Times* said, "Until the first blow fell, no one was convinced that Penn Station really would be demolished, or that New York would permit this monumental act of vandalism against one of the largest and finest landmarks of its age of Roman elegance." The loss served as a catalyst for New York City's first historic preservation statutes – laws that directly led to the authority to save Grand Central.

massive Corinthian columns in the Beaux-Arts tradition. Construction required a decade, from 1903 to 1913. This was more impressive due to the necessity of maintaining full services throughout the construction period.

### A CITY WITHIN A CITY

The railroad station was actually one part of a much larger development project. Known as "terminal city", the project included a complex with office buildings and apartments, effectively becoming a "city within a city". The monumental scale of the development necessitated the destruction of earlier urban fabric. Between 42nd and 50th Street, 180 buildings – including hospitals and churches – were destroyed. The complex's final version, nonetheless, eventually made Park Avenue one of America's most elegant boulevards. A new hotel district emerged, along with a dense concentration of new office towers around the terminal, including the Chrysler Building. By 1947 the neighbourhood was prospering, and more than 65 million people travelled through the terminal annually.

### PRESERVING AN ICON

The terminal's most recent half century has been marked by decline and renewal. Long-distance rail travel was in

*Above: The main concourse of Grand Central became Manhattan's gateway to the city during America's prime railroad era.*

steep decline by the 1960s as more Americans took to the air and freeways. Manhattan property values continued to climb, encouraging the New York Central to talk about demolition. However, in 1967 New York's Landmarks Preservation Commission interrupted the plans for demolition. Now considered one of the most significant legal battles to date in the American historic preservation movement, the fight continued when the Penn Central (successor to the New

*Below: The new terminal in 1919, which saw more than 60 million people move through the facility annually by the 1940s.*

York Central) filed an US $8 million lawsuit against the City of New York. After a ten-year battle that went all the way to the Supreme Court, the conclusion was to favour the preservationists.

More recently, Grand Central has undergone a redevelopment, taken over by the Metropolitan Transportation Authority (MTA), which has invested in extensive renovations. The terminal illustrates how an impressive historic structure has been restored and now plays a role in the new urban economy.

*Below: The Park Avenue entrance in 1947, showcasing a grand Beaux-Arts architectural masterpiece.*

# METROPOLITAN MUSEUM OF ART
## NEW YORK, NEW YORK

The final decades of the 19th century are often described as the American Renaissance, describing an unprecedented burst of interest in the arts, education and sciences. Numerous institutions were founded, including art societies, the American School of Classical Studies in Rome and new architectural departments at prominent universities. Museums proliferated across the country, all housed within Greek and Roman forms of Beaux-Arts Classicism. Their temple fronts and columned facades represented America's budding architecture, culture and taste.

America's cultural elite certainly celebrated with the incorporation of three major art museums in the United States during 1870. These included the Boston Museum of Fine Arts, the Corcoran Gallery in Washington, DC, and the Metropolitan Museum in New York

City. The latter museum, known today as the Met, was founded by a group of American businessmen, financiers, and leading artists and thinkers who sought to bring important works of art to the American people. It was to become a world-renowned facility, both for its art collection and for the imposing Beaux-Arts architecture that houses it.

### A WINDOW ON CENTRAL PARK
The extensive building that now dominates the east side of Central Park began more humbly. The Museum moved to its current site in 1880, its original Victorian Gothic structure designed by Calvert Vaux and Jacob Wrey Mould. The fledgling Museum

*Below: A monument to Beaux-Arts Classicism, the present facade and entrance structure were completed in 1926.*

expanded rapidly with the acquisition of further collections, necessitating more exhibition and storage space. Two building additions ensued, an 1888 south wing also facing the park, and a similar north wing in 1894. The architecture of both wings abandoned the original Gothic mode, and the main door to the expanded Mmuseum was changed from the west to the south side.

There had always been an intention to integrate the Museum with Central Park. The reasoning for this was practical, in part, to facilitate future expansions and to reduce the threat of fire from adjoining structures. In addition, Central Park's designer and commissioner Frederick Law Olmsted was a Museum trustee. He claimed the park would refresh "the lagging spirit and the pallid complexion" through contact with both the beauty of nature and the Museum

*Above: The newly remodelled American wing was finished in 2009.*

*Above: The Neo-classical Great Hall deliberately obscured the original brick structure and created one of the most grand interiors in New York City – "a stately bride arrayed in spotless white stands the beautiful new hall", as one newspaper reporter wrote.*

to "uplift" the eye through the contemplation of beauty made by man in both the exhibits and the building.

Renowned architect Richard Morris Hunt was hired in 1885 to develop a master plan for future expansion. It is Hunt's work that fundamentally changed the Museum's architectural style and access to Central Park. Later described as imperial by historians, his architectural scheme paralleled his highly successful Neo-classical-style Administration Building at the 1893 Chicago Columbian Exposition. His impressive, although impractical master plan called for a focus on large, open courts. His master plan encapsulated the original building and its successive additions in a new Roman temple. It consisted of a main hall with wings on each side. The wings would extend more than 457m/1,500ft along Fifth Avenue. Additional wings, joined by colonnades and pavilions, would stretch to the edge of Central Park's East Drive.

Although monumental in plan – Hunt had envisioned this as his life's work – it proved impractical. He never specified exactly how the 7ha/18 acre palace of pure white marble was to be paid for, maintained, serviced, cleaned, guarded and filled with art objects. Ultimately, the Great Hall was the only part of Hunt's plan to be completed, however, future additions would add to its intended monumentality. At the same time, the Museum instantly became oriented to the Avenue rather than the Park, and the Park aspect and entrance were thereafter abandoned. Hunt died prior to the Great Hall's completion, leaving behind only sketchy designs of the exterior plan. His son, Richard Howland Hunt, oversaw the construction and design of the interior.

Following the opening of Hunt's Great Hall in 1902, the building committee hired the architectural firm of McKim, Mead & White to prepare a new master design to complete the building. Similar to Hunt's plan, the firm proposed a symmetrical rectangular structure with a formal entrance from the Park, a grandiose Fifth Avenue facade, and a series of large open courts within the Museum. Galleries opened one by one between 1910 and 1926 as additions were completed, including the

J. P. Morgan collection of decorative arts, the great Egyptian collection, and the Greek and Roman works. All but the Morgan wing were built along Fifth Avenue in the Italian Renaissance style, which blended with Hunt's Neo-classical exterior of the Great Hall.

### THE MODERN ERA

The next master plan was devised between 1940 and 1943 and reflected America's shift away from historical architecture in favour of functional modernism. The Museum's fifth director, Francis Henry Taylor, hired architect Robert B. O'Connor to collaborate with the Parks Department. Indicative of the times, the architects sought solutions to modern problems as opposed to creating monumental architecture for its own sake. Their concerns focused on how to logically organize the collections, and provide adequate storage space, offices, seminar rooms and libraries.

In its fourth and most recent phase of expansion, a comprehensive architectural plan was approved in 1971 and completed two decades later. The Museum has now grown to occupy more than 20 times the space of the original 1880 building. Following a full century of expansions to its impressive facility, today the Museum boasts of a permanent collection with more than two million works of art from around the world. Both its imposing architecture and the quality of its collections contribute to its continued prestige.

# NEW YORK STOCK EXCHANGE
## NEW YORK, NEW YORK

For more than two centuries the New York Stock Exchange (NYSE) has played a central role in American capitalism and economic development. Formed in the 1790s to handle the first issues of government securities, the Exchange has since become the largest in the world as measured by dollar volume. It became the nation's primary securities market by the early 19th century, mirroring the growth of New York City. As the Exchange continued to grow in size and prestige, economic historian Robert Sobel claimed, "Among other things, it is the centrepiece for that great symbol Wall Street", which, until the Great Depression, "was the power centre for the land".

### ADAPTING TO CHANGE
Since 1865 the Exchange has occupied all or part of its current site, with the exception of 1901–3 during construction of its new facility. Three main buildings comprise the facility: 18 Broad Street (1903), 11 Wall Street (1922) and 20 Broad Street (1954). Only the first two structures are included within the landmark designation, given that the Exchange was leasing the 20 Broad Street building to others at the time of its nomination for landmark status.

The most notable and symbolic of the Exchange buildings is the imposing 1903 Neo-classical-style building, exemplifying America's revived interest at the time for Greek and Roman architec-

*Above: Symbolic of democracy and freedom, Neo-classical architecture was used for the facade of the Exchange building.*

tural forms. Designed by George R. Post and designed with striking exterior sculpture by John Q. A. Ward, the structure rises ten storeys, or 48m/156ft, above the pavement. Its primary facade consists of a podium for a colonnade of six massive, fluted Corinthian columns that support an elaborate, triangular pediment. This latter feature consists of

*Below: Exquisite Greek and Roman architectural forms and sculpture adorn the pediment of the main building.*

11 figures that range from 1.5–5m/ 5–16ft tall and symbolize aspects of American commerce and industry.

The younger of the two historic structures is an adjoining 23-storey, marble-faced building erected in 1922 at 11 Wall Street. It holds a portion of the trading floor and remains in good condition. It represents a conscientious effort to complement the 1903 structure. Both of the historic Exchange buildings are constructed with white Georgia marble. Additional trading floor space was added in 1969 and 1988 (the "blue room") with updated technology for electronic trading and communication. Another trading floor was opened at 30 Broad Street in 2000. Continued advances in global telecommunications led to the arrival of the hybrid market, allowing a greater proportion of trading to occur electronically. Consequently, the trading room at 30 Broad Street was closed in 2006, and in 2007 the trade rooms created through the 1969 and 1988 expansions were closed as well. As of 24 January 2007, all NYSE stocks are traded through the hybrid market.

# FLATIRON BUILDING
## NEW YORK, NEW YORK

Described by H. G. Wells in 1906 as a sailing ship, "ploughing up through the traffic of Broadway and Fifth Avenue", the Flatiron (Fuller) Building is New York City's oldest surviving skyscraper. Its distinctive triangular shape viewed from above is like a flatiron. The irregular lot on which it stands is formed by the convergence of Fifth Avenue and Broadway. Fifth Avenue was part of Manhattan's rectilinear street grid system, while Broadway was widened from an older road that cut diagonally across the island, leading to an array of irregular lot shapes. Completed in 1902, the Flatiron rises 21 storeys to a height of 87m/285ft. With its then-innovative steel-frame skeleton hidden from view, the building's exterior is sheathed in limestone and brick with terracotta ornamentation covering the structure's "skin". For ten years it remained the world's tallest building – a surprise to sceptical New Yorkers who worried its internal steel frame would collapse.

### CHICAGO INFLUENCE
The Flatiron's architect and designer was Daniel H. Burnham, commissioned by George Fuller to build an office tower for his construction company. Burnham had advanced the construction of taller buildings in Chicago with steel frames as an improvement over the heavy load-bearing walls of the past. The Flatiron symbolized the energy, optimism and imagination of architects and industrial corporations that were re-shaping American cities during the early 20th century. Burnham adopted two fundamental design approaches. The first was the steel frame construction method. The second consisted of an innovative design strategy developed by Louis Sullivan during the previous decade. Tall buildings were designed in three distinct sections consisting of a ground-level base for shops, an uninterrupted mid-

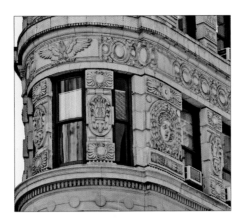

section and an ornamental cap, or cornice. The combination of steel frame skeleton and external, tripartite design was emulated throughout American cities during the early 20th century.

It was the Flatiron's architectural styling that deviated from Louis Sullivan's emphasis on modern design. Burnham championed the use of historicism. As director of Chicago's 1893 Columbian Exposition, or World's Fair, he assembled a prominent group of architects to design the Fair's main buildings. They agreed on a unity of expression to provide consistent design throughout the grounds, and the Classical (Greek) style was the theme chosen.

### BEAUX-ARTS STYLE
The Chicago fair inspired the emulation of Greek Revival architecture for decades to follow, dubbed the Beaux-Arts style. The Flatiron prominently displays the Classical design of the Beaux-Arts style. Competition between two prominent architectural philosophies ensued throughout the early 20th century. Modernist architects following Sullivan's lead preferred to discover new national styles that did not depend on historical revivals. The Craftsman style from the Arts and Crafts movement,

*Right: The Flatiron adopted the popular "tripartite" plan for organizing the vertical design of the building.*

*Left: Early 20th century skyscrapers often had exquisite exterior detailing.*

Frank Lloyd Wright's Prairie style, the machine-age Art Deco and Art Moderne styles, and the International style represented successive Modernist architecture that pointed to the future rather than the past. Simultaneous to the rise of Modernism, however, was America's continued adoration of the historical, looking to the Italian Renaissance, Classical, and related Beaux-Arts styles for inspiration up through World War II. The Flatiron Building grandly represents this latter approach.

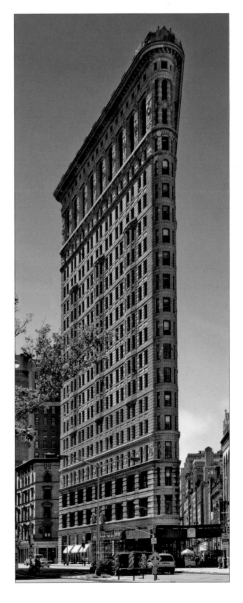

# EQUITABLE BUILDING
## NEW YORK, NEW YORK

Ernest R. Graham designed this little-altered, 40-storey, steel and masonry office structure on the site of Equitable's first home office, which was built in 1870 and destroyed by fire in 1912. The building is still indicative of the powerful position the firm attained in the insurance industry by the early 20th century. The east-west oriented office tower rises to 166m/545ft, filling the entire lot between Broadway, Cedar, Pine and Nassau streets in the heart of Manhattan. Prior to its existence, the Equitable Life Assurance Society and its founder, Henry Baldwin Hyde, played a fundamental role in initiating the country's budding life insurance industry and its tremendous growth following the Civil War. By 1886 Equitable had become the largest life insurance company in the world, and its ambitious global aspirations placed agents in nearly 100 countries.

Now dwarfed by taller skyscrapers around it, the still monumental Equitable Building is instructive on two counts: for understanding the skyscraper's early development, and as the impetus for the nation's zoning laws.

*Below: The Old Equitable Building is pictured near to Trinity Church, which was the tallest building in the area when it was built in 1846.*

*Above: The Equitable Building with shadows cast by surrounding skyscrapers, illustrating the need for zoning laws.*

### ARCHITECTURE

For the architect's part, Graham was employed by the firm of Daniel H. Burnham and Company, the world's largest architectural firm. By the time Burnham's firm became involved with New York's Equitable Building in 1914, the steel frame had already been employed outside of Chicago. Burnham had intended to design a 62-storey tower on the Equitable site in 1906, until the project got delayed. The architects provided a design typical of the Chicago School of Architecture.

Compared to eventual New York skyscrapers that would emphasize height through slender towers, Chicago architects had focused on uniform, hollow blocks, either square or U-shaped, with a continuous cornice across the top. In typical Burnham fashion, the Equitable's exterior style combines elements of the Renaissance Revival and Neo-classical styles, including a grand arched entry and Corinthian pilasters that support a one-storey-high Classical entablature. Shaped like an "H", as seen from the air, the facade extends straight up from the ground for its entire height.

## ZONING LAWS

Just as the Equitable Building encapsulates the advances of early Chicago skyscraper design, a popular movement in New York made sure it would be the last. Its prominent position in the heart of Manhattan caused outrage as the building cast a 2.8ha/7 acre-shadow over surrounding streets. The building prevented an adequate amount of light and air from reaching the streets below, and future predictions of urban "canyons" were scary. The initial concern regarding tall buildings emerged around the 1880s, resulting in a new set of height restrictions on residential buildings through the Tenement Housing Act of 1901.

With the completion of the Equitable Building in 1915 came the realization that all types of structures required some control. Rapidly expanding businesses requiring more space, rising property values that encouraged building upward and recent engineering successes allowing for steel-frame construction as well as reliable elevators all contributed to the increased interest in skyscrapers. The result was the groundbreaking Zoning Resolution of 1916. The document established a set of height and setback controls that provided for exclusive residential districts that excluded "incompatible" uses such

as industry and commerce. By the 1920s and 1930s New York's smaller buildings and iconic skyscrapers such as the Chrysler and Empire State buildings had conformed to the 1916 law, purposely incorporating periodic setbacks with height.

The implications of developing landuse zoning laws have been far-reaching. New York's space issues were not unique, leading other cities to readily adopt variations of the new zoning law. Legitimized by the Supreme Court in 1926, zoning practices soon became a fundamental aspect of urban planning. Designers of skyscrapers for the next several decades developed strategies to place more slender towers at the centre of city blocks, surrounded by pedestrian plazas or parking. Office districts through the 1980s came to be dominated with International-style steel and glass slabs that were purposely isolated and set back from surrounding city streets. While allowing for improved air and light at the ground level, traditional urban street life suffered greatly.

With time, the rationale for zoning expanded and fundamentally guided the spatial layouts of residential suburbs. Zoning had initially been justified to prevent residential overcrowding and protect people from potentially unhealthy industrial land uses. Soon the use of

zoning expanded to purposely direct where growth and development would occur. Since the 1960s critics have pointed to zoning's role in isolating neighbourhoods by economic class and ethnicity. More recent environmental and social concerns have arisen over the dependence on cars and huge freeways to practically link residential with commercial and civic areas.

Zoning is now viewed by many as the primary culprit in encouraging America's unsustainable, sprawling suburbs. Under the recent tenets of the New Urbanism, cities since the 1990s have variously revised their restrictive zoning codes to encourage urban density and mixed uses. Since the rise of the Equitable Building, then, city leaders and urban planners have sought ways to retain the clear benefits of land-use zoning while mitigating its numerous unintended consequences. This revisionary process is certainly not complete with respect to zoning and urban development in America.

*Below: New York City was the first to implement strict zoning regulations, to protect the city streets and its residents, leading to the famous building set-backs that define Manhattan's skyline.*

# CHRYSLER BUILDING
## NEW YORK, NEW YORK

The roaring twenties was a time of rampant optimism for many Americans. Although not everyone shared in the burgeoning wealth of the continuing Industrial Revolution, those who did were looking to the future. The "machine age" was upon America and newer consumption patterns led to the mass production of countless household and industrial gadgets and tools, from

*Below: Seven setbacks support a stainless steel spire on the famous Chrysler Building.*

toasters and sewing machines to streamlined railroad trains and shiny automobiles. Architects embraced this celebration of industrialism and the flowering of the so-called Modern Movement. In the 1920s the evolution of the skyscraper was at a point where structural steel and reliable elevators allowed for building heights never envisioned before. Within the context of optimism, corporate competition and image-making came the design of the Chrysler Building in New York City.

### ART DECO

Still considered one of New York's most stylish office towers, the Chrysler Building was designed to portray Art Deco architecture at its finest. In her book *Skyscrapers* Judith Dupre described the Chrysler as the "prima donna of all skyscrapers – the extravagantly topped Chrysler Building – remains the belle of New York's skyline". The structure epitomizes the height (literally and figuratively) of the Art Deco style, an abbreviation of the Exposition Internationale des Arts Decoratifs et Industriels Modernes – the full name of the 1925 fair in Paris where the style was first promoted. The style consciously strove to signify modernity through an artistic expression that complimented the machine age. Promotional literature for the Exposition clarified that "reproductions, imitations, and counterfeits of ancient styles will be strictly prohibited".

As applied to commercial and residential buildings alike in the United States, Art Deco found its expression primarily in the forms of simple and repetitive geometric designs such as chevrons, zigzags and floral or fountain imagery. Facades typically employed combinations of smooth-faced stone or metal sheathing with accents in terracotta and coloured glass. The style became popular throughout the United States by the late 1920s and survived into the 1940s. Concentrations of the style were predominantly found in metropolitan areas or districts, including New York City, Los Angeles and Miami Beach.

### CORPORATE COMPETITION

Construction on the Chrysler Building began in heady economic times in 1928 and finished during the Great Depression in 1930. For 11 months it was officially the tallest building in the world, until the soon-completed Empire State Building

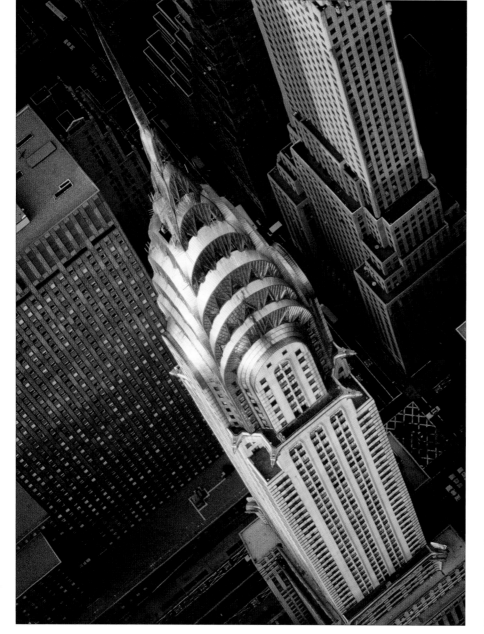

usurped that honour. This was a time when corporations competed intensely for the status attributed to owning the tallest skyscraper. Still true today, corporate owners view the image that their tall buildings present to the world as providing a distinct reflection of themselves and their companies.

The Chrysler Building was designed by architect William Van Alen for Walter P. Chrysler, founder of the Chrysler Corporation. The architect portrayed his masterpiece as a monument saying "the Chrysler Building is dedicated to world commerce and industry". The creation of this remarkable building required imagination. The development of the idea in tangible form has given New York City a most spectacular monument. Seen from many viewpoints for miles around by night or day, the Chrysler Building stands out among its fellows as a towering and glittering shaft. It rose above the street higher than any other structure ever built, up until that time creating interest and wonder. It is 319m/1,046ft from street level to the top of the pinnacle, with 77 storeys.

Van Alen's final design for the tower was dramatic enough to prompt the critic Kenneth Murchinson to dub the architect the "Ziegfield of his profession". The building's Art Deco styling was a direct reference to Chrysler automobiles, especially the building's innovative spire with its series of sunbursts. The setbacks of the building mass are adorned with the imagery of winged radiator caps, wheels and automobiles.

### THE HISTORICAL RECORD

Given the status of the building and its creators, it is surprising that little evidence was saved to document its construction or design. Neither Chrysler nor Van Alen compiled the Building's historical materials for future study.

*Right: Corporations like Chrysler used their early skyscrapers as signatures to distinguish themselves and to demonstrate prosperity through interior decor.*

*Above: The Chrysler Building was designed to celebrate the automobile and, more generally, the age of technology and machines.*

In 1979 photographer David Stravitz was introduced to an elderly colleague preparing to close his shop. Stravitz visited the shop with the intent of possibly purchasing some used equipment. He then happened upon the "treasure of a lifetime", as Stravitz himself described it. "Tucked away in the corner of the studio, almost entirely in shadow, were stacks of boxes about as high as my knee. 'What's in those boxes?' I asked my host. He replied, '…just a bunch of old 8 by 10 negatives that I'm going to

*Above: The ornamental gargoyles are modelled after the hood ornaments of the 1929 Chrysler Plymouth car.*

convert to silver in about a week'. …I couldn't believe my eyes. There, unfolding before me, were the streets of New York in the late 1920s and 1930s: the buildings, businesses, theatres, and restaurants; the advertising signage; the skyline; the people; the hustle and bustle of New York City, recorded and preserved in minute detail." There were more than 500 negatives in all. Stravitz later learned that more than 150 of the negatives he had purchased documented the day-by-day construction of the Chrysler Building.

# EMPIRE STATE BUILDING
## NEW YORK, NEW YORK

As the winning entrant in the world's tallest building contest in the 1920s, the Empire State Building ushered in one of America's most dominant eras in architectural history. The influential European Modern Movement had already attracted the attention of American architects by the 1920s, but its proliferation on this side of the Atlantic was cut short by the prolonged Great Depression and ensuing World War.

Returning economic growth in the 1950s finally allowed American Modernism, known as International style, to flourish. Prior to the construction-halting Depression, several monumental skyscrapers displaying early International architecture had been completed or were nearing completion. The Empire State Building, which rises 381m/1,250ft with its 102 storeys and two basement levels gained the most attention. When completed in April 1931 the tower was billed as the Eighth Wonder of the World and broke numerous records for its structural and mechanical engineering. It remained the

*Below: Due to cheap labour and the efficient use of materials, the building's construction cost fell US $8 million below the estimated US $50 million.*

tallest building in the world for more than four decades, until the completion of the World Trade Center in 1972.

**INTERNATIONAL STYLE**

International style was meant to became the anti-style, a style of architecture that did not allow for any revival of historical styles. It dominated commercial architecture from the 1950s to the 1970s. The Empire State Building, so named to represent the New York state nickname, became the most monumental example of the International style's first American decade.

International-style building exteriors portray one repetitive, harmonious facade from bottom to top. However, the Empire State Building represents a transition to International style, with its visual interest earned most acutely through its creative set-back design and "ziggurat" base. Although not as prominent as the shiny Chrysler Building, the Empire State Building incorporates some subtle Art Deco influences within its facade, especially noticeable on its massive crown.

The design of the world's largest speculative office tower was considered the finest work of architect William Lamb, who completed 15 initial designs before implementing the final plan.

Two weeks following the project's announcement, the stock market crashed. The financial backing came from a self-made multi-millionaire, John J. Raskob, who along with Pierre Du Pont invested wisely in General Motors stock. Just as railroad corporations had enabled the wealth to construct the magnificent Newport summer "cottages" during the 19th century, the automobile industry provided the mechanism for wealth creation that led to world-class monuments of the early automobile era, expressed through new skyscrapers such as the Chrysler and Empire State buildings.

# ROCKEFELLER CENTER
## NEW YORK, NEW YORK

Rockefeller Center is described as a city within a city. Considered one of the most successful urban planning projects in the history of American architecture, this was the only large, privately funded building project undertaken during the Depression. The Center represents the integration of skyscraper design before World War II with comprehensive urban planning. The immense construction project generated thousands of jobs during the most desperate economic times. Although most construction across the nation was halted following the stock market crash in 1929, construction on Rockefeller Center began in 1931 and ended with the completion of its 14th building in 1939.

The original three-block site was later enlarged with the construction of the Esso Building constructed in 1946–47, and the purchase of the Sinclair Oil Building in 1950–52. The grand collection of structures remains a showcase for

*Below: The ice-skating rink in the sunken plaza has become a symbol of Manhattan, but it was not part of the initial plans.*

*Above: The Art-Deco RCA Building became the dominant feature of America's last planned development inspired by City Beautiful architectural unity.*

Art Deco and the related Art Mod-erne architectural styles, which celebrated the machine age and restored the image of New York as America's premier city.

In an historical twist, Rockefeller Center may not have existed were it not for the 1929 stock market crash. The site was initially designated during the late 1920s for a new Metropolitan Opera House. Unable to afford to move locations, the Metropolitan Opera pulled out of the project and a corporate centre was envisaged instead.

Rockefeller developed a subsequent plan for a corporate office complex to house the new radio and television corporations, and Radio City was born. Given Rockefeller's increasing role in the project, it was eventually given his name. Perhaps the best known buildings in the project consist of the Radio City

Music Hall (1935) and the RCA Building (now the GE Building), the 70-floor centrepiece of Rockefeller Center. By far the tallest building in the complex, the building initially served as the headquarters for the Radio Corporation of America and served as the basis for all future buildings of the complex. The Art-Deco style tower was designed by Raymond Hood (1881–1934), who led a large design team on the project. Hood studied at the Ecole des Beaux-Arts in Paris, which clearly influenced his work on Radio City. The RCA building is also known as "30 Rock" for its address at 30 Rockefeller Plaza.

### THE LAST UNIFIED PROJECT
Public and private uses were devised for the site. A network of pedestrian passageways was laid out below street level, connecting all parts of the complex. These were lined with small shops and restaurants, effectively creating all-weather streets connecting the office buildings with the subways. Lower still was another network of tunnels for truck deliveries and related traffic congestion, separating these activities from the city streets. One embellishment to the multi-level plan consisted of a sunken plaza at the foot of the RCA Building. This component failed initially due to the inability to retain important retail tenants. It remained a design problem until a desperate experiment converted the plaza into a successful ice-skating rink.

The Center represents one of the last major projects in America to incorporate a program of integrated public art. More than 100 pieces of original art are featured here, including the famous sculpture by Lee Lawrie that depicts Atlas supporting the earth. The Center's Beaux-Arts emphasis on public space was also the first and last to reveal a sense of architectural unity.

# CHAPTER THREE

# THE CHESAPEAKE

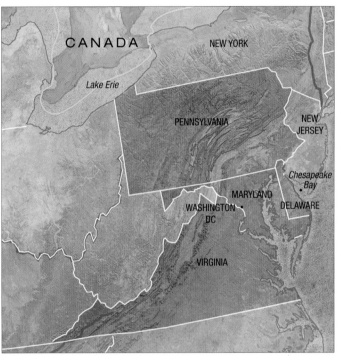

ALTHOUGH OFTEN GROUPED WITHIN THE LARGER MID-ATLANTIC CATEGORY, THE CHESAPEAKE IS INTERPRETED AS A DISTINCT REGION FOR PURPOSES OF THIS BOOK. AS ITS NAME SUGGESTS, THE REGION'S GEOGRAPHIC FOCUS IS THAT OF CHESAPEAKE BAY, AN ESTUARY OR DROWNED RIVER VALLEY OF THE SUSQUEHANNA RIVER. TODAY THE CHESAPEAKE ENCOMPASSES PARTS OF SIX STATES AND THE ENTIRE DISTRICT OF COLUMBIA. GOVERNMENT BUILDINGS AND DISTRICTS ASSOCIATED WITH THE SEAT OF FEDERAL POWER ARE THE FOCUS OF THIS CHAPTER, ALONG WITH EDUCATION ESTABLISHMENTS AND THE PLANTATION SYSTEM.

*Left: Mount Vernon, the ancestral home of George Washington, was saved from demolition.*

# COLONIAL ANNAPOLIS
## HISTORIC DISTRICT, ANNAPOLIS, MARYLAND

In 1649 the assembly of the Province of Maryland passed the Act Concerning Religion, more commonly referred to as the Maryland Toleration Act. The Act mandated tolerance for all Catholics and Protestants regardless of denomination. Taking advantage of this rare Colonial protection were 300 dissatisfied Puritans from Virginia.

The town's early street layout indicated a continuing loyalty to European central authority. Annapolis was planned as a rare example of a conscious attempt to replicate a European urban plan in North America. The town was laid out with a Baroque street plan of central circles and radiating streets. One of these hubs became the site of Maryland's capitol building. One can visit the historic district of Annapolis today to experience a watered-down version of Renaissance-era European town planning, clearly reflecting the origins of

*Below: Aside from Washington, DC, Annapolis is America's best example of European Baroque city planning, with its radial street plan.*

*Above: The permanent name of Annapolis was chosen to honour Princess Anne, the protestant daughter of James II and the future Queen Anne of England.*

those who settled there. Lining the modified Baroque street network is one of America's premier surviving collections of Georgian-style architecture, with approximately 120 surviving 18th-century buildings.

### BAROQUE PLANNING
Historically, the artistic period defined as Baroque emerged in Rome during the early 17th century and materialized in the built environment through prescribed urban layouts and architecture. Although the European Baroque city is often described through its distinctive architecture and monuments, the fundamental planning and organization of such places were important defining components. A Baroque-planned city was purposely organized to emphasize the political and economic hierarchy of European society. Perceived centres of power such as monuments, churches and royal palaces were purposely placed at the central nodes of a Baroque street plan, around which less prominent urban developments would occur.

Carefully planned avenues would radiate outward from these centres of power, creating monumental vistas along important urban axes.

### SLOW GROWTH
A relatively poor geographical situation prevented rapid commercial growth during Annapolis' early years. Its poor harbour facilities and location along a small river inlet contributed to its economic stagnation until tobacco-based prosperity came to the Chesapeake Bay region. The town served as Maryland's Colonial capital, however, which enabled its development into a regional centre of political power and cultural taste. By 1776 the place hosted 3,000 residents and 450 homes, predominantly built of long-lasting bricks.

Annapolis was economically bypassed with the emergence of a more competitive centre in Baltimore. It retained its status as state capital, however, and was infused with new life with the establishment of the United States Naval Academy in 1845. It was the slow, backwater growth of Annapolis over several centuries that actually discouraged rapid investment within its historic core, unwittingly preserving a huge collection of Colonial and early Federal structures.

# BACON'S CASTLE
## BACON'S CASTLE, VIRGINIA

One of only three Jacobean-styled buildings remaining in the western hemisphere, Bacon's Castle is an example of European Renaissance influences during the mid-17th century. Arthur Allen, a wealthy planter, built the home around 1665, employing small-scale elements of English Jacobean architecture, including a cruciform floor plan (on the original structure), curved Flemish parapets on the gables, brick construction in the English bond and towering triple chimneys. Its cruciform – or cross – plan is the earliest surviving example of this building tradition in America.

Historians tend to define English Jacobean architecture as the second or third phase of Renaissance-inspired design in England. The Jacobean style is named after King James I of England (or James VI of Scotland) and corresponds to the time of his reign. German and Flemish carvers influenced by

*Below: Bacon's Castle reveals two successive architectural styles: the original Jacobean structure and its later Federal-style addition (right).*

Italian Renaissance ideals and ornament are credited as taking the architectural style to England.

Around this time, wealthy English planters were spreading the northern European plantation model into the Americas and combined them with Renaissance-inspired Jacobean architecture on their plantations in such locations as Virginia and Barbados.

### BACON'S REBELLION

Allen's brick house became the unwitting participant in the so-called "Bacon's rebellion" in 1676. The house was seized and employed as a fort, or "castle", by the followers of Nathaniel Bacon –

*Left: Nathaniel Bacon led an uprising primarily due to the colonial governor's failure to protect the interior from Native American attacks.*

hence the name, Bacon's Castle. The home's new identity was not used until many years after the rebellion, however, and Bacon never resided there. Successive generations of owners have used the home as a private residence.

### PRESERVATION

In 1973 the property was purchased by the non-profit organization APVA Preservation Virginia, a leading promoter of historic preservation efforts in the state. Bacon's Castle has since been restored and is now open as an historic house museum. Numerous alterations were undertaken during the 19th century, including a two-storey Federal-style addition, which contrasts sharply with the original Jacobean structure. The relatively recent addition, although boldly inconsistent with the original structure, can be interpreted as historic in its own right.

*Below: The plantation economy brought wealth to the owners and Jacobean architecture to the American South, including the triple chimneys.*

# WILLIAMSBURG
## HISTORIC DISTRICT, WILLIAMSBURG, VIRGINIA

*Above: Williamsburg, including the Capitol (above), was the USA's first experiment in preserving a community as a museum.*

The city of Williamsburg is certainly best known as the site of Colonial Williamsburg and the adjacent College of William and Mary established in 1693 – the second oldest institution of higher learning in the United States.

The colonial city was the focus of one of the most ambitious historic preservation efforts of the early 20th century, under the auspices of John D. Rockefeller. As of 1975 approximately 100 Colonial-era structures had been restored, and 350 had been reconstructed on their original sites. Numerous buildings constructed after the Colonial era were actually removed in an attempt to create a more authentic Colonial reproduction of the place. Although regularly criticized by scholars for its contrived appearance and non-authentic recreations, the historic district serves today as a "living history museum", complete with historic interpreters and actors dressed in period costume. If one looks beyond the antiseptic, tree-lined, red-brick and wood-framed reconstructions, Colonial Williamsburg provides an educational treat that invites visitors to commune with the place that played a prominent role in the initial formation of the United States. Although early preservation efforts at Williamsburg remain variously controversial, it is still easy to visit these historic sites and imagine the time when the likes of Washington, Jefferson and Henry were contributing to the formation of the United States of America.

### GEORGIAN PRECEDENTS

Much of the architecture within the historic district – whether restored original buildings or newer replicas – provides a veritable clinic in the Renaissance-inspired Georgian style of architecture that dominated the English colonies along the Eastern Seaboard. Nearby at the College of William and Mary is the Wren Building, construction of which began in 1695. Scholars are still not certain if Sir Christopher Wren – one of England's greatest architects – actually designed the building. Along with the Governor's Palace in nearby Williamsburg, it nonetheless served as one of the earliest inspirations for the diffusion of English Georgian architecture in America, ushering the colonies out of their traditional Medieval building ways. Although quite visible today, both of these early Georgian-era structures were consumed by fire – numerous times in the case of the Wren Building. Both have been rebuilt or reconstructed in various guises but remain generally true to their original architectural styling.

### A POLITICAL HUB

The Colonial city's original history began with the construction of a palisaded barrier called Middle Plantation in 1633. Williamsburg assumed its current name in 1699 when it was designated the new capital of Colonial Virginia, moved there from Jamestown. Williamsburg remained the Colonial capital until 1780, after which the new Virginia state capital moved to Richmond, where Thomas Jefferson introduced the first Neo-classical public building in America. Williamsburg, the town's name, was chosen to honour William III, the king of England at the

*Below: The reconstructed Governor's Palace represents an attempt to replicate an historic structure with little information.*

*Above: Williamsburg played a pivotal role in the preservation movement in America, providing opportunities for reconstruction, rehabilitation and restoration.*

**A YOUNG WASHINGTON**

*Above: Recreated Colonial structures such as this cottage provide the setting for an outdoor museum at Williamsburg.*

time. During the 18th century Williamsburg grew in status as one of America's premier centres of refined culture and political ideology that deeply informed events of the American Revolution. The capital played host to numerous men – including Patrick Henry, George Washington, George Wythe, Thomas Jefferson and George Mason – who ultimately played leading revolutionary roles in the founding of the new nation. All of them either studied, taught or served in political office as members of the Virginia House of Burgesses.

*Below: Virginia economy, culture and politics were tied to tobacco, as was the College of William and Mary.*

Evidence of the close ties between the College of William and Mary and Colonial Williamsburg are provided by the experiences of the first president of the United States, George Washington. First, the College was provided with a seat in the House of Burgesses at Williamsburg in 1693. The role of tobacco as a Virginia export crop was paramount: it was decided that the new College would be financed through tobacco taxes and export duties placed on animal furs. Further, George Washington was issued his surveyor's certificate at the college, which led to his first public office. Together with Thomas Jefferson, Washington was elected to the

House of Burgesses that met in the Williamsburg Capitol building. Jefferson's service in the House overlapped with that of Washington for seven years. Washington rarely missed a session and religiously made the long trek from his home at Mount Vernon to Williamsburg every spring and autumn to attend most of the daily meetings of the Burgesses.

*Below: William and Mary College as it appeared in the 1700s. Today's Georgian-style Wren building is a product of a heavy restoration effort.*

# GEORGETOWN
## HISTORIC DISTRICT, WASHINGTON, DISTRICT OF COLUMBIA

Now embedded within the metropolis of Washington, DC, the settlement of Georgetown was laid out in 1751 and flourished as an interior trade centre. Known as a "fall line" city, Georgetown grew at the most interior point of navigation along the Potomac River.

Many rivers in the eastern United States flow from the Appalachian Mountains eastward, and have carved channels that "jump" off the rocky Piedmont region on to the Coastal Plain, often forming waterfalls at the boundary. Settlements such as Georgetown developed along this "fall line", taking advantage of the waterfalls for the powering of grist, flour and saw mills. The falls of the Potomac River prevented navigation upstream, necessitating "break of bulk" activities to transfer raw materials and trade goods from overland wagons or canal boats to awaiting ships.

Following the advice of George Washington, American entrepreneurs began to construct a series of canals to connect eastern cities with the Great Lakes region. Most famous and successful was New York's Erie Canal. Sometimes referred to as the "Grand Old Ditch," the Chesapeake and Ohio (or C&O) Canal linked Washington, DC via Georgetown to the inland community of Cumberland, Maryland,

*Below: Today the Georgetown portion of the C&O canal remains virtually intact and serves as a linear park that snakes through the historic core of the community.*

approximately 298km/185 miles to the west. The canal operated between 1836 and 1924 with the intent of capturing a portion of the lucrative interior trade. Coal became the principal commodity shipped along the canal. Tobacco processing became the primary economic activity, following the construction of the Rolling House in 1747.

Georgetown flourished as a shipping centre that was well connected with European and West Indies trade. The waterfront developed in turn, attracting commercial and milling activities. As the canal system was gradually opened after 1785, Georgetown became the terminal "gateway" port for western trade that extended as far as the Missouri River, Lake Erie and Mobile, Alabama.

### DECLINE AND REVIVAL

Following the decision to create a new federal capital just to its east in 1800, Georgetown became a staging ground for planning the federal city, with Suter's Tavern (no longer surviving) playing a central role. George Washington met at the tavern with the land owners of the new city, and Pierre L'Enfant spent time there devising the city's French Baroque street plan. Although not incorporated

*Above: The Historic District is surprisingly intact, contributing to its attraction to visitors and the area's expensive housing.*

into Washington City until 1871, Georgetown quickly became the social and diplomatic centre for the new federal capital.

Over time Georgetown industrialized and lost much of its trade-centre status. By World War I it had become derelict with a reputation as a slum; its homes were badly neglected. These abysmal conditions began to reverse by the 1940s, when politicians and government officials increasingly "rediscovered" Georgetown's charm and convenience. Since then the enclave has remained an upscale residential area and tourist attraction.

The Georgetown of today is a treat to visit, with much of its 19th-century residential and commercial architecture still intact. Renovated brick and wood-framed terrace houses provide character to the historic core, and its renovated buildings demonstrate the progression of American architectural styles throughout the 19th century, from earlier Georgian, Federal, and Classical housing to an eclectic array of later Victorian styles.

# ALEXANDRIA
## HISTORIC DISTRICT, ALEXANDRIA, VIRGINIA

Located within viewing distance of Washington, DC, the city of Alexandria's original street grid, now comprising the Old Town part of the city, was laid out in 1749. The town originally grew as a trading port, primarily for the export of tobacco from inland plantations.

### TRADE IN THE REGION

The earliest tobacco plantations were located along rivers, which could directly ship to England without the need for trade centres. However, it was not until African labourers were imported to Virginia as slaves that tobacco farming increased in scale and capacity throughout the region.

As the tobacco region spread inland to the Piedmont, transportation became crucial. Alexandria, located at the mouth of the Potomac River, became an official port of entry.

With its close economic ties to tobacco shipping, Alexandria played a primary and parallel role in America's slave trade prior to the Civil War. Market Square, located within the

*Above: The Port of Alexandria in 1853, more than 100 years after the town plan was first set out.*

Historic District, is billed as the oldest continuously operating marketplace in the USA, and for some time served as the nation's second-largest slave market.

Alexandria served as a Colonial trade and shipping hub for agricultural products, becoming the primary port for the export of wheat from Virginia to meet expanded market demands in England

*Below: Completed in 1753, Carlyle House was designed for one of numerous wealthy merchants.*

*Above: Duke and King streets serve as the major commercial routes through today's Historic District.*

and the West Indies. The export of wheat ultimately outpaced that of tobacco. Later clipper ships from around the world loaded and discharged cargo on Alexandria's wharves, and the resulting wealth began to make itself evident in the town. Wealthy sea captains and merchants built grand houses and supplied funds for civic projects including schools, churches and libraries.

### THE DISTRICT TODAY

A stark reminder of Alexandria's role in slave activity is found on Duke Street, at what is now the Freedom House Museum. Now part of a gentrified historic neighbourhood of 19th-century terrace houses, the museum building once served as the headquarters of the South's most successful slave trading firm, Franklin & Armfield. Between 1828 and 1841, thousands of slaves passed through this property and its adjacent facilities on their way to faraway places such as New Orleans, Louisiana or Natchez, Mississippi.

Today's Old Town area is a bustling tourism business district. Alexandria now earns its economic prosperity from its close ties to Washington, DC, essentially serving as a wealthy suburb connected by commuter rail and freeway to the federal capital.

# WHITE HOUSE
## WASHINGTON, DISTRICT OF COLUMBIA

The planning of the original District of Columbia was entrusted to French architect and military engineer Pierre Charles L'Enfant (1754–1825). In 1791 L'Enfant surveyed the tidal plain along the Potomac River and identified the two highest points for development as the two centres of government – the House of the Executive and the House of Congress. In a Baroque planning tradition adapted for the new nation, L'Enfant designed the entire plan for the new capital city around these two central nodes of government.

The original plan called for a wide esplanade stretching from the Federal House (later called the Capitol) westward to the river, lined on both sides by the residences of ambassadors and various public buildings. Later, this space would become the National Mall. Intersecting the esplanade at a right angle was a north-south lawn connected to the Executive Mansion. L'Enfant then connected the two government centres with a "bold diagonal street" called Pennsylvania Avenue. This axial and radial

Baroque plan – enhanced with a more typically American rectilinear street grid – was derived from what L'Enfant had witnessed at Versailles and Tuilerie garden in France.

### THE PRESIDENT'S HOUSE

Unlike William Thornton, who designed the Capitol, a professionally trained architect was selected to design and oversee construction of the new Executive Mansion. James Hoban was an Irishman with European training, and his plans for the mansion were heavily influenced by plate 51 in Gibb's *Book of Architecture*. This particular image greatly resembled the Leinster House in Dublin, Ireland.

James Hoban, the architect, designed and managed construction of the new Executive Mansion. George Washington approved his plans and was present for the laying of the cornerstone. Construction on the Mansion progressed slowly after 1793, simultaneous to that of the emerging Capitol building at the other end of Pennsylvania Avenue. Although

*Above: The earliest names for the White House included the Presidential Palace, The Residence, Presidential Mansion and Executive Mansion.*

still unfinished, the residence was first inhabited by President Adams in 1801.

It was considered more sophisticated and restrained than the Capitol design, and the structure consisted of a Federal-style block with a hipped roof and projecting oval office. The familiar, columned porticos were added in 1824 and 1829. The Executive Mansion relied heavily on the traditions of Georgian architecture.

Still serving the same purpose for which it was intended more than two centuries ago, the White House did not assume its popular name right away. The public began to call it the White House as early as 1811 due to its brilliant exterior of white-painted stone. It wasn't until President Theodore Roosevelt formalized the name White House in 1901 that its prior official name, Executive Mansion was retired.

# VIRGINIA STATE CAPITOL
## RICHMOND, VIRGINIA

The Virginia State Capitol building in Richmond, designed by Thomas Jefferson was the first building to purely represent the Neo-classical (or Greek Revival) Movement. The Capitol represented the first occasion that the temple form had been used for an important public building since Roman times.

### ROLES IN HISTORY

Construction on the Capitol began in 1785 and was completed 13 years later. Although minor alterations were made during the 19th century, it was not until 1904–06 when major changes were made to the structure. Two wings were added to provide new space for the State Senate and the House of Delegates. The exterior column temple remains today as it has for more than two centuries, however, little if any of the interior is original.

*Below: The Capitol ushered in the Greek-Revival Movement, a distinctive architecture that deviated from Colonial forms.*

The building has served important roles in the history of Virginia and the Southern Confederacy. It continues to house the oldest legislative body in America, which grew out of the Colonial House of Burgesses. This is also where the Virginia Convention drafted the new constitution in 1829–30. Decades later the Capitol served as the meeting place for the Confederate Congress when Richmond was the capital of the Confederacy.

### THE GREEK REVIVAL

The long-term impact of the Capitol's design on American architecture cannot be overstated. This building set the precedent for the Neo-classical Movement that shaped American architecture and symbolized democratic values for the next half century. As American interest shifted from Roman to Greek architectural forms, the Greek Revival style came to dominate the design of homes, churches, public buildings and commercial structures. Dubbed

the national style due to its popularity, the Greek Revival is considered to be the first American architectural style that deviated measurably from earlier Colonial forms. One reason for the style's popularity was the relative ease through which home owners and municipalities could apply temple-like styling to their homes and public buildings. Elaborate Greek porticos and columns could be added to otherwise modest buildings.

Other factors explained the national love affair with Neo-classical architecture. During the early 1800s the emerging educational system was focused on the Classical world, including the study of ancient architectural forms. Budding architects were trained to understand Classical architecture, and many chose to work within the confines of the style. Americans also learned of the new national style through some of the first publications of builders' guides, which spread the knowledge of Greek architectural elements to a growing readership.

# US CAPITOL
## WASHINGTON, DISTRICT OF COLUMBIA

Washington, DC, holds the honour of being the world's first master-planned capital city. The decision on the new federal city's location was acrimonious and intensely political. George Washington and Thomas Jefferson were involved in the plans for the new District of Columbia, as proclaimed in 1791, although it was French engineer Pierre Charles L'Enfant who drafted the city's master plan. Published in 1792 as a detailed street map, L'Enfant's now famous plan included diagonal avenues superimposed over a rectangular lattice of streets. His grand avenues were named after the 15 states in existence at the time, with each state expected to contribute its own monument where the avenues intersected.

The capital's final location constituted, even then, a compromise between Northern and Southern interests. As sited, the District of Columbia would be nearly central along the Eastern Seaboard between Maine and Georgia,

*Below: The wings of the original Capitol building were later added to, and the low dome was replaced.*

at the most western navigable location along the Potomac River and just downstream from the old port of Georgetown. Its interior location was strategic – both to protect the city from potential coastal attacks and oriented to the Ohio River and the potentially lucrative Trans-Appalachian West.

### AHEAD OF ITS TIME

Washington, DC, eventually set a precedent for similar projects around the world, namely more recent capitals, including Ottawa, Canberra, Brasilia, Islamabad, New Delhi, Ankara and Belise. During the early 19th century, however, both national and international sentiment toward L'Enfant's plan was unenthusiastic. The early District of Columbia was viewed as an international embarrassment throughout its first half century.

The extensive geographic scale of the plan was ahead of its time; its physical development caught up with the original plan only by the early 20th century. The Executive Mansion and the Capitol were placed a formidable 2.4km/1½ miles apart at a time when the only transport consisted of horse and carriage

or walking. Even L'Enfant's efforts to promote his own plan for the fledgling capital city were met with scepticism. He was eventually dismissed, prior to submitting his formal resignation. His plan was already entrenched, however, and the US government moved into the city by 1800. Traversing the city's early street network was more of a physical ordeal than anything else, as its location comprised a mucky, swampy environment that would only be improved much later. As such, the "unsightly young capital was desperately short of charm or symbolic prowess", described geographer Wilbur Zelinsky.

### DESIGN AND CONSTRUCTION

L'Enfant reserved the highest elevations for two monumental buildings, namely the Executive Mansion and the Capitol building. An initial competition to determine the Capitol's design resulted in less than acceptable entries and indicated that American architects had not yet matured to handle such a sophisticated project. Instead, first prize was awarded to a late entrant, Dr William Thornton (1759–1828), who trained as a physician and was educated in Edinburgh and Paris.

Perhaps ironically, Thornton's design for the upstart nation's most symbolic building relied on the English late Georgian architectural style. His scheme consisted of two symmetrical wings for the House of Representatives and the Senate, sandwiching a central section topped with a low-profile saucer dome. Like the slow emergence of the federal city itself, the Capitol's construction occurred in lengthy stages and was eventually completed by Thornton's successors – first by Benjamin Latrobe in 1803–17, and finally by Boston architect Charles Bulfinch in 1817–30. Both successors remained true to Thornton's original concept.

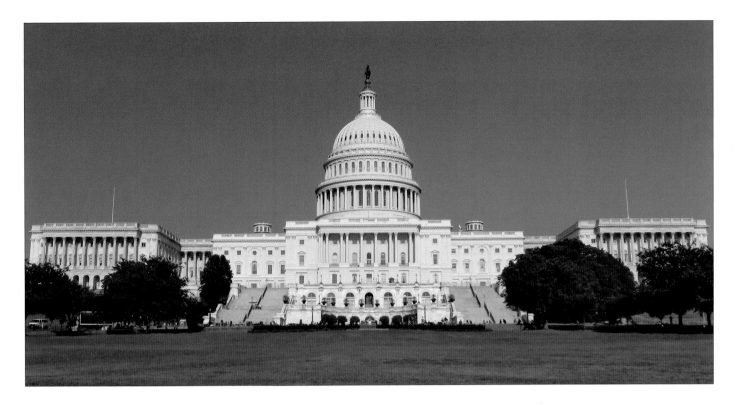

*Above: The enlarged Capitol building, complete with its third and final dome was completed in the latter half of the 19th century.*

## EXPANSION

Due to its long-term evolution, the Capitol's symbolic influence was not immediate. Domes were fashionable throughout its construction history, and the Capitol would ultimately wear three successive versions over a span of more than 50 years before becoming the "monumental symbol of world fame".

The Capitol's third and final dome was devised to balance the building's expansion project during the middle 1800s. By the time architect Thomas Ustick Walter of Philadelphia implemented the Capitol's enlargement in 1851, the Union had added 18 additional states, and the population had grown nine-fold. The original Capitol was no longer suitable. Adopting the Greek Revival style of his prior commissions, Walter provided identical wings on both ends of the original structure. His additions essentially incorporated Thornton's original Corinthian design but with additional Grecian details. The use of iron played

a prominent structural role throughout, primarily as a fire prevention strategy. With wrought iron in the roof trusses and cast iron in other sections, the Capitol used more iron than any other previous public building in the USA.

With the wings complete, Bulfinch's timber-framed dome paled in size, necessitating yet a third dome over the rotunda. Because no precedents existed for Greek or Roman domes, Walter looked to the Renaissance for

inspiration, abandoning the long-popular Greek Revival style. The enlarged dome was not completed until 1864 due to the Civil War. Its construction became a symbol for Union perseverance, with President Lincoln defending its continued construction by saying that the dome was "a sign we intend the Union to go on". As it exists today, three successive architectural styles are represented on the Capitol building, reflecting the changing tastes of successive generations – Thornton's late Georgian style, Walter's Greek Revival wings, culminating with a distinctive Renaissance Revival dome.

Following the Civil War, the Capitol's design was emulated more than any other federal building across the country, cherished for its architectural appeal as much as for its role as prominent symbol of the American democratic experiment.

*Left: Charles Pierre L'Enfant's plan for the new capital, in the District of Columbia, has a Baroque street plan similar to European town planning set over a typical American rectilinear street plan. The White House and the Capitol are clearly indicated on the grid, with stately avenues radiating out from each.*

# BALTIMORE & OHIO
## RAILROAD MUSEUM, BALTIMORE, MARYLAND

With nearly 241,400km/150,000 miles of track to the nation's credit by 1887, three transcontinental rail lines had joined the East and West coasts, and more were under construction. The technology of the railroad steam locomotive greatly improved with time and contributed fundamentally to the expanding Industrial Revolution. Only six decades earlier no railroads had existed, and inland transportation still depended entirely on horse and wagon. It was here in a southwest neighbourhood of Baltimore where America's railroad empire was effectively born.

### THE FIRST RAILROAD

Within the 16ha/40-acre site of the Baltimore and Ohio Railroad Museum, is the original point of the first commercial railroad. A variety of significant railroad structures are interpreted by the museum, including Mount Clare Station (1830), the Roundhouse (passenger car shop, 1884), Baltimore & Ohio Passenger Car Works (1869–70), and the original 2.4km/1½ mile railroad right of way. Further, the railroad's Mt Clare Shops

*Right: Mount Clare Station in 1935, the oldest passenger depot in America.*

were established here in 1829 when rail construction commenced. These are the oldest continually operating railroad shops in the world. Numerous railroad innovations occurred here, not the least being the assembly and operation of America's first steam locomotive.

The primary reason for the wave of railroad tinkering during the 1820s involved the persistent economic drive to capture Western trade. One transportation revolution after another occurred during the early 19th century, first in the form of turnpikes and wagons, followed shortly thereafter by an expanding interior canal network. On the rivers, rafts gave way to steamboats, and by the 1830s America's first steam railroads were chugging westward in direct competition with earlier canal companies. That a "railroad fever" struck the nation may be an understatement.

Amid parades and fanfare on 4 July 1828, the first cornerstone was laid for the Baltimore and Ohio Railroad,

chartered a year earlier. At precisely nine o'clock on the morning of Saturday, 22 May 1830, the first train of four cars departed from Mount Clare Station, destined for Ellicott's Mills (now Ellicott City) 20km/13 miles away. This event marked the formal inauguration of commercial rail service in the United States.

### WESTERN EXPANSION

While impressive, the overarching goal of the Baltimore & Ohio was indicated by the company's name – that of reaching the Ohio River. Businessmen were particularly fearful of New York's competition with its new Erie Canal. Baltimore's new railroad, it was hoped, would provide an alternative, much faster route for Midwestern goods to reach the East Coast. In reality, progress toward this goal occurred slowly, with the line reaching Maryland in 1842. Only in 1853 was the initial goal achieved, terminating at Wheeling, West Virginia (then Virginia) on 1 January 1853. The railroad infrastructure was well built, despite the slow progress. Not knowing how strong to construct the track and bridges, the B&O overcompensated and built much of its infrastructure with solid granite. As a result some of its earliest bridges – such as the acclaimed Carrollton Viaduct at Relay, Maryland, are still in use today.

*Left: The Roundhouse and grounds of the B&O Railroad Museum. This is where America's "railroad fever" began in the early 19th century.*

# SMITHSONIAN INSTITUTION BUILDING
## WASHINGTON, DISTRICT OF COLUMBIA

In 1846 Congress officially chartered the Smithsonian Institution, at a time when Americans increasingly viewed science and education as national priorities. The institution was made possible through a US $500,000 gift from the English scientist James Smithson. Following the successive deaths of Smithson and his nephew, the gift was bequeathed to the United States in 1838. Years of Congressional debate over the specific use of the funds followed. Smithson's intent had been to provide for "an Establishment for the increase and diffusion of knowledge…" Even Smithson could not have foreseen the Institution's eventual growth to become the largest complex of museums in the world, as it exists today.

With the Congressional Charter approved, a building committee was appointed to determine the design of the Institution's new home. Like many prominent architectural projects, this one involved a competition, advertised in the federal city's local newspapers in September 1846. The winning entry was awarded to the prominent New York City architect James Renwick, who offered a simple, less ornamental style compared to other entries. His was to be a modernized version of a 12th-century Norman castle, a design that included a combination of late Romanesque and early Gothic features.

The cornerstone was placed in 1847 and the building was completed eight years later in 1855. The Smithsonian's primary purpose was to showcase the world of science and invention. To this day Renwick's distinctive building is known to many as the Castle, due to its diverse array of towers and turrets.

*Right: Smithson's intent for his Norman-styled castle was to create "an Establishment for the increase and diffusion of knowledge".*

The eight towers, each unique in design and size, comprise the most striking Picturesque feature of the building.

### FIRE AT THE CASTLE
Every effort was made to fireproof the Castle. Prior to the building's completion, the wooden interior of the central section was replaced with a more fire-resistant one. Further precautions were numerous: no smoking was allowed, no open lights could be carried and fire equipment such as buckets and hoses were distributed prolifically throughout. Nightly inspections for fire were carried out by a watchman.

Unfortunately, all of these precautions were not enough and the worst fire in the Institution's history occurred on the night of 24 January 1865, in the fireproofed central section. The loss of irreplaceable items was staggering. All of James Smithson's original papers were destroyed, as were 80,000 letters associated with the Institution's early history. Among other treasures, a collection of scientific inventions and 200 oil paintings of Native Americans were lost. Two entire library collections were destroyed, those of the Episcopal Seminary of Alexandria, Virginia, and the town of Beaufort, South Carolina. Union troops had seized both of these collections during the Civil War. The Secretary of War, Edwin Stanton, had moved them to the Institution for safe keeping.

### THE SMITHSONIAN TODAY
Following numerous renovations, the building remains as America's most prominent example of Norman Revival civic architecture. The structure represents the epitome of Picturesque design favoured by the proponents of Romanticism during the middle of the 19th century. Its asymmetrical, unpredictable design provides a stark visual contrast to the formal, Neo-classical approach to architecture in the nation's new capital. The Institution's clear break from this formal past is enhanced by its prominent location on the south side of the National Mall at 10th Street. The structure protrudes deeply into the Mall's open space, perhaps indicating a lacking devotion to the original city master plan.

# THE PENTAGON
## ARLINGTON, VIRGINIA

As the largest office building by floor area in the world, the Pentagon is also the most recognizable. The sprawling, five-sided structure named for its unique shape was originally constructed to consolidate the expanding functions and rapid growth of the US military prior to World War II. Each outer wall of the symmetrical building is 281m/922ft in length, providing for a total coverage of 13.8ha/34 acres, including its 2ha/5 acre central courtyard. The interior courtyard was informally dubbed "ground zero" for the presumption that a Soviet nuclear missile was aimed at the site during the Cold War. Wrapped around the courtyard are five rings of offices housed on seven floors – five above ground and two below. One would need to walk 28km/17½ miles to cover all of the Pentagon's corridors. More than 25,000 employees are housed there.

### GEOGRAPHIC FACTORS
The final layout and design for the Pentagon were a product of local geographic factors combined with early influences of World War II. When the War Department asserted its need for a permanent facility in 1941, it was clear that its sheer size would prevent its placement within the boundaries of Washington, DC. The structure would need to be low and sprawling, to minimize the use of steel needed for the War build-up, and to avoid blocking prominent views of the District's monuments. Instead, it was decided to find a spacious site across the Potomac River in Arlington. The envisioned project was expected to accommodate 40,000 employees and 10,000 automobiles.

*Below: The architecture of the Pentagon represents the last of the Neo-classical Revival in America during the 1940s.*

*Above: Most Americans commuted to work by the 1940s, necessitating sprawling, shopping-mall-like car parks.*

The site was bounded by roads, necessitating that its draughtsman essentially design a square shape with a corner cut off. Although the new site did not require the irregular building shape, there was no time to begin a new design from scratch.

### THE McMILLAN PLAN
The Pentagon became the largest of greater Washington, DC's monumental structures, and was one of the last to adopt the architecture of the "stripped Classical" mode in which typical Neo-classical ornament is only implied or suggested. Its formal, symmetrical design was also one of the last projects to carry out the principles provided by the 1902 Senate Park Commission report, known as the McMillan Plan. Employing Daniel Burnham, Charles McKim, and Frederick Law Olmsted, Jr, this revised plan for Washington, DC, exemplified the tenets of City Beautiful planning and was ultimately the most successful in its implementation. The plan purposely retained and enhanced L'Enfant's earlier formal design of the city, and fundamentally led to the development of Washington's core area as we see it today. For its part the Classical design of the Pentagon revealed the persistent power of the McMillan plan four decades after its conception.

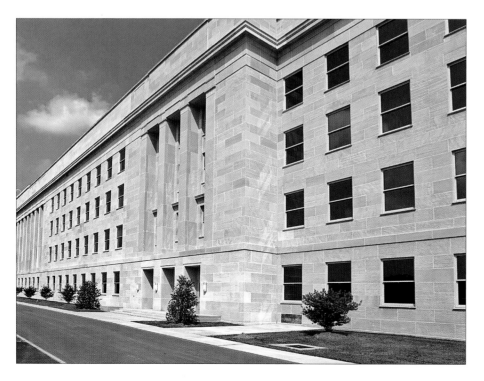

# GREENBELT
## HISTORIC DISTRICT, GREENBELT, MARYLAND

By the time of the Civil War the emerging middle and upper classes were abandoning the congested cities for the suburbs. The working-class population was left to cope with over-packed tenement houses. Social reformers made some noteworthy attempts after the Civil War to improve tenement living, but changes were slow in coming. Similar issues were being addressed in

*Left: The Greenbelt Community Center, considered one of America's most distinguished Art Deco buildings.*

England, notably by the so-called father of the garden city movement, Ebenezer Howard (1850-1928).

### A GARDEN CITY
The implementation of garden city principles in the United States occurred on a grand scale, under the auspices of President Franklin D. Roosevelt. His New Deal government sought solutions to the housing crisis. The government led what amounted to one of the boldest projects of community public housing ever undertaken in the United States. At this time a total of three "greenbelt towns" were planned and built by the federal government, all of which relied on garden city principles.

The town of Greenbelt, Maryland, was the first and largest of the three, and was designed specifically to decentralize the residential population of Washington, DC. All three towns were comprehensive with respect to their inclusion of

housing, commerce, schools and recreation. For its part Greenbelt, developed between 1935 and 1946, was designed with a highly unified architectural theme, relying particularly on Art Deco and streamlined Moderne styles, along with associated Modernistic architecture derived from Europe. Greenbelt was scientifically and regionally planned to include specialized land-use zones devoted to residential, commercial, recreational, agricultural and industrial purposes. Located 24km/15 miles northeast of downtown Washington, Greenbelt was laid out in a crescent shape that incorporated a series of "superblocks". Each superblock contains rows of multifamily dwellings constructed with wood frames or concrete blocks. Greenbelt and its counterpart towns served as powerful lessons for the future of planned communities in America, the development of which came to dominate regional planning throughout the remainder of the 20th century.

*Below: A standard, multi-family dwelling in Greenbelt.*

### EBENEZER HOWARD
Howard's ideal garden city exhibited specific characteristics and spatial layouts. Using the growing railroad network as part of his plan, he presumed that it was possible to create a system of dispersed communities linked together by regional transport. Communities could take advantage of urban living with the healthy qualities of country life. His vision went beyond the typical planned suburb of the day. Rather, his garden cities were conceived as autonomous municipalities. Each city would include a number of urban population clusters separated by rural green belts and provide railroad commuting access to industrial and commercial zones. The heart of the town would include a variety of civic and cultural institutions focused on a green open space. A second ring of houses would lie beyond a wide grand avenue, with a railroad spur encircling this residential ring.

# CHAPTER FOUR

# THE DEEP SOUTH

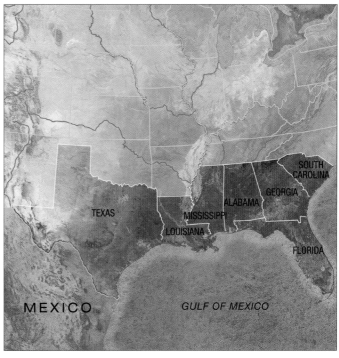

STILL ONE OF THE MOST CULTURALLY DISTINCT
REGIONS OF THE UNITED STATES, THE DEEP
SOUTH EXTENDS FROM SOUTH CAROLINA
THROUGH TO EASTERN TEXAS. NEW WORLD
EMPIRES VIED FOR REGIONAL CONTROL HERE,
NOTABLY THOSE OF THE FRENCH AND SPANISH.
BOTH GAINED STRONG FOOTHOLDS IN THE
SOUTH, PROVIDING FOR A DIVERSE ARRAY OF
SETTLEMENT PATTERNS AND CULTURAL PRACTICES
THAT STILL INFLUENCE THE SOUTHERN HUMAN
AND BUILT LANDSCAPE TODAY.

*Left: The rocket garden at Cape Canaveral is a landmark
familiar to Americans.*

# ST AUGUSTINE TOWN PLAN
## HISTORIC DISTRICT, ST AUGUSTINE, FLORIDA

Popular attention to Colonial Spanish heritage often focuses on today's America's Southwest. However, it was in Florida where the Spanish crown invested most heavily in resources and settlement. Early expeditions to Florida in the 16th century were deemed unsuccessful and did little more than ravage the Native American population. The Florida initiative was almost abandoned until King Philip II of Spain heard news of a French settlement in present-day South Carolina. Presuming their valuable coastal shipping lanes would be threatened by a French presence, the King granted the land of La Florida to his naval commander, Pedro Menendez, in 1565. His aim was to stimulate Spanish settlement with the building of three towns, each with a population of 100.

Menendez founded the town of St Augustine and then established a second port farther south, with the intention of capturing New France's Fort Caroline (present-day Jacksonville) and butchering the French force.

*Below: The Cathedral Basilica of St Augustine represents the first parish founded in 1565.*

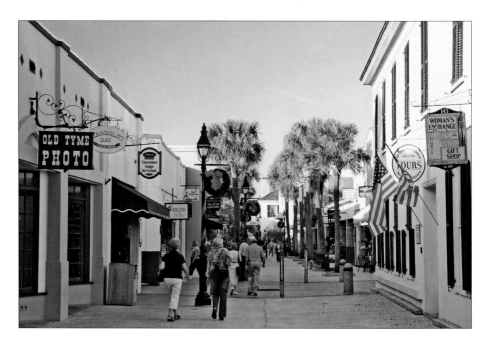

*Above: Initially settled to defend Spanish interests, today's old town is primarily a tourist attraction.*

### DEFENSIVE STRONGHOLD
Of the three standard types of Spanish colonial settlements – mission (church), presidio (fort) and pueblo (village), St Augustine evolved into a classic example of a Spanish presidio settlement. Florida had been founded explicitly for territorial defence. The fortification of St Augustine began the day before Menendez landed there with his soldiers. Following its crude beginnings, the Spanish built and improved a succession of five fortifications in the general area during the 16th century. Not until 1671 was the permanent stone fortress, the Castillo de San Marcos, begun at its present site in the town. Each of the earlier forts had succumbed through a variety of means, not the least being an attack from Native American fire arrows, a flood and a soldiers' mutiny.

As a locale settled purely for defensive purposes, St Augustine proved to be self-sufficient despite the lack of attractions that brought Spanish settlers to other Colonial regions. The soils were poor, precious metals were non-existent and sedentary Native Americans were not located nearby to provide a source of labour. Instead, the fledgling community of St Augustine endured numerous early calamities and hardships during its first century, primarily serving as a rural military outpost on the northern periphery of the Spanish Colonial empire. The settlement further developed into a point of departure for Spanish missionary work, in the ongoing effort of the Church to christianize the regional Native Americans.

### SPANISH TOWN PLANNING
Very little of St Augustine's built environment from the first two centuries still exists within today's historic district. A brutal history of fires, invaders, erosion, decay and demolition has taken its toll. Nonetheless, 36 stone houses representing the Spanish period still survive, predating the end of Spanish Florida in 1821, with 12 being built prior to 1763. More obvious from the early Spanish period is the imprint of the Spanish town plan and street layout that are of primary significance for this Historic District.

Unlike the English who relied on a more organic, unplanned approach to town settlement, the Spanish followed an orderly system of town planning more formalized and prescribed than any other Colonial power in the New World. Across the Spanish borderlands, from Florida to California, towns and cities founded under Spanish rule followed certain principles of town planning. These were first set out as early as 1513 in the Ordinances for the Discovery, New Settlement, and Pacification of the Indies. Later, the Ordinances were incorporated into the Laws of the Indies, which heavily influenced Spanish Colonial settlements in America.

The Laws included more than three dozen specifications for new town construction and layout. Most visible was the rectilinear grid of streets with a central plaza built into the plan. The rectangular plazas were placed strategically in the centre of a town to serve as the social and economic hub. Four principal thoroughfares extended out from the sides of the plaza. Lots fronting the plaza were reserved for the most important community functions including those of royal and municipal governments, hospitals, arsenals and most certainly a prominent church.

### ST AUGUSTINE'S PLAN

Two versions of the town plan existed, one designed for coastal locations, the other for inland sites. The plan for St Augustine represents one of these earlier Spanish plans for a coastal town. As

*Below: The construction of Castillo San Marcos, America's oldest Spanish presidio.*

directed by the ordinances, the plaza is oriented to the water, and prior to the 18th century only the governor's house actually fronted the plaza. The following two centuries saw an increasing number of civic and religious buildings focused there. Given that the Ordinances were drafted in parallel with the height of the European Renaissance, achieving Classical orderliness and uniformity provided the fundamental planning principles. One of the Ordinances urged officials to "try as

*Below: When Florida was transferred to the United States in 1821, Fort San Marcos was renamed Fort Marion.*

*Above: The town wall and its original entrance was constructed after the burning of St Augustine by the British in 1702.*

much as possible to have all the buildings of one type in order to enhance the beauty of the town".

Four centuries later, the streets of St Augustine provide a strong material connection to this Renaissance-inspired past. The town boasts of being the site of the oldest continuously occupied settlement in the USA. The Historic District provides a rich landscape of architectural heritage representing the nations under which it developed.

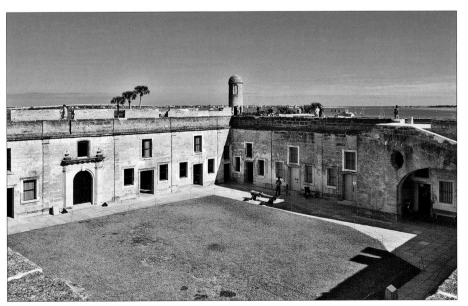

# SAVANNAH
## HISTORIC DISTRICT, SAVANNAH, GEORGIA

The British colony of Georgia was the last, and farthest south, of the 13 original colonies in America. Named in honour of King George II, the English parliament envisioned the new colony as a source of economic wealth. A committee was formed in England to determine how this new colony might provide a potential destination and opportunity for thousands of men then out of work or in serious debt. With these related aims in mind, George II granted a charter in 1732 to James Oglethorpe and 20 fellow trustees. Oglethorpe and some of his associates were genuinely motivated by a humanitarian desire to assist those experiencing religious persecution or debtors' prison. They adopted a Latin phrase as their motto, translated to "not for themselves but for others".

### A RELIGIOUS HAVEN

The king was also responding to religious groups lobbying for a new haven for religious freedom for all – except for Catholics. The Spanish threat immediately to the south was the reason to exclude the Catholics, and South Carolina to the north was more than

happy to have a new "buffer" colony established between themselves and Spanish Florida. The aim for religious tolerance attracted peoples from a variety of nationalities and ethnicities. Aside from German and Swiss settlers, the first

*Below: The Green-Meldrim House is considered one of the finest examples of the Gothic Revival style in the South. General Sherman used the house as his headquarters following the North's invasion during the Civil War.*

*Above: A statue of James Oglethorpe takes pride of place in Chippewa Square.*

colonists included a group of Sephardic Jews of Portuguese descent, desperate to escape the Spanish Inquisition.

### A SOCIAL EXPERIMENT

Oglethorpe envisioned a colony of primarily small landholders supporting themselves through a combination of agriculture and associated industries. Having chosen a location 24km/15 miles up the Savannah River for their capital city, Savannah became Georgia's foremost Colonial town. The accumulation of land was not allowed, and slavery was prohibited – the latter thought by Georgia's leaders to be morally abhorrent. Moreover, trade with local Native Americans was strictly regulated, and the importation or manufacture of rum and other spirits was outlawed. Although designed both socially and economically to be fundamentally different from the nearby South Carolina colony, conditions in Savannah deteriorated with time. The capitalist approach to wealth through slavery and land speculation proved too powerful, and the Georgia experiment was eventually diluted.

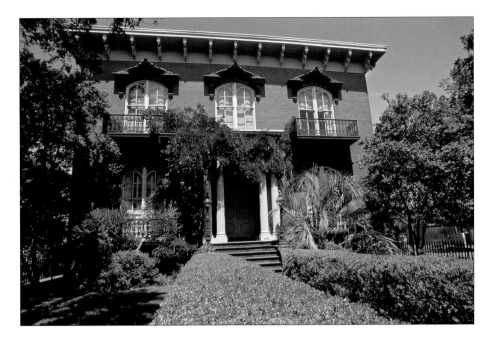

*Left: Built in 1860, the Italianate-style Mercer House was featured in John Berendt's best-selling book,* Midnight in the Garden of Good and Evil.

## THE OGLETHORPE PLAN

Proving much more permanent, however, was the unique land survey pattern developed by Oglethorpe in England for application in his new settlement of Savannah. This was only the third significant grid street plan adopted for an English town in America, the first two being New Haven, Connecticut and Philadelphia, Pennsylvania. Still, Oglethorpe's plan differed from its northern neighbours with its repetitive use of equally spaced town squares. During his ten years in Savannah, Oglethorpe personally laid out six of them, still entrenched in Savannah's historic district today. Perhaps even more celebrated by scholars and tourists alike was the continuation of this original pattern as the town grew away from the river. Prior to the disruption of the Civil War, Oglethorpe's town plan was expanded periodically with the addition of 18 more squares, for a total of 24.

Around each square, streets are orderly, numerous and short, so embedded city blocks are small by necessity. Each square had been designed to provide a centre for a surrounding ward. By plan each ward contains four "trust" lots; two on each side of the square, east and west. On the north and south sides of each square are four "tythings," two on each side, designed for the private residences of colonists. In this case the word "tything" means "ten", corresponding to the number of lots within each tything. Every square has a monument at its centre, however the names of the squares do not represent the monuments. Many of the squares were named later to honour various military heroes or victories, with their respective monuments added later during the late Victorian era.

## SAVANNAH TODAY

Modernist developments have infiltrated the historic district since World War II, but Savannah has been spared the wholesale destruction of urban renewal and freeway construction that plagued many other cities. Only two of the original 24 town squares were destroyed, in order to make way for US Highway 17 on the west side of the district.

Undoubtedly the historic appeal of Savannah lies with its extensive and well-preserved collection of 18th- and 19th-century buildings. A full two centuries of successive architectural styles can be viewed as a visual progression of American architectural history. Equally as relevant in establishing Savannah's unique sense of place, however, is the Oglethorpe town plan of alternating squares and wards. All walkable from one another, each of the remaining 22 squares offers a unique sense of place.

Today, Savannah's historic landscape, including the more recent neighbourhood accretions, provides visitors and urban planners with an exemplary model of a walking city, one that is pedestrian-friendly and multi-functional.

*Below: The most peaceful squares are those away from the riverfront, surrounded by an array of 19th-century Victorian town houses.*

# MAGNOLIA PLANTATION
## DERRY, LOUISIANA

The remaining human landscapes of Magnolia Plantation and Oakland Plantation reflect 19th-century agricultural practices in one of America's most distinctive cultural regions. Louisiana was where the French colonial influence intersected with the plantation system that diffused northward from the Caribbean. Transcending national and colonial borders, the extensive territory termed "Plantation America" includes a region that extends from the coast of Brazil through the Guianas and the Caribbean islands and into the southeastern United States.

Production methods utilized in the plantation system varied based on climate, soil and other local factors. Still, Plantation America was tied together by a large-scale agricultural system focused on the export of cash crops to Europe – a system ruled by a European elite and dependent primarily upon an African labour force. At least 10 million African slaves were brought to the Americas during the four centuries of

*Below: Humans and animals dragged crops to market. The plantation system was extremely labour intensive.*

*Above: America's plantation landscapes represented an expansion of the Caribbean plantation realm farther south.*

slave-trading activities. The continued import of African slaves into the Americas through 1870, created what geographers refer to as a neo-Africa in the Americas. Because slaves were brought from a variety of African regions, different African languages, customs and beliefs were blended into distinct regional cultures. Louisiana and

the American South were strongly influenced by this forced cultural migration. Magnolia Plantation is set in this context of slave-dependent agriculture for the production of cotton.

### THE PLANTATION SYSTEM
The plantation mode of production is distinguished by a focus on monocropping, or the growing of cash crops for profit. Successful plantations generally required the following attributes: fertile, easily tilled land available in large units; abundant, landless and cheap rural labour; bulk reduction and preliminary processing techniques; abundant, cheap transportation; and a network of factors and factoring houses to market cash crops to other regions of the world. All of these were present in the American South during the antebellum period, and are well represented at Magnolia Plantation. The plantation system continued to dominate agriculture in the South (in a modified form) in the postbellum period through the practice of share cropping, into the 20th century.

### FRENCH CULTURE
Added to the plantation production system in Louisiana was the French

colonial influence. The French Crown gained control of Louisiana in 1731, a time when black people outnumbered whites within a non-native population of around 4,000. Plantations became the primary unit of agricultural production, with French landowners turning increasingly to black slaves to meet the growing labour demand. The result in rural Louisiana by the 19th century was summarized by geographer Cole Harris: "In fact, to the extent that Old World folk cultures survived on New World plantations, those along the lower Mississippi were more African than French." Both French and African cultural influences are still reflected in the human landscape of Magnolia Plantation, providing a rare – if incomplete – window into the distinctive social attributes of this French Creole region.

### THE PLANTATION

Located along a bend of the Cane River, Magnolia Plantation traces its beginnings to Jean Baptiste LeComte II, who received some of the earliest land grants from the French and Spanish during the mid-18th century. The Plantation began at this time, but many of the surviving structures and outbuildings represent the 19th century. Officially, the Plantation was not in use until 1830. Plantations such as Magnolia

were characterized by their large collection of specialized buildings, indicating their roles as independent, self-contained communities. As one traveller once noted, "the planter has a building for everything."

Typically, only the iconic great house survives today on former plantation lands, representing only the most elite component of a complex production system. A welcome exception is found at Magnolia, however, which is significant

*Below: Slave accommodation was essential on larger plantations, but many smaller operations did not utilize slave labour.*

*Above: The subtropical climate of the Deep South provided the necessary growing season for plantation crops.*

primarily for its own collection of outbuildings and 19th-century cotton-harvesting technologies. Now part of the Cane River Creole National Historical Park managed by the National Park Service, Magnolia Plantation maintains 21 historic buildings, including a main house and its immediate dependencies, a slave hospital, a pigeonnier, eight brick slave houses, and a gin house complete with antebellum and postbellum ginning and pressing equipment. Magnolia's complement of plantation structures is impressively complete.

*Below: European demand for sugar led to the proliferation of sugar plantations throughout the Caribbean realm.*

# OAKLAND PLANTATION
## NATCHEZ, LOUISIANA

The numerous structures and artefacts preserved at Oakland Plantation provide a clear example of the French Creole (Colonial) cultural influence on the Southern plantation-based economy. The French Creole architectural tradition joins those of the Spanish and English as one of the three dominant Colonial expressions in America. Along with Magnolia Plantation, Oakland provides America's most complete collection of rural buildings and structures derived from French Creole folk traditions.

### PRESERVATION

Oakland Plantation was established by Jean Pierre Emmanuel Prud'homme in the early 19th century, after the Spanish crown granted him the land in 1789. By the beginning of the American Civil War the plantation had amassed 1,375ha/3,400 acres, 400ha/1,000 of which were worked by 145 slaves who lived in 30 separate buildings. Amazingly, the 17ha/42 acre property remained in the Prud'homme family until Jean's descendants sold it to the National Park Service in 1997. Since then the site has been opened to the public as part of the Cane River Creole National Historical Park. Impressively still intact, the plantation landscape includes the French Creole-style main house and 23 historic dependencies, or outbuildings. The Plantation exists within the heart of the Creole cultural region, in Natchitoches Parish and Pointe Coupee Parish.

### ARCHITECTURE AND OUTBUILDINGS

The impressive collection of French Creole structures located on the property provides important lessons about French Colonial construction techniques and styles. The main house is considered to be a "classic" example of French Creole plantation architecture, and the largest surviving example in the Mississippi River Valley. Raised a full storey above grade, the house features a huge, umbrella-like hipped roof, encircling galleries or porches, and the distinctive Creole floor plan.

Its central chimney and bousillage construction constitute additional French traditions. Bousillage can be compared to English wattle and daub construction and was common in colonial Louisiana well into the 19th century.

### CREOLE

The term Creole has changed in meaning over time and has multiple potential meanings. The description of a person as a "Creole" first appeared in the 16th century to identify the descendants of French, Spanish or Portuguese families living in the West Indies or Latin America. As Creole populations diffused elsewhere, the term gained additional meanings. In the Caribbean realm a Creole was a descendant of any settler of European origin, however, today certain populations of African descent also consider themselves as Creoles. In Louisiana the term identifies French-speaking populations of French or even Spanish descent, whose ancestors were upper-class whites who often owned plantations.

Oakland Plantation has the distinction of including by far the largest concentrated number of buildings featuring bousillage construction, with a total of eight. Another Creole feature was the so-called pigeonniers, used to ornament the property. Built in the form of monumental towers to house pigeons, two such pigeonniers were placed near the main house. In France, only landowners enjoyed the right to keep pigeons. Adopted in Louisiana as a status symbol, pigeonniers were fashionable well into the 19th century. Although the Plantation no longer houses the cotton production equipment, Oakland Plantation provides one of the richest environments through which to learn about Louisiana's French Creole architecture.

*Left: The Oakland Plantation house was one of several built along the Cane River Valley.*

# CHARLESTON
## HISTORIC DISTRICT, CHARLESTON, SOUTH CAROLINA

The historic district of the port city of Charleston represents the "earliest and most complete attempt to preserve an entire historic city ambience" in the United States. Charleston is considered to be the closest American equivalent to a European historic city in its character and its rigorous conservation efforts. Tourists began to discover the historic qualities of Charleston by the 1920s, when local leaders realized that the conservation of historic resources held promise for reviving the city's ailing urban economy. The Old City District, comprising 324ha/800 acres and over half of the city, was established in 1931, which made this the oldest legally designated Historic District in the United States.

### THE CHARLESTON HOUSE

Today the city provides a showcase of two centuries' worth of American and distinctly Southern architecture, reflecting Charleston's important roles in colonial seaport activities, the American Revolution, as the hub of mercantile activities surrounding rice and cotton production, and as a leader of secession. Much of the district is primarily residential and privately owned, with buildings dating from 1712. A variety of building materials still exists, including structures built of brick, stucco, or wood frame and clapboard.

Many of the residential buildings are of a form distinctive to Charleston itself, referred to simply as the Charleston house, or the Charleston "single house". These have their gabled ends to the street with tiered piazzas or galleries on the side. More elegant town mansions comprised larger variations of this theme, with sometimes three-storey galleries located on the side of the structure rather than the front. Between such buildings are long, narrow passageways leading to interior courtyards and surrounded by high walls. At the

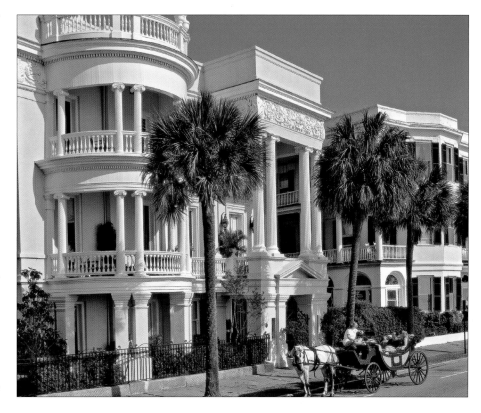

rear were "spillover" household functions including detached kitchens, slave quarters and formal gardens – essentially urban versions of the plantation lifestyle.

### REGIONAL CONNECTIONS

Charleston's urban connection to plantation life was not incidental. This was the earliest port city of note in the South, and its colonial and early American development was dependent upon the wealth generated from the surrounding plantation-based, agricultural economy. In large part the lack of urban development in the South was attributed to the focus on plantation-based agricultural production. The

*Above: The area is cherished for its collection of 18th- and 19th-century buildings, totalling more than 650.*

largest plantations enjoyed their own town-like status, remaining largely self-sufficient, even to the extent of managing their own private docks and ships that traded directly with Europe. As the plantation system spread throughout the South, away from its initial beginnings on the East Coast, Charleston lost much of its status as a hub for planter activities. More devastating was the loss of its capital status to interior Columbia, and the economic depression that followed in the wake of the War of 1812. By 1830, New Orleans had replaced Charleston as the premier port of the South, and the city's plantation wealth never returned.

*Left: The unparalleled concentration of period buildings allows visitors to gain a thorough appreciation of Charleston throughout its multifaceted historic roles.*

# VIEUX CARRE
## HISTORIC DISTRICT, NEW ORLEANS, LOUISIANA

The Vieux Carre, or French Quarter of New Orleans, was the city's first formally planned settlement along the Mississippi River. Still exhibiting a distinctive, multicultural flair in the midst of mass tourism, the city's original settlement also serves as a powerful local symbol of recovery and optimism (real and imagined) following the devastation of Hurricane Katrina. Albeit in a sweltering, subtropical climate zone, the early built environment and street layout of the Vieux Carre were essentially a transplant of French town planning.

### A NEW TOWN

In 1717 the French crown decided to fortify Louisbourg in Canada, and at the same time strengthen its control throughout the Mississippi Valley. To do so a merchant company was granted full title to Louisiana, along with a 25-year trading monopoly. New Orleans was founded a year later by this company, which began

*Below: The town plan for the original city of New Orleans was focused on the Place d'Armes. Today's Jackson Square fronts the Mississippi River.*

the process of granting large estates. Struggling to encourage the immigration of European indentured servants, the company relied more heavily on black slave labour and the plantation model of agriculture already being practiced on the French sugar islands.

*Below: The featured landmark structure on Jackson Square, Saint Louis Cathedral, was heavily rebuilt in 1850 using a mix of Renaissance and Spanish Revival styles.*

*Above: A deteriorating Colonial French building awaits renovation.*

The original town plan for New Orleans, identified today as the Vieux Carre, was essentially modelled after its northern counterpart at Louisbourg. Still intact nearly three centuries later, the original street pattern was laid out as a rectangular grid and – like Montreal – was walled on three sides. The central feature of this formal layout was the Place d'Armes, an open square that still serves as the city's historic focus. Various religious and government buildings faced the square, with commercial districts on each side. Behind the square and away from the river were the residential blocks. On the fourth side of the settlement was the Mississippi River, with the entire town sited on the river's natural levee.

The town resembled less of a fortress, however, than an imperial settlement, even though it contained all the trappings of a large garrison. It was the town's physical location that protected it more than anything else. The natural levee on which the original town sits is actually the highest elevation zone along the river. On the backside of the

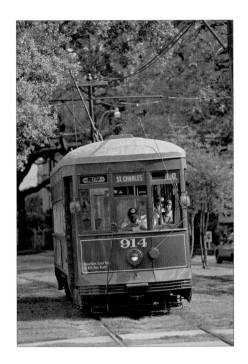

*Above: Preserved streetcars from the 1920s still shuttle visitors and residents through the historic core of New Orleans.*

settlement was the lower-level swampland of the flood plain, which resisted human development until the construction of artificial levees. Three centuries later, this quirk of physical geography contributed to the relatively minor flood damage within the Vieux Carre as a result of Hurricane Katrina, compared with the complete devastation of lower residential areas that succumbed to failed artificial levees.

### FRENCH SOCIETY

The initial decades of New Orleans were dominated by French culture, society and architecture. Cafes, ballrooms and gambling halls catered to and reinforced the French social strata, while the governor encouraged a thriving social life within the town. The stamp of French Catholicism was omnipresent, through an array of religious facilities that included churches, hospitals, offices, schools and an orphanage – all under the leadership of the Jesuits, Capuchins or Ursulines. In these ways the influence of the Roman Catholic Church on the local population was pervasive. In other fundamental ways, however, the new

French settlement could be interpreted as an outlier of St Domingue, in social, cultural and economic terms. Here was a transplant society of New France that, while resembling its northern counterparts in the material landscape, further developed into a Creole, slave-owning, tropical plantation society.

### NATIONAL INFLUENCES

The original layout of the District's street grid and square are decidedly French, as are a few select French Colonial buildings that survive. Like most cities that evolve over numerous centuries, however, this one has not only exploded in terms of growth, but has also succumbed to its share of devastating fires, floods and battles. New Orleans survived and prospered throughout the rule of three powerful nations – France, Spain and the United States. Successive phases of rebuilding and development, however, have greatly altered the city's landscape. The Vieux Carre experienced its own building boom between 1830 and the Civil War. Much of the architecture that delights visitors today is indicative of Anglo-American architecture of early Victorian times. Very little that remains is of French origin. The district's iconic wrought-iron galleries and balconies, for instance, are

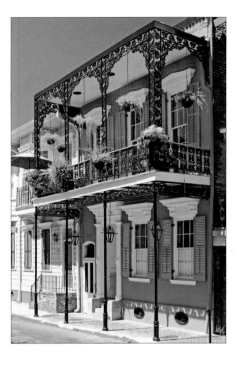

*Above: Although existing within the original French town plan, much of the architecture reflects British or American practices.*

more accurately "Southern" than "French". Still, what makes this city unique is the nature and variety of its cosmopolitan character, which makes it difficult to completely ignore the French cultural influences still imbued here.

*Below: The Vieux Carre's narrow streets contains 18th- and 19th-century properties with iconic wrought-iron galleries.*

# YBOR CITY
## HISTORIC DISTRICT, TAMPA, FLORIDA

Ybor City provides an excellent example of an ethnic enclave that thrived during the first decades of the 20th century. Described as a "city within a city", the neighbourhood northeast of downtown Tampa prospered as a multi-racial, Latin-American factory town devoted to the cigar industry. With less than 1,000 people and a struggling economy by the 1880s, Tampa gained the attention of Vincente M. Ybor, who initially planned only a small-scale development for his budding cigar business. Ybor had become a prominent Cuban cigar manufacturer when political turmoil in that country encouraged him to move his operations to Key West, Florida, in 1869. More problems there encouraged him to focus his energies farther north in Tampa. The result was the founding of Ybor City in 1886 as a planned company town, similar to others being developed throughout the industrial Northeast and booming West. Ybor wasted no time with recruitment of labour. With factories already in place,

*Below: Ybor City was founded as a planned company town complete with workers' homes such as this for a factory employee.*

he enticed 3,000 workers from Cuba by the end of the first year. About 15 per cent of them were black, which provided early impetus for the factory town's multi-ethnic character. So successful was Ybor City that Tampa quickly outpaced Key West as the leading centre for Cuban immigration in the Southeastern United States.

The company town's rapid growth by 1887 – with nearly 200 worker houses and a streetcar connection – led to Ybor City's annexation by Tampa in June, 1887. Ybor City retained its own separate cultural identity, however, and only three years later the place was home to 6,000 residents. Thus began the city's heyday, which would last up through World War II. The skilled Latin-American population turned Tampa into the world's leading city for cigar manufacturing. Tampa historian Karl H. Grismer has since described the place as a truly Latin-American city, "as though it had been in the heart of Cuba". Although immigrant Cubans and Spaniards set the cultural tone for the community, Italians, Germans, Africans, and European Jews were also immigrating here by the 1880s. A rather

*Above: Traditional handmade Cuban cigars became the economic mainstay, until demand fell during the Great Depression.*

unique multicultural community had developed – what geographers refer to as an ethnic enclave – within the otherwise deeply segregated South. English was a foreign language here, with "English Spoken Here" signs still commonly seen through the 1930s. Ybor City's cultural diversity thrived into the 1950s, however, the cigar industry reached its peak in 1929, when 500 million cigars were rolled annually within its factories.

### DECLINE AND PRESERVATION
A litany of factors external to the community dealt successive economic blows to Ybor City. Global demand for cigars decreased during the Great Depression, as consumers switched to less expensive cigarettes. Mechanization of the cigar manufacturing process led to further factory reductions and layoffs. To make matters worse, veterans returning from World War II could only take advantage

of the federal home loan program if they were buying new homes; the older housing stock in Ybor City was exempt from such incentives. Perhaps the most destructive phase came with federal urban renewal during the 1950s and 1960s. Parallelling the experiences of declining neighbourhoods nationwide, a combination of urban renewal and freeway-building initiatives ultimately led to the transformation of 93 per cent of Ybor City's historic built environment. Like many Urban Renewal projects, the demolition occurred but the expensive redevelopment did not; entire blocks of the city remained desolate for decades. Moreover, when the dust cleared, Interstate 4 cut a swath through the neighbourhood's traditional centre, physically separating the north and south sections.

Not all was lost, however. The beginnings of an Historic Preservation Movement in Ybor City emerged by the late 1950s, as summarized in an article by the American Planning Association: "Residents like Tony Pizzo, founder of the Tampa Historical Society and whose parents owned a grocery store on 7th Avenue, fought proposals that would have

*Below: The revived 7th Avenue is celebrated by the American Planning Association as one of America's "Great Streets".*

caused buildings to be levelled. Others joined in, and in 1959 the Barrio Latino Commission (BLC) was created. This was Tampa's first architectural review commission, modelled after the Vieux Carre Commission in New Orleans, and created to protect what buildings and neighbourhoods were still intact."

## YBOR TODAY

Today, Ybor City has come full circle, having continually built on these early community preservation efforts. New development has replaced vacant city blocks, and a good portion of European

*Above: The Siboney Building is an example of Spanish-style architecture in Ybor City. It features brightly coloured painted tiles around the doorways and windows.*

architectural features and buildings serve as backdrops to a vibrant community and street scene. Italian and Spanish architecture provide a European essence, and ethnic heritage is alive and well along Ybor City's primary 7th Avenue corridor. In 2008 this historic corridor gained national attention when 7th Avenue was recognized as one of the "10 Great Streets in America" by the American Planning Association (APA). The Great Streets program is part of an even larger initiative by the American Planning Association to showcase successful examples of vibrant communities – a far cry from the destructive approach of Urban Renewal that dominated urban planning decades earlier. Billed as the APA's flagship program, the Great Places in America initiative "celebrates places of exemplary character, quality and planning. Places are selected annually and represent the gold standard in terms of having a true sense of place, cultural and historical interest, community involvement, and a vision for tomorrow".

# GRANITEVILLE
## HISTORIC DISTRICT, GRANITEVILLE, SOUTH CAROLINA

Originally located in New England, the cotton textile industry expanded west to New York state and south to Georgia and the Carolinas by the late 19th century. The cotton mills at Graniteville were promoted by Southern industrialist William Gregg, who had diligently worked to convince South Carolina investors that the textile industry was the route to the state's economic future.

### THE DISTRICT
Today the Graniteville Historic District represents the beginnings of the textile industry in South Carolina, including what remains of the company town developed by William Gregg during and after 1846. Within the district is the original Graniteville canal, and the original two-and-a-half storey cotton mill, completed in 1849. Many of the residential and commercial buildings of the company-owned town remain, including 26 workers' houses, nine units of early mill housing, the 1847 Graniteville Academy, where the children were educated at company expense, and an early Gothic Revival-style methodist church.

*Above: The original cotton mill remains as part of historic Graniteville.*

Graniteville represents a regional human landscape illustrating several cultural, social and economic trends prevalent during the antebellum decades. At that time the nation had become transfixed with the suburban ideal of romantically styled homes. At the same time, entrepreneurs were learning of the trend toward company towns, whereby one industrialist or corporation essentially controlled the built environment, social conditions and labour and production within an entire community. Overlaid on these national trends of economic and cultural devel-

*Above: The social structure of the company town included the Graniteville Academy.*

opment was the regional plantation mode of cotton production throughout much of the rural South.

### INDUSTRIAL LEGACY
Cotton milling in South Carolina is traceable into the mid-18th century. When completed, the mill was considered among the best equipped in the nation, and was operating at a profit by 1852. South Carolina's development of its own textile industry lagged behind Gregg's mill town. Around 1880 cotton milling still amounted to a small percentage of the state's industrial economy. Only 18 mills were in production throughout the state by 1880, with Graniteville topping the list with 24,264 spindles. This was double the number of spindles in the second largest cotton mill. By 1907 the list of mills in South Carolina was ten times that of 1880. Further, the number of total spindles throughout the state had risen into the millions. Though requiring nearly half a century to develop, William Gregg's prediction had come true, in part due to his own personal influence.

Today's historic district provides a strong, visible testament to the early development of an industrial complex in the South associated with cotton.

*Left: Victorian house styles were adopted by company towns such as Graniteville.*

# LONGWOOD
## NATCHEZ, MISSISSIPPI

The mid-19th century was a time of innovation and experimentation with respect to building construction techniques and the adoption of exotic architectural styles. One illustrative case is with the so-called octagon mode. The idea and justification for building eight-sided houses and barns was promoted by Orson Fowler (1809–87), who published *A Home for All* in 1848. Fowler's writings focused on the utility and relative cheapness of the octagon form, and ultimately led to the construction of thousands of octagon houses and barns. Most of them were built around 1860. According to Fowler, octagons actually enclosed more floor space per linear foot of wall than the typical square or rectangular forms, making them less expensive. The octagon shape further enhanced the natural lighting through improved sunlight access and ventilation – eliminating, as he said, "dark and useless corners". His houses were also among the first to offer the most advanced household conveniences of the time, including hot and cold running water, dumb waiters, speaking tubes and indoor flush toilets.

### ROMANTICISM
The work of Orson Fowler indirectly came to the attention of Dr Haller Nutt, a wealthy cotton planter and plantation owner from Natchez, Mississippi. In 1852 the noted Philadelphia architect Samuel Sloan published his own versions of octagons. Envisioning essentially a castle of his own in Natchez, Nutt had been familiar with Sloan's book and hired him in 1859 to design an octagon house. True to the times, the home's exterior style was a combination of Italianate and Muslim Revival, essentially represented with a Byzantine onion dome on the 16-sided cupola. This combination of styling reflected the national popularity of architectural

Romanticism and exotic experimentation that flourished during the mid-19th century. The Longwood mansion is the largest and most elaborate octagon house ever constructed in the United States, and demonstrates well the dominant architectural theories and construction techniques of the time.

### UNFINISHED WORK
Unfortunately the timing of construction was poor. Longwood became known as "Nutt's folly". Construction was halted in 1861 with the outbreak of Civil War hostilities. A litany of bad luck and unfortunate circumstances ensued. Given that the main architect and accompanying artisans were from Philadelphia, they dropped the work immediately to answer President Lincoln's call to arms to support the Union's cause. Nutt used his own slaves to complete some of the work through July 1862, but was only able to finish the

*Below: The largest octagon house in America was based on an innovative house design, though its interior is incomplete.*

eight-room basement level. Ultimately, of the 32 planned rooms for the mansion, only nine were completed. The Nutt family moved into this completed section of the mansion, leaving the remaining floors vacant and unfinished to this day. The worst was yet to come, however. In the autumn of 1863 the Union forces destroyed Nutt's cotton plantations in Louisiana, the primary source of his personal fortune. His loss was tallied at more than US $1million. This was ironic, given Nutt's status as a Union sympathizer who happened to be in the wrong place at the wrong time. Dejected and financially ruined, Nutt died in June 1864, but left his widow and eight children with the house. Due to his strong support of the Union, his heirs were able to recover US $188,000 from the government as partial compensation for his loss. The mansion's interior was never completed, however, though the family used the ground floor level as its residence until 1968. Today, the home is operated by the Pilgrimage Garden Club as a house museum open to the public.

# TAMPA BAY HOTEL
## TAMPA, FLORIDA

As a reminder of the accumulation of wealth that was possible during the gilded age, the Tampa Bay Hotel served as an agent of corporate growth and as a monument to competitive spirit. The construction of the Victorian-era hotel between 1888 and 1891 was the initiative of one of America's leading capitalist entrepreneurs at the time, Henry Bradley Plant. By that time Plant had already developed the Port of Tampa as a deep-water harbour and had expanded a local steamship business connecting Tampa with Key West and Havana, Cuba. "Although the Plant Investment Company included, among other holdings, an express company, a hotel chain, several thousand miles of railroad, control of Port Tampa and associated shipping facilities and steamship lines," wrote historian James Covington, "Henry Plant was not satisfied".

Aside from desiring a first-class hotel to house his global art collection, Plant was determined to compete head to head with his business rival on Florida's east coast, Henry Flagler. As the Standard Oil tycoon who had become even more successful than Plant with the construction of his own railroads and hotels, Flagler had built his own monument to success in the form of the US $2 million Ponce de Leon Hotel at St Augustine in 1888. Although not his initial intent, Plant had the early construction plans for the Tampa Bay Hotel altered to better suit his competitive inspiration.

### CONSTRUCTION

The excessive architecture and scale of the hotel clearly matched Plant's vision, and the city of Tampa knew that it was a significant project. The cornerstone was laid on an oppressive 26 July 1888, to much fanfare and celebration, which included a city-proclaimed holiday for all of Tampa. The building was designed to be as fire, and hurricane, proof as possible. Cincinnati supplied the hotel's bricks, and its steel girders came from Pittsburgh. With the conversion of the South Florida Railroad from narrow to standard gauge, the old narrow-gauge rails were used to reinforce various concrete walls and ceilings.

For the landscaping that surrounded the hotel, gardener Anton Fiche brought back a boatload of tropical plants from the Bahamas, and Henry Plant

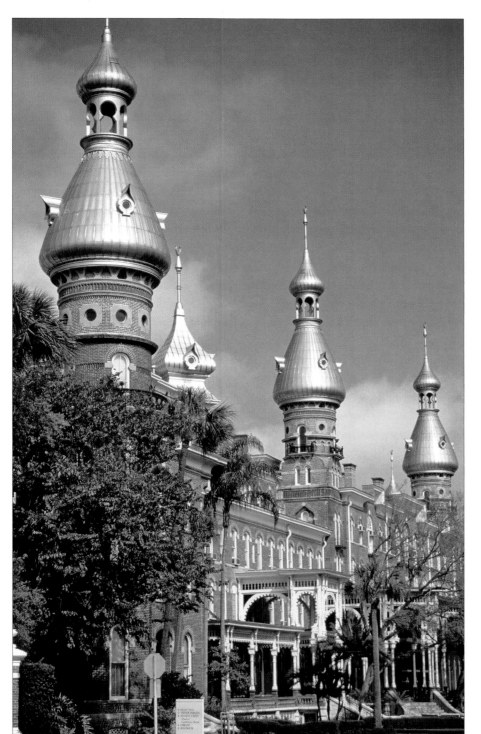

*Left: The ambitious Moorish-Byzantine hotel was never filled to more than half capacity prior to the Spanish-American War.*

supplemented these with a variety of foreign trees and plants from his own European adventures. By 1892 an inventory of specimens on the hotel grounds revealed more than 150 different species, including 22 varieties of palm trees, 13 ferns, nine cacti, three bananas, 12 orchids and a variety of citrus trees.

Inside the 511-room structure, one would find lights and telephones in every guest room. Beneath the hotel was a 61m/200ft long cistern that provided water for the hotel. Further, all of the building's windows were double thick and imported directly from France.

The hotel's exterior architectural exuberance matched the excessive scale of its construction. The Victorian era that extended throughout much of the 19th century was characterized by an interest in "revival" styles of architecture. America's continued fascination with Europe led to a variety of competing revivalist styles that reflected either European or Colonial heritage. Architects and home builders thus adopted successive architectural fads that included Gothic and Romanesque revivals, French Second Empire,

*Below: Plant Hall became the main administration and classroom building for the University of Florida.*

Renaissance Revival, and Colonial or Georgian Revival styles. In contrast architecture inspired by places not bordering the Atlantic Ocean were rare, though architects also experimented with so-called Exotic Revivals during the 19th century.

With its 13 imposing, crescent-crowned minarets and Byzantine-style trim on windows and doors, the hotel is also wildly Picturesque in its complex and irregular floor plan and layout. Its style is referred to as Moorish Revival, though historian James Covington points out that domes and minarets were more typical of Near Eastern sources rather than those of Moorish Spain. Whatever one calls it, however, the hotel provides a well-preserved, outstanding example of Exotic-Revival architecture that adorned a small share of prominent 19th-century projects.

## MEDIA HUB

The Tampa Bay Hotel gained a claim to fame attributed to far more than its architecture. The building became the headquarters for the American Army that invaded Cuba during the Spanish-American War in 1898. This is the conflict that clearly established the United States as a world power. The hotel became a hub for the media, whereby many of the nation's leading

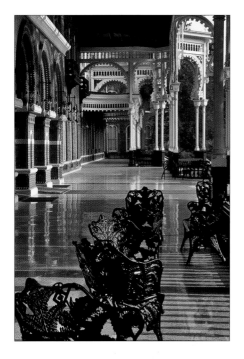

*Above: The Tampa Bay Hotel provides an exquisite example of Turkish or Moorish Revival architecture.*

news correspondents gathered there and reported to the world about the history-making developments. This became the most glorious period for the hotel. Otherwise, the premises enjoyed its share of seasonal guests each year, but generally became known as "Plant's Folly" – having never filled beyond half its capacity prior to the Spanish-American War.

## ADAPTIVE USE

When Plant died in 1899, it appeared the hotel would close permanently. The City of Tampa purchased the property in 1904 and opened the hotel again in 1906. Thus began what was perhaps the hotel's golden era, which coincided with the Florida tourist and land boom prior to the Great Depression. After declaring bankruptcy in 1932, however, the structure was turned over to the University of South Florida as its main administration and classroom building. Today the Tampa Bay reminds us of the Florida boom economic period when railroad entrepreneurs and other developers sought to attract tourists to Florida, hoping these newcomers would eventually purchase property.

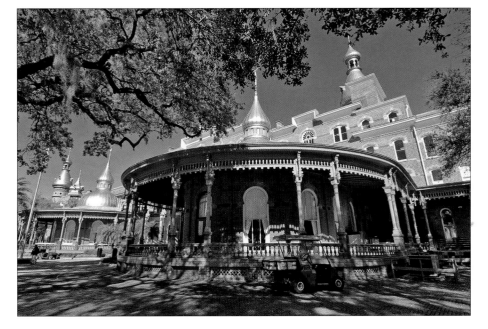

# DIXIE COCA-COLA BOTTLING
## COMPANY PLANT, ATLANTA, GEORGIA

Globalization has played an increasing role in shaping our human landscapes. One of the earliest global products was Coca-Cola, perhaps still the most recognized household name and branded image on the planet. Tracing back the roots of Coca-Cola takes one to Atlanta, Georgia, and specifically to the Dixie Coca-Cola Bottling Company Plant. Still exhibiting its Queen Anne and Italian Renaissance-style facades, the small, Victorian-era building is where the franchise concept was first applied to the soft-drink industry, under the partnership of Benjamin Franklin Thomas and Joseph Brown Whitehead. This particular building was occupied by the Dixie Coca-Cola Bottling Company between 1900 and 1901, and served during this short time as the pioneering headquarters and bottling plant. Eventually the company changed to the Atlanta Coca-Cola Bottling Company, incorporated since 1986 as a division within Coca-Cola Enterprises.

The flavourful soft drink had already been established as a global product by World War II. In 1945 *Fortune Magazine* claimed that Coca-Cola had become "the most widely distributed, undoubtedly the best known, and commercially one of the most promising mass-produced items in the world". This remarkable product, claimed New York writer E. J. Kahn Jr, has become "in the eyes of many people abroad…a fluid that, like gasoline, is indispensable to, and symbolic of, the American way of life".

### BEGINNINGS
The syrup used for Coca-Cola was first developed by a local Atlanta pharmacist John Pemberton in 1886. Soon thereafter, the drink was first sold to the public at the soda fountain of Jacob's Pharmacy in Atlanta. The famous scripted logo for the drink is credited to Pemberton's partner and bookkeeper, Frank Robinson, who first draughted the flowing letters thinking that the two "Cs" in the drink's name would be useful for advertising. By 1887 Pemberton sold his company to Asa Candler who incorporated the Coca-Cola Company a year later. Another local pharmacist, Candler successfully increased syrup

*Below: The site of the original bottling plant was a small Queen Anne-style building, since converted for other use.*

*Above Early production lines for bottling Coca-Cola were a far cry from the massive-scale organization of today.*

sales by more than 4,000 per cent between 1890 and 1900, and by the turn of the century the soft drink was already being sold throughout the United States and Canada.

### A GLOBAL PRODUCT
Although considered by many today as the epitome of the global corporation, Coca-Cola is not necessarily typical of the globalization process, for two reasons. First, the company's system of franchising is uncommon to most centralized corporations where production of a product is standardized. Coca-Cola expanded through a strategy of agreeing with local bottling plants that the company would maintain exclusivity for a particular region, and then selling only the syrup, or concentrate, to the bottler. The second reason why Coca-Cola may not reflect typical globalization was based on the uncommon, widespread consumer resistance in the 1980s, when the company changed the drink's composition to compete with Pepsi. The public essentially rebelled, and classic coke was reinstated. Regardless, the soft drink's fame as a global product is unparalleled worldwide and clearly represents the epitome of the globalization of consumer culture.

# ROHWER RELOCATION CENTER
## MEMORIAL CEMETERY, ROHWER, ARKANSAS

Human landscapes do not always evoke fond memories or recall pleasant experiences. Rather, some places serve to honour individuals or groups who suffered injustices or other hardships in the past. Such is the case with what remains of the Rohwer Relocation Center in rural Arkansas, most notably its cemetery. The cemetery features 24 concrete gravestones and two entrance markers clustered behind tall concrete monuments. The gravestones are small and provide only basic information, and the entrance markers and monuments were created by the Rohwer evacuees. Although only populated for a few years during World War II, the entire relocation site remains symbolic of the American government's efforts to relocate the entire Japanese-American population away from the West-Coast states following the Japanese attack on Pearl Harbor on 7 December 1941. Concerned that anyone of Japanese descent could pose a security risk, Executive Order #9066 was signed by President Franklin D. Roosevelt to authorize the mandatory evacuation of all persons of Japanese ancestry away from the West Coast. At least 110,000 Japanese-Americans were affected by this program of forced removal.

*Below: A thriving Japanese-American community was torn apart during the mandated removal of residents.*

*Above: The memorial cemetery provides a vivid reminder of the American government's largest forced relocation effort in the nation's history.*

### JAPANESE RELOCATION

At first there were no designated destinations for the evacuees. After a voluntary removal process was deemed impractical, full responsibility for the Japanese relocation effort was placed upon the US military. On 9 April 1942 the Wartime Civilian Control Agency (WCCA) was established to co-ordinate the evacuation process. While the locations of more permanent relocation centres were still being determined, the military decided to first move the Japanese populations out of the restricted zones to temporary quarters, known as assembly centres. Most families were given only two or fewer weeks to sell their houses and farms, with some forced to leave within 24 hours.

Within less than a year, ten relocation camps were constructed in seven states, strategically placed in rural, interior locations on the continent. California, Arizona and Arkansas each hosted two relocation camps, while Colorado, Wyoming, Idaho and Utah each had one. For its part, the Rohwer Relocation Camp was constructed in southeastern Arkansas during summer and autumn 1942, and consisted of 200ha/500 acres of wood-framed

*Above: The repetitive pattern of the relocation camps indicated the strong federal presence of its designers.*

barracks. In true military fashion, the tar paper-covered structures were organized methodically in a series of blocks, with 12 barracks per block. Within each block, additional facilities were designed for dining, laundry, bathing and toilets. Each of the barracks was divided into six apartments of varying sizes that housed 250 people.

### LESSONS

Prior to its permanent closure in November 1945, more than 10,000 Japanese-Americans were interred within Rowher's borders. The author of the nomination form for National Landmark status summarized the significance of the relocation in this way: "The decision by the federal government to discriminate against an entire race of people – most of whom were American citizens – solely on the basis of unfounded suspicions regarding their patriotism during wartime and their physical proximity to what was considered a threatened and vulnerable area has since been widely criticized by many legal and social scholars as one of the darkest and most shameful periods in the history of both the United States and the Constitution that ensures the fundamental rights of democracy and equality to all citizens."

# CAPE CANAVERAL AIR FORCE STATION
## CAPE CANAVERAL, FLORIDA

Probably more familiar to Americans than any other landmark, Cape Canaveral maintains a purpose that is singly unique in the American landscape. No other facility in North America has played such a fundamentally significant role in America's space program since it began here in the 1950s, although much of the nation's earliest experiments with missiles and rocketry occurred in the American West.

Considered the father of modern rocket propulsion, Dr Robert Goddard was an American physicist who devised approaches that eventually led to Americans landing on the moon. At a time when Henry Ford was improving his production of the Model T in Michigan, Goddard was already researching the possibilities for rocket flight in 1909. He later launched the world's first liquid-propellant rocket in 1926 and made serious proposals for future moon missions. This latter idea was ripped apart by a sceptical media at the time, and the federal government initially showed little interest in Goddard's discoveries.

*Above: Early launch attempts involved German V-2 rockets captured after World War II.*

It was World War II when the United States learned of the urgent need to build upon Goddard's work, given that German V-2 missiles that were being lobbed into Great Britain. The US government sought to consolidate its

*Below: Robert Goddard and his assistants at his laboratory in Roswell, New Mexico, with a rocket casing in 1940.*

research and test facilities at a sea range site with an island chain that could be used for permanent tracking facilities. Located in Brevard County about 250km/155 miles south of Jacksonville, Florida, the Cape Canaveral Air Force Station became the permanent home of NASA's test and launch facilities in 1947. In that year the newly formed Department of the Air Force was given authority to develop the range, with Brigadier-General W. L. Richardson named to direct the project. The geography of the Bahamas and West Indies played a prominent role, because land was acquired on these islands for the construction of tracking facilities down range.

### NASA

The first launch from the Cape occurred on 24 July 1950, in the form of a German V-2 rocket with an Army VAC Corporal second stage. The imperative for developing a national space and missile program had shifted to a focus on competition with the Soviet Union. Most notable were the successive launches of the Soviet Sputnik satellites that captured the world's attention. Soon afterward, President Eisenhower went public in November 1957 announcing the intended creation of a civilian space agency. Even by this time Eisenhower was being advised to promote a moon project, though he initially rebuffed the idea, more concerned about advancing missile technology to match that of the Soviets. Nonetheless, eight years following the first launch from Cape Canaveral, Congress passed the National Aeronautics and Space Act of 1958, which President Eisenhower signed on July 29.

Through this act, the now familiar National Aeronautics and Space Administration (NASA) was formed, the organization that would ultimately place men on the moon. The transition of the various existing elements of the space program to NASA is summarized on NASA's extensive web pages: "On October 1, 1958, NASA officially opened for business with five facilities inherited from the NACA: Lewis Research Center in Ohio, Langley Research Center and the Wallops rocket test range in Virginia, and Ames Research Center and the Muroc aircraft test range in California. That same day, Eisenhower issued an executive order transferring space projects and appropriations from other space programs to NASA. These gave NASA 8,240 staff (8,000 from the NACA) and a budget of approximately US $340 million."

### RETURN TO THE MOON

Reflecting the urgency of the emerging Cold War, the facilities at the Cape were devoted to the testing of cruise missile-type weapons. Two of the largest and most advanced launch facilities resulted from further development of the program, with the completion of NASA's Saturn IB Complexes 34 and 37. The first Saturn space vehicle was launched on 27 October 1961. It would be the Saturn V vehicle that would rocket the Apollo astronauts to the moon during and after 1969. Virtually the entire history of America's

*Above: The Vehicle Assembly Building (VAB), where the shuttles and earlier Saturn V rockets were prepared prior to launch. One of the largest buildings in the world, it covers 3ha/8 acres.*

space flight progress through NASA is directly associated with Cape Canaveral. Here is where all missions began for the manned flights of the Mercury, Gemini, Apollo, Skylab and Space Shuttle programs. Until recently, satellites and other unmanned space missions were exclusively launched from Cape Canaveral as

*Above: America's Space Shuttle program began in the 1980s and has showcased the world's only reusable space vehicle that can land like an aeroplane.*

well. Cape Canaveral is currently engrossed in the next phase of the American space program, that of Project Orion, NASA's first attempt since the Apollo missions to send humans back to the moon.

*Below: The famous Space Shuttle program came to an end in 2011.*

# CHAPTER FIVE

# THE MIDWEST

CONSIDERED PART OF AMERICA'S INTERIOR
HEARTLAND, THE MIDWEST AS DEFINED HERE
CONSISTS PRIMARILY OF THE TALL-GRASS PRAIRIE
STATES SURROUNDING THE GREAT LAKES,
BROADENING OUT TO THE STATES ALONG THE
MISSISSIPPI RIVER. WITH THE OPENING OF THE
MIDWEST TO ANGLO-AMERICAN SETTLERS
DURING THE 19TH CENTURY, THE NATION'S SIZE
HAD INSTANTLY DOUBLED IN AREA. CHICAGO
BECAME THE NEW GATEWAY TO THE WEST. WITH
THESE NEW TOWNS CAME MAIN STREET,
ANOTHER AMERICAN INNOVATION, WITH
ORDERLY ROWS OF BRICK COMMERCIAL
BUILDINGS LINING THE PRIMARY COMMERCIAL
STREET. TODAY THE LARGE FARMS OF
AGRIBUSINESS DOMINATE THE PRODUCTION OF
CROPS THAT NOW FEED THE WORLD.

*Left: Gateway Arch in St Louis.*

# ASTOR FUR WAREHOUSE
## PRAIRIE DU CHIEN, WISCONSIN

The colonial French economy in North America focused primarily on the trade of two commodities: fish and fur. Prior to the 1850s beaver skins were in high demand throughout Europe. The French fur trade relied heavily on Native American labour for hunting and supplying the beaver skins to French traders. In return the French provided European goods, from metal knives and guns to blankets and porcelain beads.

The fur trade reached its peak during the 1750s. During this decade the French controlled 80 per cent of the fur trade in North America, drastically reducing the native beaver population.

Prairie du Chien, and especially St Feriole Island, served for a long time as a major fur-trading rendezvous point. Every spring and late autumn, tribes would gather here from throughout the Mississippi Valley and Wisconsin to swap goods with French, Spanish, British and, later, American traders.

The Louisiana Purchase in 1803 effectively ended French control west of the Mississippi, and encouraged American business ventures into the region to reach the Pacific Ocean. Without the French, the British and French-Canadians dominated the trade.

*Above: Tribes gathered throughout the Mississippi Valley and Wisconsin to swap goods with traders.*

Seeing an opportunity, John Jacob Astor formed the American Fur Company in 1808. His business plan involved an annual shipment of trade goods and supplies from New York via Cape Horn. It involved the collection of furs throughout the Columbia River interior and their export to China. In turn Chinese products would travel eastward to America and Europe, thereby realizing the long-standing dream of Thomas Jefferson and others to open up American trade directly with Asia.

*Below: The Astor Fur Warehouse is a reminder of an extensive fur trade network.*

### PRAIRIE DE CHIEN

The American Fur Company struggled to trade during the War of 1812, and after it, a federal law in 1816 provided a new opportunity for Astor's company. The law specifically excluded foreign traders from the large fur market of the Louisiana Territory. Acting quickly to tighten control over the trapping areas of the upper Mississippi Valley, the firm established a permanent post in Prairie du Chien. As Astor's company created subsidiary firms throughout the Louisiana Purchase, it created what is considered to be the first business monopoly in the United States.

### FUR TRADE DECLINE

Named for a Fox Native American chief (named *chien*, or "dog" in French), Prairie du Chien became the gateway to the Mississippi River trade network. The Astor Fur Warehouse in Prairie du Chien was constructed in the heyday of the firm's operations. This is the only known original fur-trade warehouse that survives in the upper Mississippi Valley today. It is located on St Feriole Island. The Astor Fur Warehouse building is a two-storey, rectangular, gable-roofed structure, built in 1828 on the site of an earlier log building. The company's good fortunes – due in part to ruthless business tactics – provided the funds for Astor's land investments that propelled him to become the world's richest man. The American Fur Company's business empire was nonetheless short lived. Astor recognized the decline of all fur-bearing animals, and competition ramped up from other sources during the 1830s. He retired in 1834.

Since the decline of the fur trade in the 1850s the warehouse has been adapted variously as a business and residence. It is little altered from its original appearance and was eventually restored and converted into a museum.

# BEGINNING POINT
## OF THE FIRST PUBLIC LAND SURVEY, EAST LIVERPOOL, OHIO

One of the more distinctive elements of the American landscape is the national grid, or more formally the township and range land survey system. Although the survey lines are invisible, they provide a rectilinear framework into which many other human developments exist, including farmsteads, town sites, transportation networks, utilities and many other features of the built environment.

### LAND SETTLEMENT

It was the Northwest Ordinance of 1785 that, when passed by Congress, dictated that the United States be systematically surveyed and organized around square-mile sections of land, each consisting of 259ha/640 acres. In turn, a township was defined as 36 contiguous sections, constituting a 93km/36 mile square block. Survey lines were to follow the cardinal directions, north-south and east-west, intersecting at 90-degree angles. This was the world's first-ever mathematically designed method for the partition of land in advance of settlement. Thomas Jefferson and his contemporaries had realized that the previous colonial European system of surveying land would not be sufficient to facilitate the sale of western lands. The colonial metes and bounds system had been brought to the colonies from Europe, basically comprising an ad-hoc process of arbitrary surveying that relied on physical features such as trees, streams and cow paths.

The ordinance was precisely three months old when the Beginning Point of the public land survey was established. Although the exact location of the original survey conducted is likely under water, the Beginning Point is represented by a granite marker with a 2m/6ft square area located on State Route 39, 3km/2 miles east of East Liverpool, Ohio. This marker and site are maintained by the East Liverpool

*Above: The township and range survey system is typically highlighted by farm roads dividing the square-mile sections.*

Historical Society. It was near this point that the geographer of the United States, Thomas Hutchins, assembled his surveying party and began the task of marking out the first seven ranges of the township and range system. The system was subsequently expanded across the continent over the next century.

Perhaps the national square-mile grid is most prominent in the Midwestern farming landscape. Farmhouses and outbuildings are typically oriented to the cardinal directions, as are their characteristically straight row crops and access roads. Since the 1850s farm structures had two organizing rules: square to the road, and hogs to the east. Since interior rooms of the house were also rectilinear, this meant that furniture, beds and other household items were aligned north-south and east-west. Midwesterners consequently lived in a social system where they ate, slept, shopped, ploughed and recreated in alignment to the national grid; "even the dead are settled on the grid system" with graves facing the cardinal directions.

The growth of western cities since World War II has only reinforced the grid's existence, and its power to "discipline" the developments within it. Flying over the Phoenix metropolitan area makes this strikingly clear, where former farm section roads outlining the square-mile tracts now comprise the region's major suburban roadways and shopping corridors. Consequently, what the modest marker near East Liverpool lacks in grandeur is more than compensated for by the extensive impact of the township and range system on the ordering of America's vast territory.

*Below: The manifestation of the land survey is most pronounced from the air at Phoenix, where a landscape resembling a vast chequerboard plays out on the ground.*

# MADISON

## HISTORIC DISTRICT, MADISON, INDIANA

Settled on a shelf of land along the Ohio River, the city of Madison prospered as a major pork-producing centre during the 19th century. Growth was further assured with the city's status as the region's dominant "break of bulk" point for trade with an expansive interior hinterland. Break of bulk refers to the raw materials and agricultural products sent overland to Madison, where they are transferred to riverboats for shipment eastward. Madison commanded a large trade territory prior to the construction of railroads, and served for some time as Indiana's largest city with 10,700 residents by 1870. It was the terminus for Indiana's first overland road to Lake Michigan (named the Michigan Road), and eventually for Indiana's first railroad. With these profitable industries came wealthy capitalists from the East seeking new opportunities in what is now known as America's "Old Northwest Territory".

The city's prosperity gradually withered during the late 19th century as additional east-west railroads cut through Madison's former trade territory. With rail links to eastern markets from nearby Louisville, Cincinnati, and Indianapolis, Madison's hinterland was

*Left: The Annual Regatta Parade in Madison represents a typical social function for American main streets.*

substantially reduced, coinciding with a decline in riverboat traffic. Still, a smaller building boom following the Civil War sustained the development of housing and commercial buildings in town.

Continuous growth through the century was reflected in the construction of fashionable Italianate and Second Empire-style commercial buildings and homes. Commercial buildings along Madison's main street (originally Main Cross Street) displayed new plate-glass windows and cast-iron store fronts, intermixed with earlier Georgian and

Federal-style structures from the city's first building boom. With a spattering of 20th-century Modern commercial buildings thrown into the mix after World War II, Madison's commercial district exhibits the entire history and development of American commercial architecture. Practically the entire built landscape of main street remains intact today, and provides the first dominant impression that one receives when visiting the town. Main street has, since the 1980s, become the community's premier visitor attraction for this reason.

### THE REDISCOVERY

As Madison's economy sagged during the 1960s and 1970s, the town ironically benefited from a process referred to in historic preservation circles as "benign neglect". A lack of interest in local investment discouraged the otherwise common bulldozing of historic properties to make way for new developments. Madison's historic housing stock and collection of commercial architecture consequently sat undisturbed for decades. Property values decreased.

By the 1980s, the nation's re-awakened interest in national heritage and historic preservation provided a new economic rationale for Madison's historic residential and commercial areas. Wealthier people "discovered" Madison's historic resources and bought up many of the historic properties to renovate as second homes or to sell for a profit. An active historic preservation movement in town further contributed to the community's

*Left: Madison has preserved one of America's most complete main street commercial scenes, including this row of Italianate-style buildings,*

rebirth, and an increasing number of visitors flocked to Madison by the 1990s, informed about the place by a blitz of recent media attention. Once left behind economically by surrounding cities, these metropolitan places were supplying many of Madison's urban-oriented newcomers and private wealth. Previously derelict housing has been transformed into trendy second homes and bed-and-breakfast establishments.

Madison has, therefore, capitalized on its historic resources to attract a new generation of relatively wealthy suburban newcomers, retirees and day-trippers to the revitalized Historic District. This is the recently "reinvented" Madison that one will find when visiting today. Like many towns of similar size across the nation, Madison has been transformed from a place of industrial production to one oriented more toward middle-class consumption and tourism development, providing a whole new host of successes and challenges for the local population.

Madison's unrivaled historic commercial district earned a special recognition during the 1970s. During this time the National Trust for Historic Preservation was seeking alternatives for systematic bulldozing of historic buildings. The Trust embarked on an adventurous pilot project known initially as Main Street USA. Three inaugural "pilot towns" were chosen to employ experimental approaches to revive ailing historic downtowns. What was learned in Madison between 1977 and 1980 helped set the stage for the development of the popular National Main Street Program, in which hundreds of communities have since participated nationwide. Preservation of a community's historic resources is now considered a necessity for reviving small-town economies and engendering a sense of place.

## RESIDENTIAL ARCHITECTURE
Beyond Main Street, Madison displays one of America's largest collections of Federal-style residences, numbering more than 400. These properties illustrate the prominent interest in Classical architecture during Madison's initial period of prosperity. These homes take on numerous sizes and shapes, including banks of English-inspired terrace houses, narrow townhouses and stately mansions. Interspersed within these homes are more than 200 simple frame residences reflecting the working class. Many of these are so-called "shotgun" houses, a folk type that originated in the Caribbean and diffused throughout the American South. The Preservation Movement has had an impact on these modest homes too, with newcomers having renovated many of them.

## GEORGETOWN
Beyond its architectural history, Madison further played a pivotal role in the Underground Railroad and the growth of African-American communities. The Georgetown neighbourhood in Madison may represent the most intact pre-Civil War urban area directly involved with free blacks and their freedom-seeking movement. Historic African-American homes and churches still remain from the pre-Civil War period. Georgetown recently became the first Underground Railroad Historic District in the country to be listed as part of the Network to Freedom.

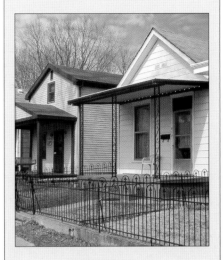

**SHOTGUN HOUSES**

*Above: Shotgun houses line one of Madison's former working-class streets.*

Despite its northerly location, Madison's inclusion of so many shotguns reflects the extensive range of the American South as a distinctive cultural region. Such houses were so named for their long, narrow proportions designed for skinny urban lots. It was said that one could open all of the doors and fire a shotgun through the long axis of the house without hitting anything.

*Below: The James Lanier mansion, a national example of Greek Revival architecture, is now a State Historic Site.*

# QUINCY MINING COMPANY
## HISTORIC DISTRICT, HANCOCK, MICHIGAN

As industrialism drove urban growth and manufacturing, the demand for minerals and metals skyrocketed. The output of American mines grew twice as fast as the output of manufacturing during the late 19th century, primarily because metals such as iron, copper and steel were replacing traditional wood construction techniques. While core manufacturing regions focused on earlier Midwestern and Northeastern trade centres, the locations of metallic ores were often far removed from where they were needed. To extract these distant ores and transport them to the urbanized east required expansive rail networks into these rural territories and the establishment of entire communities focused on mining activities. A colonial type of economic system consequently developed, whereby the rural hinterlands sent raw materials to the industrialized cities, in exchange for manufactured products.

One instructive example of this economic geography involved the copper industry, which shifted geographically from England to Michigan, then to Montana and ultimately Arizona during less than a century. Located on

Michigan's Upper Peninsula, the Quincy Mining Company played a significant role in the evolving and profitable story of copper extraction.

### COPPER BOOM

Prior to the 1880s copper had become a valuable metal due especially to its indestructibility. Copper was in demand as a key ingredient in the alloys brass and bronze, and the red metal could be found in a wide range of manufactured

*Above: Hoist houses raised and lowered miners and ore from the mine.*

products such as clockworks, jewellery, roofing, cookware and the protective sheathing on ship hulls. With the advent of electricity during the 1880s, copper became immensely valuable for its electrical conductivity. The price and demand for copper reached meteoric levels by the 1900s, primarily for its use in copper wire.

The isolated Keweenaw Peninsula constitutes the extreme northern part of Michigan's Upper Peninsula, and is the location of the world's most extensive deposits of copper. Prior to its large-scale extraction by industrial capitalists, the copper here had been mined for 7,000 years by Native Americans. Hundreds of ancient diggings from prehistoric miners led 19th-century explorers to these massive deposits of nearly pure copper. The first "modern" mines of the 1840s triggered a copper boom that spurred the settlement of the

*Left: Ruins abound in abandoned communities that moved quickly through an extractive boom-bust cycle.*

Upper Peninsula. Experienced miners were recruited from Cornwall, England, then the world leader in copper production. Copper extraction in Michigan soon outpaced that of Cornwall. Between 1872 and 1920 approximately 400 mining companies operated within this lucrative area.

The Keweenaw Peninsula gained a rich ethnic heritage during this period, as substantial populations of Cornish immigrated here following widely published accounts of the copper deposits. The Finns came later, during a time when Finland was a colony of Russia.

### LEADERS IN MINING

Despite popular folklore that portrays rural miners as rugged individuals striking out on their own, the copper industry was by necessity heavily capitalized by the late 19th century. The bulk of America's mining activities were dependent upon large-scale corporate operations and their massive infrastructure of railroads, mine shafts, digging equipment, company buildings and workforce accommodation. Such derelict mining infrastructure and associated community buildings provide the human landscape of the Quincy Mining Company Historic District today.

The Quincy Mining Company was a leader in mining technology, continuously adapting its hard-rock mining equipment to meet the demands of the deposits. The company replaced its antiquated ladders with man engines by 1850, for instance, and introduced the first use of power drills in its Pewabic

Mine. In 1873 Quincy further introduced the "shaft-rockhouse", which served as a model for all of Michigan's copper industry. The company's growth and autonomy expanded greatly with the construction in 1898 of the Quincy Smelting Works. Instead of contracting with independent smelting companies to process the mined ore, the company erected its own facility on Portage Lake at the foot of Quincy Hill. The two fundamental components of the smelter were the reverberatory and cupola furnaces, which first separated the copper from the rock and then from the slag.

### SHIFT WESTWARD

Michigan's Upper Peninsula remained the nation's leading copper supplier before 1880. The depletion of the best ore deposits in Michigan encouraged the next major shift in copper production, first to Butte, Montana, and soon thereafter to various copper districts in Arizona. Montana and Arizona already accounted for 43 and 14 per cent, respectively, of national copper production by 1889. At that point, Michigan accounted for 39 per cent. By 1919

*Left: Large-scale copper mining operations required complex machines, buildings, shafts and communities, all controlled by large corporations.*

*Above: The tall smelter, where the copper metal is extracted from the ore.*

Arizona had become the leading producer accounting for 47 per cent of the nation's total, while the Montana and Michigan districts had declined to 16 and 19 per cent, respectively. By 1920 the American West was supplying 80 per cent of the nation's copper, despite its distance from eastern manufacturing belts. Mining operations ceased in 1957 after years of declining production, though the reclamation plant produced copper for an additional ten years.

Although much of the historic mining infrastructure and equipment remain in ruins today, much of the company's built environment is still visible and, in some cases, in very good condition. The mine and its environs now constitute a popular tourist attraction, all part of the Keweenaw National Historic Park. The integrity of the mining facilities and remaining community structures is strong, and still provides a sense of the corporate-scale activities that occurred here. Smokestacks from the boiler houses, abandoned railroads, mine shafts, company housing and Victorian-style homes all remain to indicate the full scope of community and company life that surrounded this particular extractive industry.

# MISSOURI BOTANICAL GARDEN
## ST LOUIS, MISSOURI

The expanding interest in science during the Enlightenment in Europe provided an opportunity for the flourishing of natural history and horticulture during the 19th century. The American Colonial and Federal periods saw an array of cultural and scientific exchanges between Europe and the Americas, and exchanges of plant specimens were no exception. This interaction set the stage for an explosion of 19th-century botanical and horticultural interest in the United States. At first it was European enthusiasts who traversed America's wilderness to collect plant specimens, of which early American and European botanists were eager recipients. These pioneer explorers wisely followed along the routes of others – along the paths of fur traders, on planned expeditions into the Rocky Mountains and elsewhere, or along new trails through the Louisiana Purchase on the heals of the Lewis and Clark Expedition.

### EARLY BOTANY

As the world's pre-eminent Colonial power at the time, England aspired to lead the world in the area of natural sciences. In this pursuit Sir Joseph Banks (1743–1820) served as the botanical advisor to King George III and as de

*Above: The knowledge of botanical gardening was brought to the rural Midwest by the tireless enthusiast Henry Shaw.*

*Below: As one of two world-renowned botanical gardens in the United States, the facility documents and grows plant species from around the globe.*

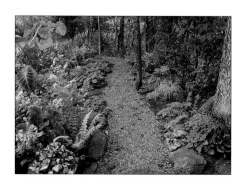

facto director of the Royal Botanic Gardens at Kew, near London. Banks convinced members of England's royal and aristocratic society to sponsor English naturalists to accompany ships and expeditions overseas. The gardens at Kew became a global repository for foreign specimens and botanical data provided by England's colonies. England's ambitions were further assured with the founding of the Horticultural Society of London in 1804, an organization designed to advance botanical science and provide new specimens for English gardens. The society also funded collectors to explore foreign lands and thereby add to the scientific knowledge of plant communities around the globe. By the 1820s the society was sponsoring plant-collecting expeditions to all reaches of the planet, venturing into Asia, Africa, Central and South America, and the western United States.

Making the arduous transport of living specimens easier was the fortuitous discovery of the greenhouse principle in 1838 by Nathaniel Ward. He had buried a glass jar that held a chrysalis within some soil. He noticed that seeds in the soil had germinated due to condensation that produced a self-sustaining environment. The greenhouse has ever since become a standard apparatus for collectors and botanical gardens alike.

Benefiting greatly from England's leadership and knowledge were early American naturalists who ultimately contributed in their own right to botany and horticulture. Among the most prominent of these was Andrew Jackson Downing, who promoted the Picturesque principles of landscaping and gardening prior to the American Civil War.

### HENRY SHAW

By the time St Louis businessman Henry Shaw (1800–89) envisioned his own botanical gardens, he was able to learn from a host of European and American predecessors. Born and raised in England, young Henry accompanied

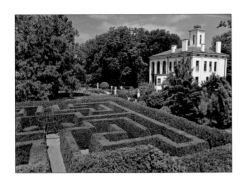

*Above: Henry Shaw's Italian villa, called Tower Grove, became the focus for the future botanical gardens near St Louis.*

his father to America on business and eventually struck out on his own to take advantage of Mississippi River trade. The vast Louisiana Purchase had been added to the United States a decade earlier, and Henry settled appropriately within the expanding French village of St Louis. Capitalizing on the place's budding status as gateway to the west, Shaw operated a hardware outlet and provided goods and services to soldiers, farmers, immigrants and pioneers heading west. So successful was his business that Shaw was able to retire by age 40. He had become one of the city's largest landowners and an influential local citizen. The next, longer phase of his life would be devoted to his greater loves of travel, botany and philanthropy.

Following two lengthy stays in Europe, Shaw built an estate for himself in the St Louis countryside, named Tower Grove. The grounds surrounding his stylish Italian villa would become the acreage for the Missouri Botanical Gardens. It was during his third European trip that he became convinced to begin a garden of his own. His main intent on this 1851 trip was to visit the Great Exhibition in London, essentially a world's fair that marked England's political and cultural prominence around the world. He likewise paid a visit to Chatsworth, the ancestral home of the Duke of Devonshire. Shaw was introduced here to the influential work of Joseph Paxton and his gardens, fountain, cascades and conservatory.

This was considered the most magnificent private residence in Europe at the time. Strolling the grounds, Shaw wondered if he could start his own garden in St Louis. He further visited the Royal Botanical Gardens at Kew, and upon returning to St Louis began a written correspondence with Kew's renowned director, Sir William Hooker. In establishing communications with Hooker, Shaw had accessed the mind of the most qualified person in the realm of botanical gardening.

Hooker recommended that Shaw scour the London catalogues to find relevant books at reduced prices. Shaw complied in this and other ways, ultimately acquiring voluminous amounts of literature on the subject of gardening and horticulture. The Missouri Botanical Gardens, therefore, evolved through Shaw's vision, but importantly, reflected the prevailing standards for botanical gardens in both Europe and the Eastern United States. In large part due to Shaw, the knowledge of botanical science diffused from these core cultural areas to the emerging American Midwest. As in England, Shaw designed his expanding

*Below: The principle of the greenhouse effect was discovered by accident and quickly made use of in the world of botanical gardening.*

gardens to be ornamentally pleasing as well as scientifically significant. By 1859 Shaw had added a museum that housed the garden's library, herbarium and administrative headquarters.

**THE GARDENS TODAY**

Although Shaw preferred that his institution be called the Missouri Botanical Garden, the property is referred to informally as Shaw's Garden more than a century later. Shaw would undoubtedly be pleased to see how his creation has expanded its public educational role today. Seasonal shows are still regularly held, as they were during the garden's earliest years. The garden has further developed an extensive educational program for both youths and adults.

In the realm of science, the Missouri Botanical Garden continues to serve as a world-renowned centre for the advancement of botany in the USA. It is the oldest remaining botanical garden in the nation, and it takes pride in its prestige as one of only two American gardens that rank among the finest in the world. Today the mature combination of the garden's physical landscape, publications, library, herbarium and educational programs provides a thorough documentation of botany in the USA from the mid-19th century to the present day.

# MARK TWAIN BOYHOOD HOME
## HANNIBAL, MISSOURI

Promoted as "America's Hometown" by city boosters, Hannibal sits on the west shore of the Mississippi River and exhibits a fairly typical Midwestern small-town landscape. Setting it apart from hundreds of other smaller communities, however, is the fact that it was the boyhood home of Samuel Langhorne Clemens (1835–1910), known best under the pseudonym of Mark Twain. Clemens grew up to become America's foremost humourist during the latter half of the 19th century, and later became more widely renowned as a successful novelist. He is one of America's best-known literary figures of the 19th century.

Having lived in Hannibal between 1844 and 1853, it was here where Clemens gained much of his literary inspiration for later novels, including his best-known works such as *The Adventures of Tom Sawyer* and *The Adventures of Huckleberry Finn*. His own boyhood experiences in Hannibal greatly influenced the now-legendary events within his novels. Numerous characters were likewise derived from his boyhood acquaintances. Most prominently, Tom Sawyer's sweetheart, Becky Thatcher, resembled the real Laura Hawkins. The character of Sid

*Below: Clemens returned to his hometown in 1902 and confirmed his boyhood home.*

Sawyer was based on Clemens' brother, and "Negro Jim" resembled a slave acquaintance known as Uncle Dan'l.

### A MIDDLE-CLASS HOME
Now restored as a museum, the dwelling in which Clemens resided is an unpretentious two-storey frame house that was typical for middle-class Missouri homes of the time, and represents a Pennsylvania-derived example of folk architecture. Clemens' boyhood dwelling most closely resembles a variety of common housing known as "Pennsylvania Georgian". The only major change to the dwelling since its construction was the second storey, added in 1851. Its six rooms have been decorated to mirror what one might expect to see during the times of Tom Sawyer's family. The museum comes complete with Tom Sawyer's infamous whitewashed fence connected to the side of the house.

### THEME TOWN DEVELOPMENT
Perhaps more important than the house museum itself is the cultural identity it has engendered for the entire town. Hannibal provides an excellent exam-

*Above: Some consider the dwelling of Clemens to be the Midwest's most outstanding literary shrine.*

ple of what geographers refer to as "theme towns," where a distinctive local trait or historic event has been consciously promoted as a theme to a wider audience. In the face of economic decline and outmigration since the 1960s, America's rural communities have been driven to "reinvent" themselves as appealing to outsiders. Attaching their locale with a distinct theme has been a common approach for improving local economies and sense of place. America is now replete with visitor-oriented theme towns that have succeeded and gained name recognition nationally or globally. In Hannibal, one finds a transition from a once sleepy, Midwestern river town to a nationally known tourist attraction that provides numerous images and experiences associated with Mark Twain. As a distinctive type of place, then, the Hannibal community has learned to improve its local economy and cultural identity through the fortunate existence of one prominent author's boyhood residence.

# RIVERSIDE
## HISTORIC DISTRICT, RIVERSIDE, ILLINOIS

Famous from its recent success with designing Central Park in New York City, the team of Frederick Law Olmsted, Sr and Calvert Vaux were given free reign to design a new suburban community 14km/9 miles west of downtown Chicago beginning in 1869. They were employed by the president of the Riverside Improvement Company, Emery Childs, who intended to subdivide 650ha/1,600 acres of farmland into housing tracts.

The location for Riverside was determined by its planned location as the first station stop outside of Chicago, along the Chicago, Burlington & Quincy Railroad. Steam trains would provide transportation for suburban Riverside residents to and from Chicago. Olmsted further wished to construct a separate, suburban "parkway", or pleasure drive, to better link Riverside with Chicago. Although added to the masterplan, the parkway was never completed.

### NATURALISTIC TOWN PLAN
Olmsted and Vaux successfully brought together the emerging American real estate development process with landscape design for social and recreational purposes. They strategically adapted Picturesque landscaping principles similar to those in Central Park. Prior to the 1860s, American cities and towns had been laid out on rectilinear street grids that ignored existing natural topographic features such as hills and streams. Nature was viewed as an inconvenience to be subdued. With Riverside, however, Olmsted established a more Picturesque approach to suburban design. Streets were not straight, but curved, allowed to flow around the natural topography. In this case the primary natural feature of the site consisted of the meandering Des Plaines River, the land along which Olmsted reserved for public parks or commons. The

deliberately curved residential streets were intended "to suggest and imply leisure, contemplativeness and happy tranquility." His flowing street plan long served as the classic guide for later suburban developers, and would remain the standard approach for planned suburbs in the 20th century.

Picturesque landscaping principles were incorporated into the site's unbuildable wetlands for a park, and the dammed Des Plaines River became a public lake. Reminiscent of Central Park, Olmsted devoted nearly a third of the site's total acreage to public spaces, including a 65ha/160 acre park on both sides of the river, enhanced with various smaller commons, groves, fields and even a croquet ground. Streets were lined with trees to visually break up the monotonous view of the natural prairie. Houses were set back at least 10m/30ft from the roads. Underneath Olmsted's

*Below: Avery Coonley House was designed by architect Frank Lloyd Wright, and built in 1907–08.*

landscaping was the now-standard infrastructure of drains and sewers, and gas and water lines – technologies that had matured recently for suburban developments. By the early 1870s, 50 framed homes had been completed, many in the still popular Gothic Revival style. Approximately five are still standing.

Perhaps amazingly, only minor alterations have occurred to Olmsted's initial plan. Gas street lamps still exist in all residential areas, and many of the homes constructed after the 1870s continue to reveal the succession of popular American architectural styles as Riverside slowly built out through the 1960s. Of course, metropolitan Chicago has long since expanded outward from downtown. All of the Riverside Historic District and its planned open space are now surrounded by unplanned suburban development. Olmsted's initial design remains intact, however, providing a powerful residential memorial to the advent of the modern-day suburban community. Riverside is one landmark that has most influenced American society and suburban living.

# PULLMAN
## HISTORIC DISTRICT, CHICAGO, ILLINOIS

A quintessential entrepreneur of the Industrial Revolution, George M. Pullman became one of the richest men in the country by 1876. Pullman was trained initially as a cabinet maker and later realized that America's expanding railroad network had not yet provided decent sleeping accommodation for overnight train travel. He first entered the railroad industry through several experimental conversions of regular passenger cars into sleeping cars. He formed the Pullman Palace Car Company in 1867, appointing himself as president and general manager. Competing successfully with numerous other upstart companies, Pullman secured lucrative contracts with the railroads as he pursued his steadfast dream of revolutionizing overnight train travel. The Pullman name became associated with luxury as dozens of his sleeping cars entered regular passenger service. At its peak the Pullman company had 10,000 of its railroad sleeping cars in service across the country.

*Right: Named for George Pullman's daughter, the Florence Hotel in Pullman still survives.*

*Above: The company town of Pullman was celebrated for its design to support a working-class community.*

### PORTERS
The Pullman company became a primary employer of freed slaves. Recognizing the availability of cheap labour in the South, Pullman recruited African-Americans to serve passengers on his sleeping cars. Referring to them as "porters", the company provided them with one of the most promising, though gruelling, career paths. Although praised by historians for providing employment for African-Americans following the Civil War, Pullman was first and foremost a cunning businessman.

Working conditions improved over time, however, early porters were poorly paid and worked excruciating hours.

### A COMPANY-TOWN MODEL
By the 1870s some industrialists realized it was in their best interest to provide a minimum set of amenities for their employees, even if their primary aim was to prevent labour strikes and to discourage unionization. Earlier companies had designed their own employee housing, eventually experimenting with the creation of entire company-owned towns. On the positive side, the trend toward company towns for large industries provided an alternative to overcrowded tenements. Companies sought to gain rental income from their tenants while improving their overall living conditions. In turn, it was hoped, companies would encourage a more stable work force by reducing the transience of employees.

Pullman adopted the company town model for his own business of producing luxurious railroad sleeping cars. At Lake Calumet, 19km/12 miles south of Chicago, Pullman built an entire community between 1880 and 1884 that included free-standing houses, public parks, recreational facilities, retail outlets, churches, a library and even a music hall. Still surviving today, many of Pullman's houses were designed in the Gothic Revival and Queen Anne styles of the Victorian era. Approximately 1,750 dwellings were constructed, all of them with brick that was manufactured from clay on the site. The architect Solon S. Beman was responsible for the design.

In 1885 Richard Ely published a review of the new community. He raved about the housing, which he believed was expected more from middle-class suburbs than company towns. A variety of architectural styles and designs were employed, including French or square roofs, dormers, turrets and other Victorian-era features. Ely reported that: "Desirable houses have been provided for a large labouring population at so small a cost that they can be rented at rates within their means and yet yield a handsome return on the capital invested."

Ely was less enthused with the town's social conditions. Working families were not able to own property in the town of Pullman. He further noted a lack of emotional attachment, contending that families considered themselves no more than temporary residents. Ely ultimately described the town as "un-American" in that the place represented the "absolute power" of industrial capital and the "repression of all freedom". His concerns were validated in 1894 when a violent workers' strike and riot led to the deployment of federal troops to the town. According to architectural historian Leland Roth, the incidents at Pullman served to discredit the idea of corporate-controlled communities. More important than public perception, the bloody and violent turmoil drastically affected the progress of the American labour movement.

### PULLMAN STRIKE

Known as the "famous Pullman strike of 1894", the incident began when the company laid off one-third of its men

*Above: Rioters burn 600 freight cars during the famous Pullman strikes of 1894.*

due to the deepening economic depression, and it cut the wages of everyone else from 30–40 per cent. Even worse, no reductions were made to the monthly cost of rent or retail goods. The American Railway Union quickly supported the Pullman strikers, and the strike soon spread nationwide. A year later the Pullman Company was ordered by the Illinois Supreme Court to sell off all land, houses and buildings not used strictly for manufacturing. This signalled the beginning of the end for the company's control over Pullman, Illinois. The

*Below: Despite its shortcomings, the town of Pullman represented an impressive advancement from the more typically overcrowded, unsanitary and makeshift living conditions faced by the working class throughout much of the 19th century.*

*Above: A poster advertises the comforts of travelling by Pullman carriage.*

population declined from 12,000 in 1895 to about 10,000 by 1905. Both Pullman and Hyde Park community were annexed by the City of Chicago.

### PULLMAN'S LEGACY

Historians continue to credit Pullman with envisioning and realizing America's first master-planned company town designed to provide ideal living conditions for employees and their families. This was a pioneering urban social achievement at the height of America's Industrial Revolution. Although some of the larger structures no longer exist, much of Pullman's built landscape remains intact today, including more than 1,600 of the original dwellings, the four-storey hotel, the company administration building, church, stables and numerous other structures.

# PILLSBURY "A" MILL
## MINNEAPOLIS, MINNESOTA

Now a household name throughout America, Pillsbury helped Minneapolis to grow into the "milling capital of the nation" between 1880 and 1930. The city was settled and grew around St Anthony Falls along the Mississippi River, a natural feature that figured prominently in its economic development. Emerging first as a regional hub for the timber industry, 17 saw mills eventually co-existed around the falls, from which they derived power. The city soon became the centre for the milling of flour from wheat, grown by farmers on the Great Plains and shipped in by rail. No less than 34 flour mills provided Minneapolis with its foremost industry, with Pillsbury and General Mills serving as leading processors. Nearly ten per cent of the nation's flour and grist was processed through Minneapolis by 1905.

*Below: Costing US $500,000 to build, the limestone structure of the Pillsbury "A" Mill soars to six storeys high, not including its basement. The foundation sidewalls measure 2.6m/8½ft thick, and the rough ashlar (stone) walls are 75cm/ 2½ft thick at the top of the structure.*

**PILLSBURY'S DREAM**
Originally from New Hampshire, Charles Alfred Pillsbury (1842–99) made his way to Montreal, Canada, and eventually to Minneapolis to take advantage of St Anthony Falls. Pillsbury had experienced the processing of grain in Montreal, which drew him to join the industry in Minneapolis. For five years, Pillsbury secretively planned to build the largest and most technologically advanced flour mill in the world. He travelled widely to learn the most effective techniques for handling large-scale milling. He fulfilled his dream in 1881 with the completion of the Pillsbury "A" Mill along the Mississippi River. Designed by architect LeRoy S. Buffington and several engineers, the full complex included two units: the East "A" and the West "A", with two independent streams of wheat flowing into the mill.

The mill's initial capacity was approximately 4,000 barrels a day, which was a staggering amount for that time. Pillsbury's detractors thought that the mill was much too large, given the level of demand for flour. Initially, they were correct, because several years passed

*Above: Construction of the West Side Canal begins to the side of Pillsbury "B" Mill and Excelsior Mill in the flour district.*

before the "A" actually reached capacity. Eventually, the mill's capacity was increased several times over, given newer technologies. A capacity of 17,500 barrels a day was gradually realized. As the largest, most advanced mill in the world for some time, it served as the standard in the industry and gained much attention for its design.

Two 1,500 horsepower water wheels initially powered the mill until its conversion to electricity during the 1950s. Of all the former mills in Minneapolis, this is the only one that survives today. Fires and explosions were common for flour mills, to which several of the Pillsbury A's neighbours succumbed. Having avoided such a disaster, the remaining "A" mill retains its original wooden frame. The old mill race that shuttled water to the wheels also remains, as does the water power machinery in the sub-basement. Production continued until 2003.

Three years later Shafer Richardson, a local developer, acquired the property and began a massive historic rehabilitation project dubbed "East Bank Mills", converting the old mill into a residential loft complex. The project demonstrates a common trend in America's post-Industrial era.

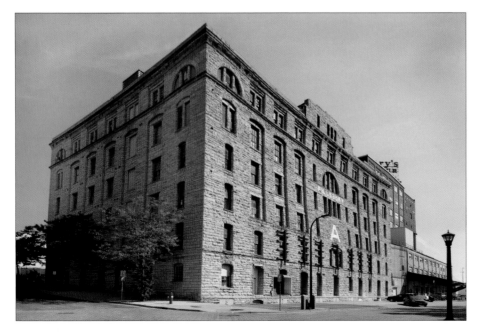

# PEAVEY-HAGLIN
## GRAIN ELEVATOR, ST LOUIS PARK, MINNESOTA

Not a typical tourist attraction, this otherwise drab, concrete tower nonetheless helps to explain one of the Midwest's most striking landscape features. The cylindrical grain elevator is a central function of hundreds of small towns and cities throughout America's prairie region. Such elevators are grain storage bins located periodically along railroad lines or river routes. Farmers drive their trucks full of food crops to the nearest elevator and sell their product to the grain storage company. The grain is periodically loaded from the local elevators on to awaiting railroad hopper cars. From there it moves along rail routes to larger urban centres for processing and milling, or overseas to faraway markets. Because the local elevator traditionally became a central hub for surrounding farms, main-street business districts often developed along the tracks beneath the building, providing farm and town populations with goods and services. Residential neighbourhoods developed around main street.

### VERTICAL EXPERIMENT

The earliest grain elevators were rectangular wooden structures covered with tin siding to repel sparks from steam locomotives. Some still survive at rural railroad junctions, but most have been replaced with the towering, concrete types. These towers have their roots in one experimental project, the Peavey-Haglin Grain Elevator outside of Minneapolis, Minnesota.

The nation's first cylindrical concrete elevator was developed by Frank H. Peavey (1850-1901) who was the owner of a leading grain company, and Charles H. Haglin (1849-1921), who had ascended to become a prominent civil engineer and local contractor. Haglin was responsible for the Globe Building and the Minneapolis City Hall and Courthouse. Together, these two inno-

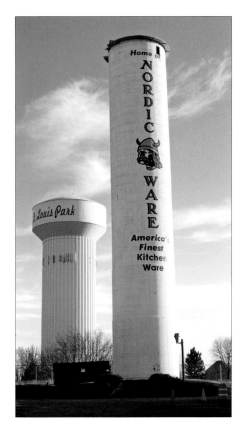

vators aimed to determine the feasibility and limitations of a grain storage unit built entirely of concrete on the outskirts of Minneapolis. At the time of

*Below: Earlier grain elevators had wooden frames with tin plating. The most common, looming threat for wooden grain storage structures was sparks from passing locomotives.*

*Left: The Peavey-Haglin grain elevator is now owned by Nordic Ware.*

construction in 1899–1900, Minneapolis had grown to become Minnesota's "grain metropolis". Their demonstration structure was completed in two phases, as a precautionary measure. Round, wooden forms braced with steel hoops were used to pour the concrete for each section. The forms were moved upward as each section hardened. Engineers ordered the first part of the elevator to be capped at 21m/68ft because no one knew how much force or pressure the structure would withstand. The first attempt to fill the elevator with grain was a success, which encouraged the extension of the tower to its final height of 38m/125ft.

Because it was built with the sole purpose of proving its strength, the structure never held grain again. It did become rather famous, however, at least as far as grain elevators go. This slender, silo-like structure became the prototype for larger and more complex grain elevators that became ubiquitous throughout the grain growing regions.

*Below: Modern grain elevators are concrete and usually much larger than Peavey-Haglin's model.*

# WAINWRIGHT BUILDING
## ST LOUIS, MISSISSIPPI

A ten-storey office building in downtown St Louis, the Wainwright Building, was the first to demonstrate all of the design and structural elements of the modern-day skyscraper. Designed by Louis Sullivan and constructed in 1890–91, the office tower was built for Ellis Wainwright, a wealthy St Louis brewer.

Sullivan advanced the Wainwright to the next level of structural building form, following lessons learned in Chicago. This was the first-ever tall building to incorporate an iron and steel structural frame. Its load is supported entirely by its steel frame and is sheathed with fireproof brick and terracotta. A concrete "raft" foundation supports the building's column load.

### EXTERIOR DESIGN

The exterior design of the Wainwright is innovative, and served as a prototype for early 20th-century skyscraper facades. The building was organized around three visible sections, including a lower block of street-level store front, a vertical block of office floors and an upper section with the requisite mechanical equipment. Essentially, Sullivan divided the building into a tri-partite system of base, shaft and capital of a Classical column. This vertical design scheme was subsequently adapted for skyscrapers nationwide and allows one to easily identify the first generation of office towers.

Sullivan believed "that the appearance of an office building should reflect the activities within". The lower floors were visually distinctive from those above them, with the first two floors sheathed in brown sandstone. In contrast the office floors above were designed to be visually and functionally uniform. Thus, the next seven storeys above the store front rose with continuous, red brick piers, and the uniform windows were set back and separated with uniform panels of terracotta.

### INTERIOR DESIGN

Inside, this uniform structure allowed the identical office floors to be sub-divided in numerous ways, depending on the needs of the occupying tenants. Such flexibility on each floor was also enabled by the lack of space-hogging masonry pillars and walls that once accompanied load-bearing buildings.

Sullivan envisioned the attic storey to terminate the building visually while housing the functional mechanical equipment now necessary to operate such a spacious structure. The tenth and final storey is therefore distinctive in its own right, essentially a frieze of inter-twined leaf scrolls framing circular windows. The whole building is capped off with Sullivan's characteristic over-hanging roof slab.

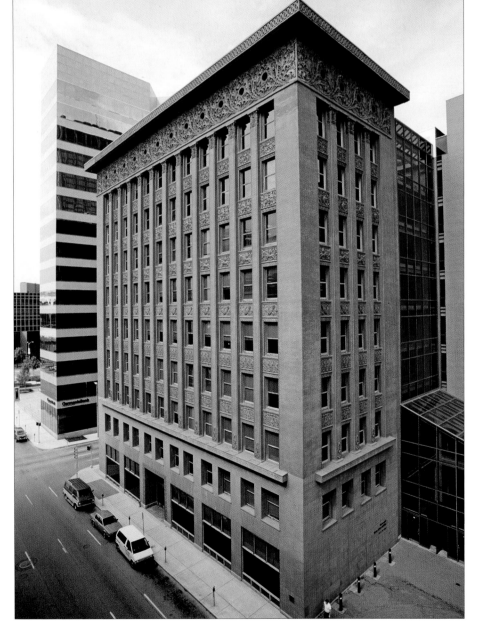

*Left: The Wainwright was the first office tower to completely employ steel-frame construction, freeing up the space inside.*

# AUDITORIUM BUILDING
## CHICAGO, ILLINOIS

Designed by the prestigious team of Chicago architects Dankmar Adler and Louis Sullivan, the Auditorium Building represents both an unprecedented engineering feat and the genesis of skyscraper development. When completed in 1889 the monumental structure was the tallest and most culturally important building in Chicago. A coalition of businessmen envisioned the construction of a grand auditorium primarily for opera productions. The city needed not just an opera house, however, but a multi-use space for political conventions, charity balls and other civic purposes. Desiring a financially self-sufficient facility, the architects were asked to surround the 4,300-seat auditorium with commercial, office and hotel space to support the opera's expenses. Although not intended as a commercial building, the final structure covered 59,000 sq m/ 63,500 sq ft of land fronting Michigan Avenue and included 136 offices, a 400-room hotel and stores on the ground level. The masonry, load-bearing building rose ten storeys with an additional 17-storey tower incorporated into the main block.

### CONSTRUCTION
With steel frame construction yet to be perfected, the design plans challenged the engineering skills of Dankmar Adler and his associates. No bedrock existed beneath the auditorium, or beneath any of downtown Chicago for that matter. Instead, increasingly heavy city buildings had to be engineered to prevent sinking into the soft clay below. In conjunction with engineer Paul Mueller, Adler conceived of an innovative "raft" foundation that would simulate the stabilizing attributes of bedrock. They designed a floating mat of criss-crossed railroad ties and added steel rails over the top, embedded in concrete. The weight of the auditorium's massive walls

would consequently be distributed more evenly throughout the raft assemblage. Although successful for its time, the building has settled with age. The raft has been slowly deformed by the relatively heavy outer walls as compared to the lightweight interior. Portions of the structure have settled as much as 74cm/29in, an effect noticeable in the theatre lobby where the floor slopes downward toward the outer walls.

The weight of the 15,000-ton office tower required similar creative techniques. Adler solved this engineering dilemma by employing a cast-iron interior frame with wrought-iron trusses to support the tower. The basement provided yet another problem, which was 2m/7ft below the water level of Lake Michigan. Adler successfully made it water tight. The auditorium itself was designed to accommodate 4,237 guests, requiring that it occupy a full third of the building's interior space. The seating was designed to enable a full view of the stage from anywhere in the auditorium, and the acoustics ended up

*Above: The Auditorium Building played a significant role in the evolution of the American skyscraper.*

nearly perfect, even in the highest balcony. The vast enclosure was cooled by air tempered roof sprays, making this the first air-conditioned structure.

### RECENT HISTORY
The facility suffered hard times when the opera moved to the new Civic Opera House in 1929. Coupled with the lengthy Depression, the theatre closed for some time, and the office and hotel facilities showed their age. Bankruptcy came in 1940. The Auditorium Building's second chance arrived in 1946 with its purchase by Roosevelt University, which embarked on a massive restoration effort. Still a prominent architectural icon along Chicago's Michigan Avenue, the building continues to serve as the university's downtown campus, and the theatre remains open to the public as an excellent example of adaptive use.

# UNION STATION
## ST LOUIS, MISSOURI

With the 1871 construction of Vanderbilt's first Grand Central Station in New York City, America's "age of the grand terminal" had begun. In the highly competitive industrial economy of the late 19th century, railroad companies forged intense rivalries that led to increasingly grander and ornate railroad terminal buildings, or "union stations". By the 1880s cities nationwide were championing their own union terminals, which compared favourably with, and sometimes rivalled, huge civic buildings such as city halls and cathedrals. Such terminals were designed to be monumental in scope, serving as stately symbols and, more practically, as the "gateways" into their respective cities. A wave of grand terminal construction occurred between 1880 and

1930, paralleling America's "golden age" of railroad travel, prior to the common use of aeroplanes or automobiles. The construction of such terminal buildings was considered an important high-water mark for the booming railroad companies at the height of America's Industrial Revolution. Never had the travelling public been lavished with such grand architecture and services before as they travelled.

### COMPETITION

St Louis's Union Station remains today as America's finest surviving example of high Victorian railroad architecture, in this case representing a blend of French chateau and Romanesque styles. Erected in 1892–4 and designed by architect Theodore C. Link, the terminal illus-

*Above: A blend of French chateau and Romanesque styles, Union Station was designed to put St Louis on the map as a cultured Midwestern city.*

trates the culmination of the so-called Picturesque Eclectic mode of Victorian railroad architecture. On the heals of this, Union Station saw a fundamental shift in architectural preference for such structures, which thereafter moved away from Victorian Eclecticism into the trendy Classical Beaux-Arts mode associated with the emerging City Beautiful Movement.

St Louis did not escape from the competitive vigour of the period. By the time planning began for its own grand terminal, those of other Midwestern cities had already been constructed. Already well aware of their unique status as "gateway to the west", St Louis sponsored an international competition to determine the best design for its own new terminal. The intent was clear: that of outdoing all of its Midwestern counterparts. Entrants for the competition poured in from both sides of the Atlantic, but ultimately it was a local St Louis architecture firm that took the prize. Link & Cameron presented a design that celebrated the French heritage of their home city, effectively combining a Richardsonian-Romanesque form with the style of a magnificent French chateau like those along the famous Loire Valley. The final product proved a powerful cultural symbol: that a Midwestern city had finally risen to a level of sophistication and population growth comparable with older cities farther east.

### TRAINSHED

Also of note for its monumental scale is the Union Station's adjoining train shed, the largest of America's single-vault train sheds erected during the 19th century. This one exceeded all others in both area and linear dimension, and covered the largest number of tracks (originally

*Below: Replacing the 32 tracks under the enormous train shed are a hotel, restaurant and plaza-type attractions.*

32). The tin-covered wooden roof was constructed on top of a steel framework of transverse Pegram trusses, so named for the shed's designing engineer, George H. Pegram. The final train shed measured 183m/600ft wide, 192m/630ft long and 22.5m/74ft high. Reflecting the height of demand for rail travel by the 1920s, this massive structure became inadequate to handle the volume of rail traffic. The terminal was so congested by the 1920s that the railroad company expanded its facilities. Most notably, a two-storey baggage building was added in 1928, and ten more tracks with separate canopies were added in 1929.

*Above: The late Victorian concourse served as a grandiose gateway for travellers into and out of the city.*

### ADAPTIVE USE

Perhaps the lowest point in the terminal's history arrived in the 1970s with the image of a lone Amtrak train departing for the last time, surrounded by abandoned terminal tracks and weed-covered rights of way. Union Station fell into disuse. It would be up to the forward-thinking participants of the emerging Historic Preservation Movement to bring together the resources and expertise to revive these great monuments to the railroad era. The effort in St Louis required US $140 million in grants and loans for the restoration of Union Station, which made it the most expensive rehabilitation project to date. Both station and train shed survive today, though now serving as a shopping mall. Underneath the shed one now finds a multi-storey hotel that fits without even touching the train shed roof. Perhaps out of place, this transformation does represent the dominant urban trend to convert historic landmark attractions into tourist and shopping venues. The St Louis version has clearly become a success story, and has allowed this magnificent set of structures to survive as a St Louis icon.

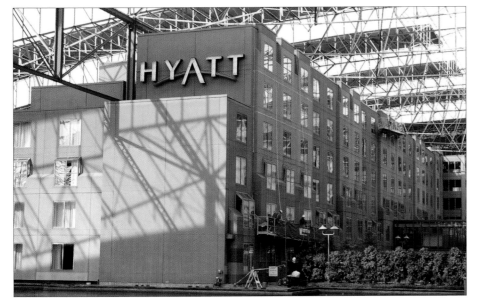

# MILWAUKEE CITY HALL
## MILWAUKEE, WISCONSIN

During the 19th-century Milwaukee welcomed German immigrants, making it the most consciously German-influenced city in the United States. This city became America's centre of ethnic German culture, politics and society, earning it the nickname "Deutsch-Athen". Why Milwaukee? A combination of political and economic turmoil, and the failed German Revolution of 1848 provided a collective reason for millions of Germans to begin new lives in America. Further, many of these immigrants had been actively recruited in Europe by Midwestern railroad companies eager to sell their federal land grants to farm families. Native German speakers were even sent to Europe to promote land sales. The young states of Illinois, Minnesota and Wisconsin were anxious to grow quickly and to generate a solid tax base from producing farms, stimu-

*Below: The bell tower at one end of City Hall was nicknamed Big Ben due to the sound of its massive 11-ton bell.*

lating even more active recruitment in Europe. These promotional campaigns were successful. Along with millions of other immigrants from northwestern Europe, Germans arriving prior to the 1890s concentrated within the Mid-Atlantic and Midwest regions. In the northern Midwest, including Wisconsin, Germans were as highly represented as the Irish were in New England.

Many immigrants from Northwestern Europe continued to settle in Ohio, Michigan and Illinois in the decades surrounding the American Civil War. However, the largest population gains occurred in Wisconsin, Minnesota and the Dakotas. Wisconsin was one of the more popular destinations for immigrating German farmers due to familiar climate and soil characteristics similar to those of their homeland. By 1910 about 17 per cent of Milwaukee's population consisted of German immigrants, by far the largest proportion of Germans in any American city.

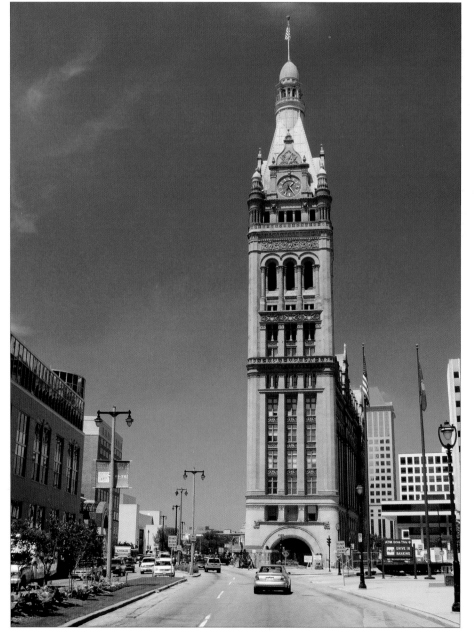

### GERMAN INFLUENCE

It seems appropriate that Milwaukee's City Hall is the only one in America designed in the German Renaissance Revival style of architecture. With its soaring masonry bell tower, it is also one of the largest. Symbolically, it is considered the "capitol building" of the city most associated with German immigrant culture in America, and has served more than a century as the seat of city government. City Hall also played a key role in Milwaukee's socialist movement during socialism's "golden age" before World War I. The influence of socialism in the United States is likewise linked to German heritage, as anti-socialist laws in Germany had encouraged the emigration of socialists to America. The Germans established America's first-ever socialist party in 1867, and German immigrants constituted a large propor-

*Above: Imagery of Milwaukee's industry and heritage decorates this intricate glass window in City Hall.*

tion of its members. The party witnessed some of its greater successes in Milwaukee, which in 1910 became the first among large American cities to be run by socialists. Other cities looked to Milwaukee's socialist political victories as models for their own future successes.

The Renaissance Revival architecture of City Hall further reflects the city's dominant German cultural heritage. Although the so-called American Renaissance of the late 19th century looked primarily to Italy for architectural inspiration, Milwaukee's new City Hall in 1896 revealed a purposely German flair. In 1891 the City Council held a nationwide competition for the structure's design, which gained 11 responses. Eventually, the contest was narrowed down to two applications: a Gothic-style design by Chicago architect Henry Ives Cobb, and a German-oriented Renaissance design by Henry C Koch, a German-born Milwaukee architect. The final decision was made with extensive debate, but the council ultimately voted for the latter design that reflected both German and Milwaukee precedents. By this time the steel frame had become feasible based largely on precedents in Chicago and was employed here, though its masonry walls still bear the load. Placed on an

irregularly shaped lot, the wedge-shaped structure was comprised of two dominant elements – a clock and bell tower at the south end and the main building block to the north. The main structure includes eight storeys plus basement and attic, with its distinctive tower rising to a height of 120m/393ft above ground level.

## THE BELL

The tower itself has gained its share of local and national attention, due especially to the story of its impressive bell. As described by a city of Milwaukee history briefing, *Treasure in the Tower*, the massive bell attracted 1,000 tourists a month who nimbly climbed the tower to see it, and some couples were even married beneath it. It rang for the first time on New Year's Eve in 1896. The 11-plus ton bell was the largest ever made by Milwaukee's Campbell Centennial Company, and it ranks today as the second largest ever produced nationwide. In 1925 the mayor Daniel Webster Hoan had the bell silenced because it was reputedly causing structural damage to the tower. This claim is highly disputed, however, only adding to the folklore surrounding the bell's history. A Milwaukee tradition was begun in 1945 when the bell was rung on Independence Day. Thanks to

donations from prominent Milwaukeeans, the bell was returned to service on Thanksgiving Day in 1999 by a group of bell ringers that gained an international audience on CNN. An automatic ringing system has since been installed, though the bell can still be rung manually on special occasions. The names of the mayor, council members, and other 1896 city officials are inscribed on the bell, along with the following message:

*When I sound the hours of day*
*From this grand and lofty steeple,*
*Deem it a reminder, pray,*
*To be honest with the people.*

As for City Hall, the structure has been immaculately restored through a US $70 million facelift project, completed in December 2008. This was the first-ever major overhaul of the building and its bell tower. One need not travel to Milwaukee to hear the deep sound of the tower's bell, originally nicknamed Big Ben given its comparable size and tone. A City of Milwaukee website allows virtual travellers to hear the bell from their own computers.

*Below and below left: The Renaissance-inspired City Hall has undergone a recent transformation.*

# CLEVELAND ARCADE
## CLEVELAND, OHIO

Considered one of the first indoor shopping centres in America, the monumental 1890 Cleveland Arcade represents the convergence of at least three dominant innovations from the 19th century – namely the European arcade, the glass skylight and Richardsonian-Romanesque architecture. The entire complex consists of two separate, nine-storey office buildings that face Euclid and Superior avenues, both connected by a five-storey, iron and glass skylight over the Arcade. The Arcade's facade on the Superior Avenue front displays its original Romanesque style. The facade on Euclid Avenue was remodelled in 1939. Both avenues are connected by the 91m/300ft-long glass-covered Arcade, with a total of 100 commercial store units originally designed into the two lower levels. The third and fourth balconies provided office space for rent. As one of the grandest urban shopping arcades in America, the Cleveland Arcade was designed to accentuate the vastness and height of its interior space, which reaches up 30m/100ft to the pointed arch of the skylight.

### PRECEDENTS
The interior shopping arcade began modestly during the early 19th century and reached its zenith with the most striking arcade in Europe, the Galleria

Vittoria Emanuele in Milan, Italy. As commercial buildings became taller and bulkier, during the decades prior to electric lighting, light courts or skylights became popular features that took advantage of natural lighting. The Cleveland Arcade represents the fashionable European arcade with American light-court construction techniques.

### CONSTRUCTION
Built by the Detroit Bridge Company, the Arcade opened its doors on Memorial Day, in 1890 following a rather complicated construction process. The fact that Superior and Euclid avenues are neither parallel nor level with one another presented some initial engineering and design challenges. The arcade axis, therefore, leads creatively to a rotunda at the Euclid Avenue entrance that is offset 23 degrees from the main structure, allowing both facades of the arcade to sit flush against their avenues.

*Left: In 1975 the Arcade became Cleveland's first building to be listed on the National Register of Historic Places.*

*Left: In 1978 a food court was added beneath the Euclid Avenue stairway and much-needed restoration was completed.*

Moreover, the Superior entrance is 3.6m/12ft lower than the Euclid one, necessitating a series of staircases that connect the two main floors. A wide variety of construction materials and techniques were used. The nine-storey entrance towers on both facades had load-bearing walls, representing the last decade when this masonry construction approach would be necessary. The advent of steel frame technology in Chicago did influence the Arcade's design. The masonry facades are carried by I-beams resting on steel columns. Unlike the facades, the floors and roofs of the Arcade's two office buildings are supported through a network of iron columns and a combination of oak, wrought iron and steel.

### RESTORATION
The structure that was once known as Cleveland's Crystal Palace has seen various changes to its interior function and its ownership. Most recently, an impressive public-private partnership was created between Cleveland's mayor and economic development team, and Related Midwest and Hyatt Development Corporation. Together they conceived of a creative financing scheme for a US $60 million restoration that was completed in May 2001. Today the Arcade's atrium and two towers house the Hyatt Regency Cleveland Hotel, while boutique retail shops, dining and services occupy the lower two levels that are open to the public. The Arcade has been reinvented to appeal to today's consumer- and visitor-oriented downtown economies. Given the Cleveland Arcade's original design as an elegant shopping and office complex, it still retains that function 120 years later.

# OHIO THEATRE
## COLUMBUS, OHIO

Hollywood's Golden Age effectively began with the opening of America's first movie palace in New York City, the Regent Theatre, in 1913. The next three decades would see the production of films and the sizes of audiences rise accordingly.

More than 4,000 movie palaces were constructed nationwide between 1915 and 1945, with thousands of smaller theatres built in appropriately smaller towns and cities. While not one movie palace existed prior to 1900, they were commonplace fixtures on America's main streets less than three decades later. Never before had the spectacle of opulence been promoted to this extent, with the aim of attracting people from all walks of life. Along with Hollywood, the golden age of the movie palace had arrived. Opened in 1928, the Ohio Theatre represented the height of this magical period of American social history.

The most glamourous movie palaces such as the Ohio Theatre were prominently located in the heart of a city's downtown business district. Often they were clustered within existing entertainment districts and tied to upscale shopping venues. By definition the main purpose of a large-city movie palace was to launch and promote new Hollywood films. Smaller versions took the form of neighbourhood movie houses found in outlying cities and smaller towns. These more rural theatres were generally not as glamourous architecturally and were designed as second- and third-run outlets. Thus, it was in the largest urban centres where the initial reputation of new films was established, appropriately showcased within elegant movie palaces.

### INTERIOR STYLING
The movie palace quickly became a distinctive architectural type in America. Both its interior environment and exterior facade were purposely designed to appeal to self-esteem and fantasy. Designers created elaborate schemes often rooted in historic themes or ideals, the fundamental goal being to essentially "transport" the audience into a magical time and place.

With the orientation toward fantasy in mind, the Scottish-born Thomas Lamb envisioned the Ohio Theatre as a "palace for the average man". Its exterior, columned facade resembled a Neo-classical temple, common for prominent buildings of the time. Conversely, its interior was designed as a Spanish-Baroque masterpiece, utilizing this European style as the requisite fantasy world for its audiences. The Ohio's decorations and furnishings were further elaborated upon by New York decorator Anne Dornan, a graduate from the Columbia School of Architecture. Her travels took her around the world in search of appropriate art and furniture, including a safari in Africa. It is reported that more than US $1 million was spent to furnish the Ohio so lavishly, which was more than the cost of the theatre construction itself. Perhaps completing the interior spectacle was the inclusion of a Robert-Morton theatre pipe organ, which is among the finest in the nation and remains in use today. Patrons of the Ohio during its heyday enjoyed the newest movies and a variety of stage shows that included performers Milton Berle, Cab Calloway, Ray Bolger, Buddy Ebsen, Martha Raye, Jean Harlow, Ginger Rogers and Jack Benny.

### THE OHIO TODAY
Like similiar venues around the nation, the Ohio was threatened with destruction after its closure in 1969. Although many movie palaces were lost forever, the Ohio was saved and restored for a glorious second life. It was purchased by the Columbus Association for the Performing Arts (CAPA), which still manages the facility today. The original building was completely restored during the 1970s, while additional modern lobby, office and stage facilities were added in the 1980s. This was one of the earliest attempts to restore a movie palace of the Ohio's calibre, and it has served as a model for later renovations elsewhere. Today the Columbus Symphony Orchestra enjoys the Ohio as its home, as do BalletMet, the Broadway Series, Opera Columbus and the CAPA Summer Movie Series. The Ohio is clearly back in business.

*Below: Early American theatres adopted dazzling marquis signs and entryways to promote their sentiments of fantasy.*

# HIGHLAND PARK FORD PLANT
## HIGHLAND PARK, MICHIGAN

Henry Ford is most often associated with his famous Model T automobile. According to historian Daniel Boorstin, however, his most unique achievement "was less in designing a durable automobile than in organizing newer, cheaper ways to make millions of one kind of automobile". After the Ford Motor Company was founded in 1903, Ford and his engineers made significant advances in auto assembly methods to increase the speed of production. They continuously developed new machinery and altered the placement of workmen on the factory floor to reduce bottlenecks and improve efficiency. It was after the Ford Motor Company moved its operations to the new Highland Park plant in 1910 however, when the fundamental principles of mass production were developed and refined. Men, machines and materials were constantly rearranged to maximize productivity, to reduce unnecessary motions and to reduce costs.

Ford's crowning achievement was his development of the modern assembly line in 1913, allowing the company to

*Right: Mass production reduced the price of cars such as this 1915 Model T Ford for consumers, encouraging our current automobile age.*

realize economies of scale never seen before. After five years of development, the company could concentrate on the production of one model of automobile to drastically reduce the unit cost. In 1908 the price of a Model T had been US $850. This had dropped to only US $260 by 1924. On 21 October 1925, Ford's efficiency of production reached its peak, when a new model T rolled off the assembly line every ten seconds. This was a far cry from Ford's first plant on Mack Avenue in Detroit, where his men could assemble a maximum of about 15 Model T's per working day. It was the inexpensive Model T, according to Ford's biographer William Greenleaf, that "put the nation on wheels, enormously accelerated the urbanization of

*Below: The engine of a Model T is being lowered into the body of the car on the innovative production line.*

America and ultimately brought the motor transportation revolution to other countries".

### PIONEERING PRODUCTION
With his pioneering of the mass production of automobiles, Henry Ford is now primarily credited (along with his engineers) with his effective development of a division of labour, the use of interchangeable parts (dating back to gun maker Eli Whitney) and the moving assembly line. So influential were these advances on 20th-century industry that economists have dubbed the term "Fordism" to describe this mass production approach. Ford's methods

### DIVISION OF LABOUR
The concept known as division of labour became a primary feature of Ford's assembly process at the Highland Park complex. Workers who are trained to perform only one operation in the production process are much more efficient than those responsible for all aspects. This strategy further enabled the hiring of unskilled labour, because a worker could learn one simple task in a short time. The division of labour was instrumental for the early success of Ford's assembly line process, and over time for the growth of the automobile industry in America and elsewhere.

were widely copied around the world by numerous industries throughout the 20th century and dominated the manufacturing process around the globe.

An added benefit of mass production was increased wages for Ford's employees. Ford introduced the "Five Dollar Day" on 5 January 1914, which made him world famous. According to historian Roderick Nash, Ford became "an international symbol of the new industrialism". The increased wages may have compensated many of Ford's workers who complained about the relentless monotony of their specialized duties.

## HIGHLAND PARK

When operations were transferred to the Highland Park Ford Plant in 1910, the plant consisted of a four-storey factory building, a massive power plant with five smokestacks, an administration building and various other structures at different stages of completion. The complex was continuously expanded from 1910–22 as Ford and his colleagues developed new production techniques and refined older ones. For this reason

*Below: The body of a car is lowered on to the chassis of the vehicle in this early production line.*

the Highland Park Ford Plant was never considered complete, as Ford was on a constant search for more efficient production methods. Like his own production approaches, Highland Park was always a work in progress. Eventually, all of Highland Park had become obsolete according to Ford, especially due to its limited potential for expansion and its inadequate water and sewage facilities. He was already setting his sights on the new and gigantic River Rouge Plant (also a national landmark) west of Detroit in the city of Dearborn.

*Above: Highland Park, where Ford production techniques were advanced.*

River Rouge ultimately surpassed Highland Park in size and importance, and in 1927 the final assembly line was moved out of Highland Park to the more modern facility. However, the complex continued to play a role in the production of automotive parts. In 1947 it was designated the principal facility for the production of Ford tractors and served in this capacity until 1974. The main buildings are now used for document storage for the Henry Ford Museum and the Ford Motor Company but are not open to the public. What remains of the Highland Park complex is well maintained. Some of the structures have been destroyed, but several still exist in decent condition.

One implication of Ford's advancements is not often considered – that of America's improved capacity for production during World War II. Historian Roger Burlingame has asserted that Ford's work at both facilities "made it possible for the United States to become the 'arsenal of democracy' in World War II…with the manufacture of 20 million cars over 40 years Ford had evolved a pattern for all large-scale production including that of the atomic bomb".

# WORLD WAR MEMORIAL PLAZA
## INDIANAPOLIS, INDIANA

War memorials constitute a common form of memorial landscape, designed specifically to "locate the remembered or imagined past in the present landscape", as historian David Lowenthal put it. The Indiana World War Memorial Plaza was designed to recall a victorious past and is now preserved as an historic landmark in its own right. The Indiana World War Memorial Plaza provides a distinguished example of a commemorative tribute, in this case to Indiana's veterans who fought and suffered or died in war. More than a memorial, it serves as the national headquarters of the American Legion, the largest organization devoted to military veterans and their families. The Plaza complex includes five buildings designed primarily in the Neo-classical style, composed with various smaller structures, open space and sculptures. The entire composition was designed by architects Frank B. Walker and Harry E. Weeks in 1923, though construction occurred in phases until its completion in 1950. The idea for the complex was conceived as a way to attract the American Legion to the city in 1919, the year the legion was formed.

In addition to the War Memorial Building, the Federal Building and the Indianapolis Central Library structures earned much attention. The Federal Building compliments the Indianapolis Central Library, completed in 1916, and was considered to be one of the more imaginative interpretations of the Greek Doric style. The Library was designed by prominent architect Paul Cret. The grand structure gained wide attention and was highly praised by America's foremost Gothic Revival architect in America at the time, Ralph Adams Cram. Believing it was America's best example of Classical architecture in the country, Cram commented in 1918 "The whole thing is not only Greek in form but penetratingly Greek in spirit... the most notable qualities in the exterior are scale and surface. It is not a large building, yet the scale is so delicately preserved that one does not think of dimensions.... Nothing is overdone or wasted, and the enormous success of the result follows from proportions that are fine and sensitive to the point of perfection...one of the most distinctive and admirable contributions to architecture that have been made in America."

*Above: Cities and towns across the country have added their own local memorials to commemorate fallen war veterans.*

### CITY BEAUTIFUL

The Indiana World War Memorial Plaza provides a dramatic example of City Beautiful planning that had its origins in the Chicago Columbian Exposition of 1893. The City Beautiful Movement sought to provide order and grandeur to America's otherwise chaotic and unplanned cities. Classical formality and its associated Classical Revival (or Neo-classical) architecture became prominent features of City Beautiful designs. For its part, the Memorial Plaza in Indianapolis is characterized by majestic Classical Revival buildings, of which the War Memorial Building itself is considered to be the grandest of the ensemble. The Plaza's spatial layout is likewise quintessential City Beautiful, with its formally designed open spaces and north-south vistas that strategically focus on the War Memorial.

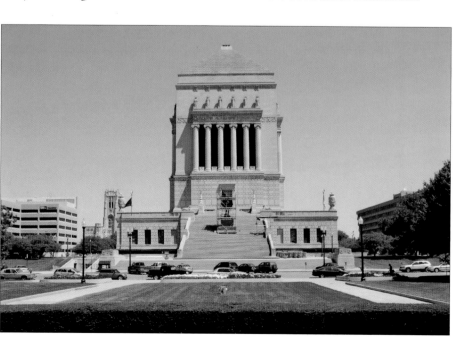

*Left: The War Memorial Building provides the central focus for the Plaza and complex of surrounding structures.*

# INDIANAPOLIS MOTOR SPEEDWAY
## SPEEDWAY, INDIANA

The ingenuity that accompanied the Industrial Revolution allowed the fledgling auto industry in America to catch up quickly with what was happening in France, a country that dominated automobile technology, production and auto racing. Auto racing arrived nearly in parallel with the earliest self-propelled automobiles. Competitions for speed and endurance provided opportunities to test and improve early designs, powered at that time by petrol or electricity.

### DEVELOPING A TRACK

America's first auto race took place as early as 28 November 1895 on a 50-mile course in Evanston, Illinois. The earliest races were hosted on public streets in Europe and the USA, though they were eventually deemed unsafe for spectators and drivers. Instead, oval-shaped horse-racing tracks were promoted as offering better safety and viewing conditions. Such tracks have been the norm ever since.

Land for the Speedway was developed in 1909 by four businessmen involved with manufacturing automobiles in Indianapolis. The first track was constructed with crushed stone and tar,

*Above: Early auto races were held to test new car designs, though attention turned quickly to competitive racing.*

but it was soon replaced with 3.2 million 4.5kg/10lb brick paving blocks. It was eventually covered with asphalt as it is today. The most significant historic component of the Speedway is the 4km/2¹/₂ mile track, featuring two long stretches (1005m/1,100yds each), two short straight stretches (201m/220yds each) and four turns. The maximum banking of the turns is just over nine degrees. This unique configuration became the model for newer speedways

*Below: The Speedway's 4km/2.5-mile track served as the model for today's standard American race tracks.*

*Above: Today's race cars, such as this Formula 1 vehicle, have come a long way since 1911, now reaching speeds of 369kph/229mph.*

following World War II. This particular track served as America's primary proving ground for the automotive industry, because private test facilities were not developed by automobile manufacturing companies until after World War I. The track is still regularly used for testing purposes, but the original focus quickly turned to competitive racing.

Automotive racing has become one of America's most popular spectator events since the inaugural Indianapolis 500 race held on 30 May 1911. One source ranks the National Association of Stock Car Auto Racing (NASCAR) alone as the second most popular professional spectator sport based on American television ratings.

### GREATEST CAPACITY

The Indianapolis Motor Speedway features a seating capacity of more than 257,000 people, compared to the world's largest stadium that seats 220,000 spectators. With the Speedway's additional infield seating, total capacity is raised to a staggering 400,000 people, making it the highest-capacity sporting facility in history. Designated as a National Historic Landmark in 1987, the speedway remains the only such landmark associated directly with automotive racing history in America.

# ARTHUR HEURTLEY HOUSE
## OAK PARK, ILLINOIS

Frank Lloyd Wright (1867–1959), America's most influential architect of the 20th century, focused primarily on the design of residential architecture. He was obsessed with the horizontal line, shifting the proportions of the American house from a vertical to a horizontal box. The flat, open and horizontal appearance of the Midwestern prairie strongly influenced his designs. A house should incorporate a simplified floor plan with a minimum number of rooms, Wright believed, while expressing an overall essence of simplicity and repose. Shaping his dominant philosophies of design were the American prairie landscape, Japanese architecture and the Shingle style of the late Victorian era. All of these influences contributed to Wright's determination to incorporate nature and natural materials into his work. What Wright termed "organic architecture" has henceforth been called the Prairie style.

### PRAIRIE STYLE

It is his 1902 Arthur Heurtley House that is recognized as one of the first fully mature expressions of the Prairie style.

*Below: The Heurtley House is acclaimed internationally as a critical contribution to the development of modern architecture.*

*Above: The exterior of the Arthur Heurtley House is neat and compact, with understated architecture.*

Its low-pitched, hipped roof with overhanging eaves is a defining component of the style, coupled with horizontally grouped windows and a variety of terraces and balconies. The Heurtley House was considered the most revolutionary form of avant-garde Modernism in recent Western history. The stylistic patterns established served as precedents for all of Wright's great houses.

With his aim to blend architecture with the surrounding Midwestern prairie landscape, Wright purposely raised the major spaces of the house well above the surrounding terrain. He understood that such elevated vantage points would be necessary to enjoy any sort of view over the surrounding low lands. The Heurtley House was the first residential structure to abandon the traditional relationship of rooms and floor levels, consequently the living and dining rooms are on the upper floor instead of at ground level.

The floor plan is open, allowing uninterrupted views from the living room to other parts of the home. Rejecting traditional wall partitions, Wright employed some trickery to divide up various spaces, including wooden screens and a colonnaded wall in the living room. Glass and glazed doors were placed on the walls distant from the interior fireplace and chimney.

### THE FOURSQUARE HOUSE

Between 1890 and 1930 the American foursquare, or prairie box, became the dominant house type of choice. Sharing numerous features with Wright's upscale Prairie-style homes, the foursquare is so named for its cubical shape, with two-and-a-half floors, symmetrical facade, with four rooms up and four rooms down. After World War II, Wright's prior emphasis on horizontal design and open floor plans was adapted across the country in the form of single-storey ranch homes that dominated American suburban development for decades.

*Below: The two-and-a-half-storey house is inspired by the Heurtley House.*

# MERCHANT'S NATIONAL BANK
## GRINNELL, IOWA

Louis Sullivan is lauded as the father of Modern architecture in the United States. He is considered the visionary and creator of the modern commercial skyscraper in Chicago. He played an instrumental role in designing the Chicago Auditorium Building through the firm of Adler & Sullivan. The full expression of his work was displayed with his Wainwright Building in St Louis, built in 1890–91. Sullivan's views on the relationship between a building's form and its function were demonstrated in that building. In 1918 he wrote that "if a building is properly designed, one should be able…to read through that building to the reason for that building".

### LOUIS SULLIVAN PROJECTS
The Depression of 1893 found Sullivan down on his luck, as the number of commissions for Adler & Sullivan were drastically reduced. Striking out on his own, Sullivan received fewer and fewer commissions. It was during these troubling times when his philosophies matured and he produced some of his finest work. Such examples are not found in major cities such as Chicago, but instead scattered around the Midwestern prairie region in smaller communities. Many of them are small town banks. Perhaps the most often cited of these later Sullivan projects is the National Farmers' Bank in Owatonna, Minnesota (1907–08). His other smaller banks were similar Modernist boxes, "with clearly expressed banking rooms, colourful textured materials and pockets of dense intricate ornamentation", as described by architectural historian Leland Roth. Although modest in scale, they effectively demonstrated Sullivan's drive to have form follow function.

*Right: Sullivan's striking cartouche and rose window.*

### SULLIVAN IN IOWA
One of Sullivan's later, post-Depression projects is the Merchant's National Bank, constructed in 1914, toward the end of his bank-building phase, between 1909 and 1914. What would otherwise have been another ignored bank building in a small town attracted outside attention through the architect's reputation. The Merchant's Bank consequently received national coverage, including an article in the *Western Architect*'s February 1916 edition, which

*Above: Smaller Midwestern towns, including Grinnell, benefited from Sullivan's commissions outside Chicago.*

read in part, "at Grinnell, Iowa, there has been completed recently, a bank building, which not only brings distinction to that city, but adds another interesting example to the list of those unique banking institutions designed by Louis H. Sullivan of Chicago". The bank is composed of a simple cubic plan, but with a magnificent ornamental cartouche and rose window embedded on to the facade above the main entryway. Although functionally simple, the effect of the bold and solid brick cube is striking, especially within a smaller community like that of Grinnell. Not only does Sullivan's Merchant's Bank and related projects display his mature principles of design, but it stands as a monument to the beginning of America's 20th-century Modern Movement in architecture and urban planning.

# JOHN FARSON HOUSE
## OAK PARK, ILLINOIS

The Farson House (also known as the Pleasant Home) was one of the earliest expressions of the Prairie style in the USA. Its architect was George Washington Maher (1864–1926), who was already established by the time he finished the plans for Farson House in 1897. His Farson House is recognized as one of the most distinguished examples of the Prairie style, which was heralded internationally as one of America's greatest contributions to architecture. The house type proved extremely popular and was adopted across the nation.

### THE PRAIRIE SCHOOL

Early in the 20th century, architects and writers sought an appropriate term to describe the innovative, modern architectural work that was emerging in the Midwest. The term Prairie School was finally accepted, adequately describing the collective response of architects to the geographical features of the Midwestern prairie. Not only did they adapt the imagery of the broad prairie landscape, they also incorporated native flora into their designs. The emphasis on the horizontal lines of the prairie manifested in the incorporation of low-pitched, hipped or gable roofs, horizontal window bands, and ornamental work inspired by native plants and geometric designs.

As for the Farson House, Maher identified the honeysuckle as the home's dominant natural image. The pattern appears within the medallions embedded within the porch's piers, in the art glass, in carved pilasters at the entrance and in the ornamental, iron fence that surrounds the grounds. The repeated use of the honeysuckle exemplified what Maher called his "motif rhythm theory", a deliberate attempt to unify the prominent decorative details of the house and its furnishings.

### AN AMERICAN STYLE

Like Frank Lloyd Wright, Maher primarily designed homes for wealthy Midwestern clients, and he considered the Farson House as an ideal type. Photographs of the home were published in the *Inland Architect and News Record* in November 1899, in which the editor wrote that "the architect submits this design as a type for an American style". Maher's vision was quickly fulfilled, as his design influenced other Prairie School architects after 1900, and the model became enormously popular for other architects and builders nationwide. The house type was simplified by general builders across the Midwest, some of which offered "Maheresque" houses by mail order. Certain signature features of Maher's house style were considered vital: a low-hipped roof, cubic massing and floor plan, prominent roof dormers and detailed ornamentation. Ultimately, the Farson House type remained highly popular for more than two decades, and it established Maher as one of America's prominent designers. Of all Maher's large estates, only the Farson House and the Frederick T. Gates House in Montclair, New Jersey, survive intact.

*Below: Several features of the Farson House became American standards, among them cubic design and a hipped roof.*

# S. R. CROWN HALL
## CHICAGO, ILLINOIS

The peace and economic prosperity that returned to America following World War II enabled an unprecedented national building boom. The population boomed as well, necessitating the expansion of schools and universities. Between the 1950s and 1980s college students would spend much of their educational experiences within college buildings designed purely for function, constructed of varying combinations of masonry, steel and glass. Just as the International style of modern architecture flourished across the country during these decades, educational institutions were no different, largely adopting the popular building modes and forms of the day. Campuses that expanded during the post-war Modern era, therefore, still remain dominated by classroom and dorm buildings that represent variations on the International-style theme. Good portions of many college campuses still depend on these Modernist, functional buildings from earlier decades.

### INTERNATIONAL STYLE

The campus of the Illinois Institute of Technology (IIT) not only exemplified the national expansion of higher education, but also helped to shape it. Out of 19 buildings designed there by architect Mies van der Rohe (1886–1969), the S. R. Crown Hall building was his last and most influential. Completed in 1956, the Hall represents the epitome of International style architecture, which is ironic because the primary idea was to promote functionalism over the use of stylistic or historic themes. Mies considered the building to be the clearest statement of his own design philosophies. He and his fellow modern architects were searching for a universal building type that would transcend international boundaries and cultures – leading to its common

"International style" description over time. Unlike his other functional buildings on the IIT campus, the S. R. Crown Hall – initially named the Industrial Design and Architecture Building – is the only structure composed entirely of steel and glass, with no visible masonry walls. It served as the precedent for even more notable buildings that Mies designed during his career. The Hall is considered one of the most influential Modernist buildings of the 20th century. It was the leadership of Mies in the IIT Department of Architecture and throughout the campus that helped transform the campus into one of the most progressive and experimental of the time. Although rarely constructed

*Below: The entrance lobby of S. R. Crown Hall, like the rest of the interior open space, features movable partitions.*

*Above: Organized on two floors, the building's main floor is raised up about 2m/6ft from ground level, allowing natural light and ventilation into the lower level through clerestory windows.*

exclusively with steel and glass, colleges and universities would be dominated by International-style building projects for the next three decades or longer.

### INTERIOR FEATURES

Just as noteworthy is the S. R. Crown Hall's interior design, considered an innovative departure from more traditional spaces for learning. In this case, the 2415 sq m/26,000 sq ft of interior space was designed to be fully flexible and unobstructed. Rather than the common set-up of isolated, self-contained classrooms accessed through a central hallway, the space within the Hall is almost entirely open. The philosophy of this design was to enable and promote an open and collaborative exchange of ideas through co-operative learning. This was an influential experiment in American education at the time, though the idea would ultimately decline after a brief flourishing. Still, Crown Hall represented one of America's first full-scale examples of a totally flexible interior space.

# GATEWAY ARCH
## ST LOUIS, MISSOURI

The Jefferson National Expansion Memorial in St Louis was conceived in 1935 during Franklin Roosevelt's administration. It includes 37ha/91 acres of land along the Mississippi River and is maintained by the National Park Service. The site is located near the point of origin of the famous Lewis-and Clark Expedition.

The Gateway Arch was established to commemorate three historical events: the Louisiana Purchase, the first cathedral in St Louis (the Basilica of St Louis) and the Dred Scott Case.

The debate for where to place the Gateway Arch began in 1947. The original plan placed the arch close to the

*Below: More than a half century after it was built, the arch remains America's largest monument and serves as the dominant icon and tourist attraction for St Louis – America's earliest geographic "Gateway to the West".*

banks of the Mississippi River, though the site was determined to be too hazardous. By the mid-1950s the current location on higher ground was finalized, and construction began in 1963.

The competition to design the project attracted national media attention and submissions from 172 architects. First prize was unanimously awarded to the designer Eero Saarinen, the son of the prominent Modernist architect, Eliel Saarinen. Eero was clearly prepared for the challenge, even though the Arch was his first commission. As the only structure in the world based on the catenary arch, the monument as completed stands 192m/630ft tall and the exact same width at its base. The Arch was constructed in triangular, stainless steel sections that grow progressively smaller toward the top. Inside both legs are unique trams with capsule-type cars that transport people to the small observation room above. Such a massive

structural system had never been attempted prior to Saarinen's design. At the Arch's bases are two entrance ramps that lead into the subterranean visitors centre and the Museum of Westward Expansion. The tunnel entrances are carefully integrated into the park layout below grade to make them seemingly invisible from ground level.

The stainless steel arch design was a monument to westward expansion, an engineering feat and an icon of Modernist architecture. The conception, design and construction of the gateway extended from the New Deal to Mission 66, the ten-year park development program founded in 1956.

### THE LOUISIANA PURCHASE
Regularly identified as America's "gateway to the west", the city of St Louis began as a trading post within the Colonial empire of New France. At a time when the French Crown

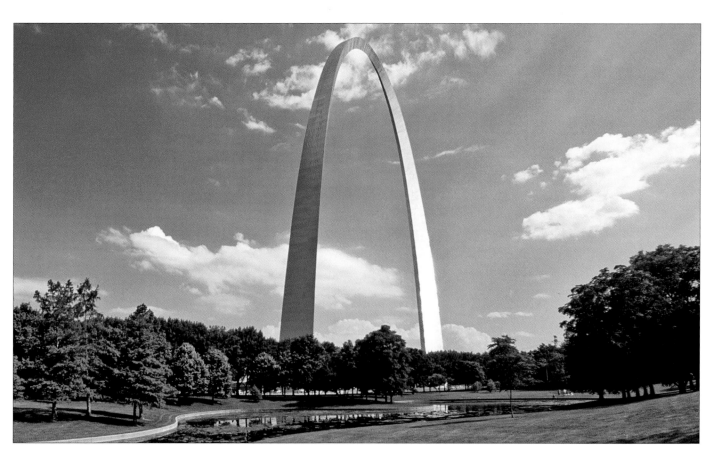

controlled the entire Mississippi Valley, a New Orleans merchant named Pierre Laclede obtained a franchise for trade with Native Americans. Laclede chose a site for his trading post on a low limestone rise just south of where the Missouri and Illinois rivers joined the Mississippi. The post became an instant town, due to the fact that the entire eastern side of the Mississippi River was controlled by the British. Numerous French residents moved from the east side to the new trading post, favouring French soil. By 1803 St Louis could boast modestly of 200 dwellings and about 1,000 residents. The town was poised to become a leading trade centre on the American frontier.

In 1803 the French foreign minister startled everyone by asking if the USA would be interested in purchasing Louisiana outright, including 2,144,520 sq km/828,000 sq miles of land. Regardless of the numerous indigenous tribes and foreign settlers, this was an unprecedented opportunity from the American perspective. With the stroke of a pen, the world's largest republic was nearly doubled in size, now reaching west to the Rocky Mountains and up through Montana. President Jefferson learned of the treaty's signing on 3 July and announced it to the public the next day, on the 27th anniversary of the Declaration of Independence. Not only was the nation's security enhanced by removing powerful France from the continent, but the Spanish claim retracted to that of Florida and Texas. Now in American hands, the town of St Louis was at the eastern edge of the entire Louisiana Purchase, making it the obvious point for westward exploration.

## LEWIS–CLARK EXPEDITION

For centuries Europeans had sought westward routes to the Indies, with the primary goal of accessing lucrative Asian markets by travelling west. The early Americans were no different, also hoping to secure the elusive northwest passage overland to the Pacific Ocean.

Thomas Jefferson was perhaps the idea's greatest champion, having sponsored a plan for a French naturalist in 1793 "to find the shortest and most convenient route of communication between the US and the Pacific Ocean, within the temperate latitudes". Although this effort never materialized, Jefferson refused to give up. Prior to any thought of acquiring Louisiana, he asked Congress for approval to send an expedition up the Missouri River, across foreign-controlled territory. Support was granted, and so Meriwether Lewis and William Clark prepared to embark on their westward journey only a few weeks following the unexpected transfer of Louisiana to the Americans.

Their primary mission was to find the legendary "interlocked" rivers that would apparently transport them easily to the Pacific and, as in centuries past, the exploration's rationale was economic. Following 28 months of now legendary adventures, Lewis and Clark arrived triumphantly back in St Louis to inform the president of their success. They had found a practical route along the branches of the Missouri and Columbia rivers. Although clearly an inspiring success for the nation, the reality was more daunting than initially reported. Their idea of a practical route westward involved a land passage of 547km/340 miles over treacherous mountains. They had also only survived

*Left: The curving, metallic surface of the arch has inspired artistic photographs.*

the ordeal due to the generosity of numerous Native American tribes along the way. Regardless, they had made history, and opened up the western part of the continent for future trade and immigration routes. American commerce responded in kind, as Jefferson had hoped.

## GATEWAY TO THE WEST

As for St Louis, the city grew and continued to enjoy the status as gateway to America's western frontier. As historian William Cronon points out, however, a place's gateway status is necessarily temporary, as settlement and transportation routes continue to move west. The frontier transitions into regions with their own trade centres, which ultimately reduce the earlier importance of previous gateways. This was indeed the fate of St Louis, the vast western hinterland of which was carved up into smaller trade areas of newer cities. With the railroad came Chicago's turn to serve as the gateway to the west, as more transcontinental rail routes ultimately converged there than anywhere else. Chicago's prime position on Lake Michigan only enhanced its ability to link America's entire western hinterland with eastern markets. Although diminished to a second-tier metropolis, St Louis still became a major railroad centre and remained the second or third largest railroad hub in America throughout the late 20th century.

*Below: The observation deck.*

# CHAPTER SIX

# THE UPLAND SOUTH

THE UPLAND SOUTH IS CONSIDERED, FOR PURPOSES HERE, A TRANSITION ZONE BETWEEN THE MIDWEST AND CHESAPEAKE REGIONS AND THE CULTURAL CORE OF THE DEEP SOUTH. IT IS GENERALLY A RURAL AREA WITHOUT ANY DOMINATING URBAN ECONOMIES. THE CULTURAL CHARACTERISTICS OF THE REGION WERE A PRODUCT OF MIGRATION STREAMS AS WESTERN LANDS WERE OPENED TO SETTLEMENT DURING THE EARLY 19TH CENTURY. THIS CHAPTER REPRESENTS A DIVERSE COLLECTION OF LANDMARKS WITH INNOVATION AS THEIR KEY. GOLF, MOTOR RACING, FORESTRY MANAGEMENT AND FLIGHT, AS WELL AS LEISURE AND ENTERTAINMENT, FEATURE HERE.

*Left: Biltmore Estate and Forestry School.*

# STATE CAPITOL
## RALEIGH, NORTH CAROLINA

Determined to replace the earlier capitol destroyed by fire, the North Carolina General Assembly appropriated an initial US $50,000 in 1832 to build a new structure. The new State Capitol was designed as an enlarged version of the previous one, including a cruciform (cross-shaped) plan and a central rotunda covered by a copper dome. By this time Greek Revival architecture was at its height of popularity.

A new generation of professional architects had emerged in America by the 1830s, many of them having studied Greek and Roman forms for use in the USA. Most prominent among them were Ithiel Town (1784–1844) and Alexander Jackson Davis (1803–92), whose firm was commissioned to complete the design of the new State

*Below: One of America's finest examples of Greek Revival architecture is found in the North Carolina State Capitol.*

Capitol in Raleigh. Town and Davis received some significant assistance from an architect from Edinburgh. At Town's suggestion, David Paton took charge of the Capitol's construction and brought with him skilled stonemasons from his home country and elsewhere.

### GREEK REVIVAL STYLE

Both the interior and exterior of the structure serve as a virtual clinic on the distinctive features of the Greek Revival style. Ornamental details employed throughout the capitol, such as those used for mouldings, plasterwork and columns, were meticulously based on a collection of ancient Greek temples. The columned porticos on the east–west axis of the structure were modelled after the fully developed Doric order of the Parthenon in Athens. The screen of fluted Ionic columns in each wing were based instead on the Ionic order taken from the Temple of Ilissus, also in

Athens. Perhaps most intriguing is the D-shaped seating area that constitutes the chamber of the House of Representatives. The chamber features a full height, semi-circular colonnade with a straight row of four columns placed behind the speaker's desk. This spatial layout is reminiscent of Latrobe's similar design within the US Capitol and most likely inspired by ancient plans for Greek theatres.

### DECORATIVE DETAILS

A wide array of talented people from both sides of the Atlantic ultimately contributed to this Greek Revival masterpiece. Philadelphia supplied much of the Capitol's ornamental ironwork, marble mantels, hardware and other interior design features. Furniture such as desks and chairs came from a local Raleigh cabinetmaker, and records indicate that local slaves contributed to the State Capitol's construction.

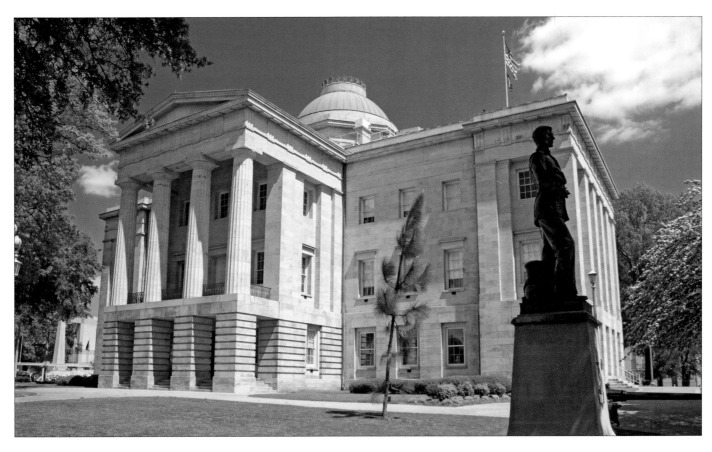

# WHEELING SUSPENSION BRIDGE
## WHEELING, WEST VIRGINIA

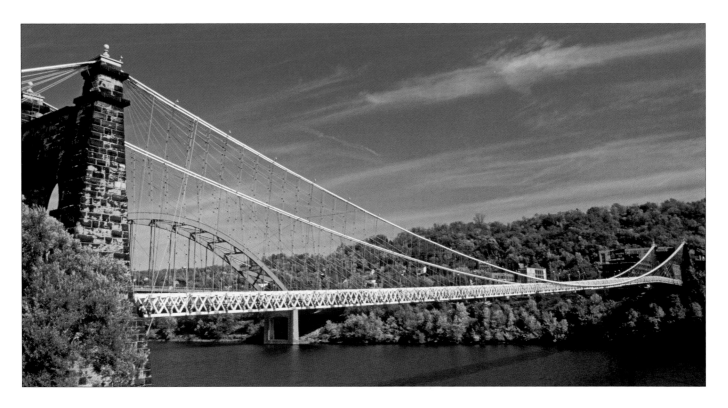

*Above: Today the bridge serves as America's oldest vehicular suspension bridge in the country that is still in use, albeit with weight limitations similar to the horses and buggies it was designed to carry.*

During the early 1800s came a concept to link the Eastern Seaboard with the fledgling state of Ohio by constructing an artificial, overland route. The National Road, as it would be called, was authorized by the federal government in 1802 to serve that purpose. This was one of the few road projects that received federal support, as much of America's budding transportation network relied instead on private entrepreneurial risk.

### A VITAL LINK
The National Road (corresponding with today's alignment of US 40) began as an attempt to bring the Ohio country under the control of the republic, and to encourage western settlement and trade. The route would be operated as a turnpike, and funded through the sale of western lands from the Federal Reserve. Ultimately, it became a significant westward migration and trade route across the Appalachian Mountains.

A significant improvement to the National Road came with the comple-

tion of the Wheeling Suspension Bridge in November 1849 to great public fanfare. Reaching more than 304m/1,000ft across the main channel of the Ohio River, this was the longest suspension bridge in the world at the time of its construction, and the first bridge to cross the Ohio River. The bridge provided a vital link in the National Road. Today's bridge deck is not the original. On May 17, 1854 the original was destroyed by a freak wind storm when most of the span crashed down into the Ohio River.

### CHARLES ELLET JR
The bridge's long and successful history masks the project's early challenges. A charter had been granted to construct a bridge over the Ohio River as early as 1816. Numerous factors contributed to

construction delays, however, and the project wasn't revived until 1836, when engineer Charles Ellet Jr submitted a sketch of a possible bridge design. Eleven years passed before a new bridge charter was obtained and a new board of directors was elected. Invitations were then sent to two of America's renowned designers of suspension bridges, Charles Ellet and John Roebling. A competition ensued between them and Ellet's design won. Charles Ellet Jr is still recognized today as the father of the modern American suspension bridge. Given his skills as an engineer, Ellet was further involved with proposing improvements to transportation, water resources and flood control for the entire Mississippi and Ohio rivers system. As for John Roebling, he and his son would gain fame through their efforts on the Brooklyn Bridge and other related projects. Today's Wheeling Suspension Bridge retains the general appearance it first had in 1849. Its massive stone piers, anchorage housings and island approach all consist of the original masonry.

# BATHHOUSE ROW
## HOT SPRINGS, ARKANSAS

For thousands of years the springs that now supply the water for Bathhouse Row were enjoyed by local Native American tribes. Their mythology instructs that the hot springs were considered neutral ground, a sacred space in which warring tribes set down their weapons to take advantage of the healing waters. The first permanent American settlers arrived in the area by the early 19th century, following the Louisiana Purchase. A tradition of developing early resorts and spas had already taken hold farther east, especially within the Catskills and Adirondacks mountains of New York State. First the canals, and later the railroads, encouraged inland tourism and resort development prior to the Civil War. The emerging bathing industry became a focus for the American spa, and the thermal springs at Arkansas became increasingly popular.

### HOT SPRINGS RESERVATION
The establishment of the Hot Springs Reservation came with little government oversight or management until decades later. Congress had set aside the land in 1832. The reservation was modest, encompassing a 10 sq km/4 sq mile preserve that contained the bulk of thermal springs. An organic process of resort development emerged around the springs, led by entrepreneurs intent on taking advantage of the natural resource. By the Civil War an unorganized collection of primitive bathhouses were

clustered around the springs. Although the Civil War stalled further resort development, the city of Hot Springs could boast in 1873 of hosting six bathhouses and two dozen boarding houses and hotels. The arrival of the city's first railroad connection spurred more luxurious developments, notably the construction of Arlington Hotel in 1875. As Richard Sellars explains, "The enthusiastic promotion of recreational tourism in the parks generated a tradition that the Park Service would eagerly embrace." Places such as Hot Springs, set the precedent for a greater economic rationale in the development of national parks – that of tourism promotion.

The earlier bathhouses, along what is today Bathhouse Row, consisted of crude buildings of shoddy construction

*Above: A federal makeover in the 1880s encouraged a redevelopment of the earlier Bathhouse Row.*

that frequently burnt or collapsed. Many simply rotted prematurely due to constant exposure to water or steam. The central drainage channel of Hot Springs Creek became an eyesore and presented an increasing flood hazard. In 1884 the federal government assumed more control of the earlier reservation and promptly covered the creek with a masonry arch. A road was laid down on top, encouraging development of formal walkways and landscaping along what is today Bathhouse Row. Now integrated into the heart of downtown Hot Springs, Bathhouse Row constitutes the largest collection of 20th-century bathhouses in the nation. The Row includes eight bathhouses along Central Avenue, the main street of Hot Springs, representing the height of recreational activity here from the 1920s through the 1940s.

*Left: The hot springs were the first federally protected area within the National Park System and played an influential role in National Park history.*

# PERRYVILLE BATTLEFIELD
## BOYLE COUNTY, WEST OF PERRYVILLE, KENTUCKY

Few memorial landscapes are more poignant for visitors than those of America's Civil War battlefields. As historian Reuben Rainey reflects, "There is something about the experience of the physical reality of the place, of being there, of walking over the grounds, that admits of no substitute." Numerous organizations and government authorities have attempted to restore natural landscapes to accurately portray the Civil War battle landscapes that they commemorate. Without human intervention, the agricultural fields that served as stages for clashes of Northern and Southern armies would have quickly returned to forested ecosystems. Many of them did. Later efforts to manage and preserve such natural landscapes have halted much of this ecological succession, allowing future generations to gain a clearer perspective of what the soldiers encountered. Consequently, "At Gettysburg it is July 1–3, 1863 forever; at Antietam it is always September 17, 1862". At the battlefield at Perryville, now managed as a Kentucky State Park, the special character of the place is

*Below: American preservationists have attempted to restore environments such as battlefields to their original appearance.*

promoted to potential visitors as "one of the most unaltered Civil War sites in the nation; vistas visible today are virtually those soldiers saw on that fateful day in 1862".

### HIGH STAKES

The "fateful day" was 8 October, when Confederate and Union forces clashed just outside the village of Perryville. Kentucky had desperately tried to remain neutral after 11 Southern states had formed the Confederacy. All hopes of neutrality had vanished by the summer of 1861, however, because the state was occupied by Northern and Southern forces. Southern sympathizers had created a Confederate government in Kentucky, in contrast to the pro-Union state legislature. The Confederacy invaded Kentucky in 1862, hoping to arouse Southern sympathies to drive the Union forces out of the state. Four days prior to the battle, the Southern army occupied Frankfort and attempted to install a new Confederate governor. Before the conclusion of ceremonies, however, the Union cavalry approached Frankfort, causing the southerners to retreat to Lexington. As 58,000 Union men marched toward the Confederate position, the Confederates proceeded

*Above: Fields and open spaces at places such as Perryville are managed to preserve landscapes as they would have appeared.*

toward the town of Harrodsburg via Perryville. It was here where the two forces clashed in one of the most intense battles of the Civil War. Essentially, the winner could claim Kentucky for its own.

Following initial skirmishes on the morning of October 8, intense fighting began after noon. In the short span of five hours the Battle of Perryville became one of the War's bloodiest fights. Heavy casualties were tallied on both sides. Bragg's losses included 510 killed, 2,635 wounded and 251 missing. Casualties on the Northern side were even greater, with 845 of Buell's men killed, 2,851 wounded, and 489 taken prisoner. By the end of the day, the battle incurred a total of more than 7,000 casualties. It was Bragg who ultimately decided to retreat from Kentucky to Tennessee. The Union claimed a victory and kept Kentucky within its fold. Not long after the Perryville battle, advancing Union forces re-acquired Tennessee as well. The Confederate General Basil Duke saw the implications of Bragg's retreat from Kentucky, stating that "On the 10th of October more than fifty thousand Confederate soldiers were upon the soil of Kentucky…the first of November they were all gone, and with them departed all hope, perhaps, of Southern independence".

# PINEHURST
## HISTORIC DISTRICT, PINEHURST, NORTH CAROLINA

The truth about the origins of the game of golf may remain unclear, but Scotland was the scene of the first permanent golf courses, club memberships and the first written rules. The first club outside Scotland is credited to Blackheath, England, formed in 1766. From England the game diffused throughout the rest of the world. The earliest known record of the game in Colonial America involved Albany, New York, when the game was banned from the town's streets in 1659.

It wasn't until the 1870s and 1880s when organized golfing came to North America, oriented to the social elite. Although a matter of some dispute, the first permanent golf club in the United States was founded in Yonkers, New York, in 1888. The origin of golf in this country is typically traced back to that event. From Yonkers, golf diffused rapidly, first through the Northeastern and North-central regions. Since the 19th century, the sport of golf has enjoyed two distinct periods of growth.

The first boom occurred during the 1920s, considered by historians as the golden age of sport. This period coincided with a rapid increase in personal wealth and prosperity, and in turn an increase in leisure activities and interest in sports. More than 4,000 golf courses were created during this time. The second boom occurred during and around the 1960s, when increased visibility of the game encouraged a much wider segment of society to take up the sport.

This so-called democratic revolution encouraged a parallel development of public courses inexpensive enough to attract the general public. During this period 6,000 golf facilities were constructed nationwide, and television viewers were treated to the likes of Hogan, Snead, Palmer and Nicklaus.

### DONALD ROSS
One of the foremost contributors to golf was Donald J. Ross (1872–1948), who was born in Scotland and moved to America in 1899. A year later he was hired as the golf professional at North Carolina's new Pinehurst Resort, launching his career as a professional player and prolific course designer. Throughout his career, Ross either designed or revised more than 400 courses. He is further credited with single-handedly improving the sport's prominence in North America; prior to his arrival at Pinehurst, golf had yet to receive much national attention. Under the stewardship of Donald Ross, not only did Pinehurst represent the height

*Left: Pinehurst enjoyed early fame as the first and only resort in the world by 1919 that included four courses with a total of 72 holes of quality golf. Today it is part of a larger historic district.*

*Above: Pinehurst was to golf what Churchill Downs was to horse racing, both providing new leisure landscapes.*

of recreational resort development in America, but it set the standard as a national model.

### HEALTH RESORT
The story of Pinehurst, now preserved as a Victorian-era Historic District, began as a planned recreational resort community focused more on health than on golf. Boston soda fountain magnate James W. Tufts first conceived of Pinehurst as a winter health resort, having purchased 2,225ha/5,500 acres in 1895. His Holly Inn opened on New Year's Eve, and the resort's first golf course was completed by 1898. The resort's landscaping was entrusted to the firm of Frederick Law Olmsted, though Olmsted claimed ill health and relied heavily on his colleagues, particularly Warren H. Manning. Considered one of America's most prominent landscape architects, Manning served at Pinehurst for 46 years. Similarly, three generations of Tufts retained control of the resort until 1970, however, it was the decades prior to World War II when Pinehurst enjoyed its most significant period of history.

# CHURCHILL DOWNS
## LOUISVILLE, KENTUCKY

Known internationally as home of the Kentucky Derby, Churchill Downs officially opened on 17 May 1875 with four scheduled races. A horse named Bonaventure won the historic first race, however, it was a three-year-old chestnut colt named Aristides who won the featured race of the day—the Kentucky Derby. In 1883 the first reference to Churchill Downs was published in an article in the *Louisville Commercial*, in which it exclaimed: "The crowd in the grandstand sent out a volume of voice, and the crowd in the field took it up and carried it from boundary to boundary of Churchill Downs."

Home to the largest horse-racing grandstands in North America, Churchill Downs is still the site of the Kentucky Derby, which serves as the first phase of the highly coveted "Triple Crown". Status came quickly to Churchill Downs, as the Derby rapidly acquired prominence in racing and attracted the most highly-skilled jockeys, trainers and horses.

Throughout much of the 19th century Americans continued to look to Europe and particularly to England for instruction on matters of culture and society. The early enthusiasts of horse

racing were no different. Motivated to reinvigorate the thoroughbred industry then in decline, a respected breeder named colonel Meriwether Lewis Clark travelled to England and France in 1872–73 for instruction on European racing. At the age of 26, Clark met with several prominent racing leaders and learned from existing facilities. He then began to develop his own racetrack, intent on displaying the Kentucky breeding industry.

### ENGLISH LESSONS

Clark's track was modelled after Epsom Downs in England and was constructed with funds raised by selling 320 membership subscriptions at US $100 each. Clark's uncles, John and Henry Churchill, leased the necessary land for the track, about 5km/3 miles south of downtown Louisville. In addition to the track, a grandstand, a clubhouse, stables and a porter's lodge were added to the site. Clark's three major stakes races, namely the Kentucky Derby, Kentucky Oaks and the Clark Handicap mirrored

*Below: The twin Victorian spires built in 1895 provide the most recognizable feature of Churchill Downs.*

*Above: The success of Churchill Downs as an acclaimed horse-racing venue owes many of its features to precedents set in England.*

the three premier English races, the Epsom Derby, Epsom Oaks and the St Leger Stakes. Professional horse racing had finally arrived in America. Beyond his formation of the Jockey Club and Churchill Downs, Clark was the first to introduce pari-mutuel betting to the USA from France. Naturally, he further supported state legislation passed in 1878, which legalized this form of betting at recognized horse-racing venues.

The grandstand at Churchill Downs has undergone numerous expansions throughout its existence, though it was the 1894–95 addition that created the most lasting visual appeal. Intersecting the roof are two gables, each of which is topped with an octagonal cupola crowned by a Victorian-era spire. The twin spires have become the visual trademark of Churchill Downs and are synonymous with the Kentucky Derby. More recently, the facilities have undergone a series of renovations, including the 2002 addition of 64 luxury suites and meeting areas built on top of the existing grandstand. The new balconies provide impressive views of the twin spires. Even more comprehensive was the second phase of renovations that began in 2003, signalling the continued growth and status of Churchill Downs. The US $95 million project increased seating capacity to 52,000.

# WRIGHT BROTHERS
## NATIONAL MEMORIAL VISITOR CENTER, KILL DEVIL HILLS, NC

In 1931 the National Park System had hosted between three and four million guests. By 1948 that number had increased eight-fold. Neglected from years of inattention and upkeep, the parks were overwhelmed.

Following increased publicity in the national media, the national park problem attracted the attention of the federal government and in response a decade-long program of capital improvements was proposed in 1955. The intention was to improve Park facilities throughout the nation in time for the 50th anniversary of the National Park Service in 1966.

### MISSION 66

The Mission 66 program was born; its fundamental goal was to expand the services offered within the national parks. Initially organized as a series of planning committees, the Mission 66 staff was charged with studying the most pressing needs and determining the problems

*Below: The Wright brothers memorial landscape is based on modern design philosophies to encourage park visitors.*

faced by the parks. A list of priorities was ultimately presented, and a plan to standardize park services was devised. Every park would include a uniform entrance sign, lists of park resources, paved trails, a minimum number of staff, and similar facilities that visitors could count upon. Most important, however, would be the Visitor Center, which served as the core planning and design component of Mission 66. The Visitor Center was to be the main point of contact between the park service and the public, a facility designed to provide a wide variety of amenities.

### THE NEW VISITOR CENTER

Built at the official site of America's first flight, the Wright Brothers National Memorial Visitor Center was completed by 1959. It was considered an important Mission 66 project, and remains an excellent example of Mission 66 goals and architectural values. Prior to the Visitor Center's construction, the site of Orville and Wilbur Wright's experiments during 1900–03 had been designated as a national monument in

*Above: The world's first recorded flight occurred near the memorial center, later designated a national monument.*

1927. One year later a granite marker was installed to indicate the approximate take-off site for the first recorded flight. This was followed in 1932 by the construction of an 18m/60ft high pylon nearby, on Big Kill Devil Hill. The National Park Service assumed control of the monument in 1933 to continue the development of visitor facilities.

The new Visitor Center represented a fundamental reorganization of how the Wright brothers site would be interpreted and experienced by visitors. Designed strategically as the focus of visitor activities, the new building was placed to encourage viewing of the two monuments. Most striking was its unfamiliar Modern architecture at the time, the success of which set a precedent for the park service throughout the nation. Unlike the strict formalism promoted by the International style that dominated urban development after 1950, the Visitor Center better exemplifies the work of the Philadelphia School of Modern Architecture. Still following Modernist tenets, the Philadelphia architects were inspired more by Louis I. Kahn and his contemporaries. The Visitor Center consequently became an important showcase for this benchmark project of the Philadelphia variant of Modern architecture.

# BILTMORE ESTATE
## AND FORESTRY SCHOOL SITE, ASHEVILLE, NORTH CAROLINA

Distinctly a product of America's gilded age, the Biltmore Estate combined European Revival architecture with a budding national interest in science during the late 19th century. During the 1880s, George Vanderbilt, William Vanderbilt's youngest son, became enthralled with the Asheville, North Carolina, area and visited regularly. He decided to create a summer estate in similar grand fashion to those already built by family members in Newport, Rhode Island, and Hyde Park, New York. Envisioning his own European-type working estate, Vanderbilt hired prominent architect Richard Morris Hunt to design a house in the manner of the French Renaissance, incorporating the style of Loire Valley chateaux specifically the Chateau de Blois. Vanderbilt's mansion included 1.6ha/ 4 acres of floor space, 250 rooms, 34 bedrooms, 43 bathrooms and 65 fireplaces. Frederick Law Olmsted, America's "father of landscape architecture", was commissioned to design the grounds. Together the house and grounds demonstrated 19th-century interests in Renaissance Revival architecture and Picturesque landscape design through the esteemed team of Hunt and Olmsted.

### FORESTRY – A NEW SCIENCE
Little did anyone know that, when George Vanderbilt purchased 50,585ha/ 125,000 acres of farmland and forested mountains for his estate in 1888, he was enabling the birth of modern forest science. Biltmore ultimately became the "home of conservation" in the USA. First it was Frederick Law Olmsted who assumed direction of the estate's development, planning to incorporate a large arboretum, game preserve and a managed forest. The estate grounds were designed as a demonstration of a profitable business. In 1891, Gifford Pinchot was

*Above: Architect Richard M. Hunt designed George Vanderbilt's summer estate in the style of a French chateau from the Loire Valley. The Chateau de Blois was the inspiration for the design.*

appointed to manage the estate. Pinchot had studied at the French National Forestry School where he learned that little progress with managing American forests could be made until it was demonstrated that a scientifically managed forest could be commercially profitable. Pinchot returned to America determined to convince the timber industry that the nation's forests provided only a limited resource and required long-term management.

In 1895 under Pinchot's successor, Carl A. Schenck, new scientific and practical forestry approaches were implemented. Over time, Schenck discovered an increasing amount of local interest in his work. Encouraged through this experience to begin a forestry education program, he gained permission from Vanderbilt to found the Biltmore Forest School in 1898, the first of its kind in America. At this time less than a dozen trained foresters existed in the country, all of whom had been educated in Europe. The Biltmore School provided a one-year program that focused on a combination of theory and

practical forest management training. The life of the School was short lived, and discontinued prior to World War I. By that time, however, it had trained many of the nation's first-generation foresters who came to dominate the field of forestry for years to come. Since 1930 the main house and gardens of the Biltmore Estate have been opened to the public.

*Below: The azalea garden at Biltmore is open to the public, a large visitor attraction on this self-sufficient estate.*

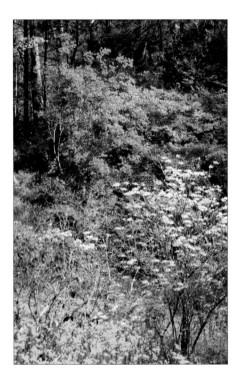

# BEALE STREET
## HISTORIC DISTRICT, MEMPHIS, TENNESSEE

Beale Street's historic appeal lies with the vibrant African-American culture that prospered here by the 1920s. The Beale Street corridor is often touted as the "birthplace of the blues". It was here that this regional musical form developed and ultimately had an impact on American rock, jazz, pop and even symphonic music. W. C. Handy focused his career on Beale Street and elevated the blues to new heights in American culture. While working in Memphis, Handy wrote songs including *Memphis*

*Blues* and *St Louis Blues* that earned far-reaching appeal. Beale Street served as the headquarters for Handy's band. This backdrop of musical development along Beale Street enabled a thriving multi-cultural community to develop as a place where African-American music traditions and their associated business interests flourished. With the mayor's 1959 announcement of the city's plans

*Right: W. C. Handy's home is characteristic of the Southern region.*

to transform Beale Street into a tourist attraction, the federal urban renewal process commenced.

### REDEVELOPMENT

Targeted as a redevelopment zone financed through both federal and city funding, the first urban renewal project began by the late 1960s. More than 60ha/150 acres of land and 14 city blocks were included in the project, which officials proclaimed would be focused on the construction of housing for the elderly, low-cost public housing, rehabilitation of some historic buildings and the renewal of the blue light entertainment district on Beale Street. Ultimately, much of this never happened. Plans were scrapped, funds were cut and the once-vibrant Beale Street neighbourhood became an urban wasteland. According to research conducted at Rhodes College in Memphis: "Empty lots replaced razed, historic buildings. Five years after the start of the project, Beale Street resembled 'removal' more than 'renewal'." Black and white business owners and families were forced to decide between keeping their livelihoods in place or selling out to the city government. Both the heritage and future of a vibrant African-American community were in jeopardy, and many argue today that it has never been the same. By the

## URBAN RENEWAL

Until just after World War II, America's cities focused their social, economic and cultural energies within their traditional downtowns. With the construction of freeways and suburban developments oriented to car travel and shopping centres, however, traditional downtown areas became decentralized and left primarily the poorest residents behind. With the earliest signs of urban decay came America's first political and economic efforts to revitalize ailing downtown cores. Although initially intended to improve impoverished residential areas described as blighted or deteriorating, a federal program known as "urban renewal" became a popular approach by the 1950s that ultimately reached far beyond its intended goal. One loophole to the federal program – passed as part of the Housing Act of 1949 – enabled cities to simply demolish slum housing near downtown areas, regardless of what was built in its place.

Predictably, those with an economic stake in downtown areas viewed urban renewal as a method through which run-down neighbourhoods could be eradicated to be replaced with flashy, new development projects oriented to middle-class consumers. Whether such

blighted neighbourhoods were still socially and economically vibrant was unimportant. What constituted "blight" was also open to interpretation, thereby encouraging city renewal directors to consciously search for "the blight that's right" – places run-down enough to clear but also marketable enough to attract developers. The impact on urban neighbourhoods across the country was staggering. By 1967 more than 400,000 families had been displaced from their homes, forced to move elsewhere with little compensation. Entire swaths of historically rich housing and downtown commercial architecture had likewise been razed, often waiting decades for developers to show interest in the new "urban deserts".

*Below: Beale Street in 1978.*

*Right: Beale Street comes alive at night once again, because Memphis has redeveloped its downtown based on entertainment.*

1960s much of downtown Memphis resembled a ghost town, along with Beale Street – one of numerous urban renewal efforts in the city.

Over time, two redevelopment efforts occurred through the initiatives of largely white-owned companies, both of which failed. The African-American community viewed the redevelopment project as a civil rights issue, claiming that their own cultural heritage was being destroyed to make way for a tourist district oriented to the white middle class. Only by the 1980s did the third redevelopment attempt take hold, one led this time by a culturally sensitive developer named John Elkington. He developed strong ties with the community and interviewed nearly 100 African-American residents before the project broke ground. Further, he actively recruited African-American businesses, managers and employees to relocate back to Beale Street.

## A VIBRANT STREET SCENE

Not only had the vibrancy of Beale Street returned by 2006, but 35 per cent of the businesses there were owned by African-Americans. Although considerably altered since the glory days of the blues, Beale Street emerged from urban renewal as a vibrant downtown community and historical attraction, much like the stories of similar urban neighbourhoods across the country. It was the lessons learned through urban renewal that ultimately encouraged America's ongoing historic preservation movement since the 1970s, with communities forming renewed appreciation for their historic building stocks and heritage. Smaller communities such as Madison, Indiana, sought to revitalize older mainstreet districts rather than bulldoze them, a movement that led to the now-famous National Main Street Program. For larger cities such as Memphis, revived neigh-

bourhoods such as Beale Street now thrive once again and provide important lessons for future development and community cohesiveness.

Today the Beale Street district is a major tourist attraction, a mix of new and old, with themed restaurants adjacent to vibrant local businesses. This recent success story of economic redevelopment masks the challenges and threats that Beale Street faced during the urban renewal era. What has occurred

*Above: Celebrated B. B. King began his career as a performer on Beale Street.*

here reflects the most recent trend for downtown redevelopment across the country, that of reinventing commercial districts into themed entertainment areas dubbed as "fantasy cities".

*Below: Tourism in Beale Street is now thriving after earlier challenges with urban renewal.*

# CHAPTER SEVEN

# THE GREAT PLAINS

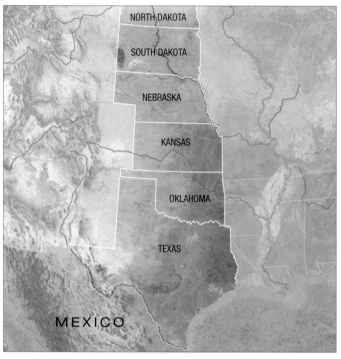

ONCE THE REALM OF NOMADIC INDIGENOUS
TRIBES, EARLY SETTLERS HAVE CULTIVATED
THESE ONCE MARGINAL LANDS SINCE THE
GOVERNMENT OPENED UP THE AREA FOR
SETTLEMENT. THE REGION SPANS THE
MISSISSIPPPI RIVER TO THE ROCKY MOUNTAINS
AND INCLUDES NORTH DAKOTA, SOUTH DAKOTA,
NEBRASKA, KANSAS, OKLAHOMA, TEXAS, AND
PARTS OF COLORADO, MONTANA AND WYOMING,
(THE LATTER THREE STATES ARE INCORPORATED
INTO OTHER REGIONS FOR THE PURPOSES OF THIS
BOOK). THE RURAL LANDSCAPE IS
CHARACTERIZED BY STEPPE, PRAIRIE AND
GRASSLANDS.

*Left: The small school house at Spring Hill Ranch, part of the
Tallgrass Prairie National Preserve.*

# FORT LEAVENWORTH
## LEAVENWORTH, KANSAS

Americans associate the city of Santa Fe, New Mexico with the southwestern USA, but the political geography of the region was quite different before 1848. Prior to the American acquisition of northern Mexico during the Mexican-American War of 1848, Santa Fe was part of New Spain and briefly under the jurisdiction of Mexico.

### TRADE ROUTE UNDER THREAT

The Arkansas River served as the international border between the USA and Mexico. First established during Spanish Colonial times, the Santa Fe Trail became a vital trade corridor between isolated New Mexico and the Americans to the East. Long ignored as part of the remote Mexican northland, Santa Fe and the upper Rio Grande Valley desperately sought American manufactured goods – and those traders were eager to comply. Another presence was just as eager to disrupt this lucrative trade route, the collective indigenous inhabitants who had inhabited the Plains long before the arrival of American or Mexican settlers. The Native Americans were perceived as trouble makers who occasionally led attacks on the seasonal wagon trains destined for the famed Santa Fe plaza.

*Below: Fort Leavenworth was established to protect the Santa Fe Trail.*

### ESTABLISHING A FORT

The calls for military protection grew louder in the 1820s. An early proposal to place an American fort along the Arkansas River was turned down by the army due to issues with staffing such a remote location. Eventually decision makers in Washington, DC, approved a camp on the Missouri River, and Cantonment Leavenworth was established in 1827 by its namesake, Colonel Henry Leavenworth, then in command of the Third US Infantry. Located strategically on a 46m/150ft bluff on the river's west bank, the cantonment officially became Fort Leavenworth in 1833 when all American cantonments were ordered to be called forts henceforth. The Santa Fe Trail was located several miles south of the fort. As an indicator of the traffic seen on the Trail each spring, the first trade caravan

*Below: The wagon train was the transport of choice before the railroad was built.*

*Left: Horses were once the primary mode of transportation on the Great Plains.*

protected by soldiers from Leavenworth departed in 1829 and involved nearly 40 wagons of merchandise with 70 men. Accompanying the traders were almost 200 soldiers on foot with 20 of their own supply wagons hauled by oxen. Buttressing their stock of weaponry was a mule-drawn carriage loaded with a 2.7kg/6lb cannon.

With its early establishment to protect the Santa Fe Trail from Native Americans, Fort Leavenworth became what is considered today as the oldest, continuously active army post west of the Mississippi River. The Fort became the hub of army activity that ultimately protected additional routes westward, including the Oregon Trail. During the war with Mexico, Leavenworth served as the outfitting post for the army of the West. The fort gained political status as the first capital of Kansas Territory in 1854. Then, when the American government turned its attention to the Plains Indians following the Civil War, Leavenworth played a key role in the final removal of Native Americans from their homelands that allowed the proverbial floodgates to open for American settlers.

The historic district of contemporary Fort Leavenworth contains more than 110 buildings and structures that represent certain facets of the base's long history. Though many buildings have been altered as a byproduct of continuous use, the district still exhibits its appearance as it existed during the late 1800s and early 1900s. Perhaps the most amazing survivor of all consists of the still-visible wagon ruts that led from the old river landing for the Santa Fe and Oregon trails. The Fort's parade ground is another survivor, having remained in continuous use since its founding.

# WOUNDED KNEE BATTLEFIELD
## WOUNDED KNEE, SOUTH DAKOTA

One of America's most poignant memorial landscapes is located in rural South Dakota near the Pine Ridge Indian Reservation. Wounded Knee – at once a symbolic place and historical event. The events of 29 December 1890 constituted the last American military engagement with indigenous people. Wounded Knee is considered to be a watershed that reflected the end of Native-American freedom and their final resignation to life on federally designated reservations.

### SYMBOLIC LANDSCAPE

Prior to 1890, the majority of indigenous peoples had been subdued, generally through military force, with their leaders either killed or captured. The once powerful Sioux Nation had been reduced to barely being able to feed itself and – prior to his assassination – their last great leader, Sitting Bull, had been exiled to Canada.

Simplified here from Dee Brown's 1970 account, the chief of the Minneconjous, Big Foot, learned of Sitting Bull's death and began to move his people to the Pine Ridge Reservation in South Dakota. En route, Big Foot fell ill of pneumonia. On 28 December they were approached by four troops of American cavalry led by Major Samuel Whitside. Upon their approach, Big Foot had ordered a white flag to fly above the wagon that carried him. Whitside told the chief that he had orders to remove him to a cavalry camp on Wounded Knee Creek. Big Foot stated that he and his people were already headed in that direction. For the continued march to Wounded Knee Creek, two troops of cavalry took the lead, with Big Foot's people, 120 men and 230 women and children, herded behind them. The remaining troops and a battery of two Hotchkiss guns brought up the rear.

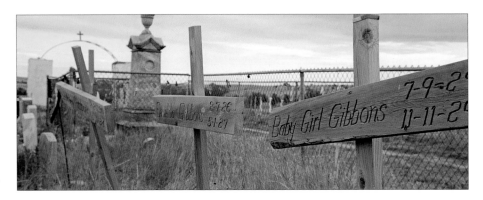

*Above: The Wounded Knee events of 1890 signalled the end of an indigenous way of life on the Great Plains.*

The following morning, the military men surrounded the encampment and proceeded to disarm the Indians. Teepees were searched and bundles of personal belongings were ransacked. Only two rifles were found, including one held by a young Minneconjou named Black Coyote, who was reported later to have been deaf. He raised his rifle above his head, prompting soldiers to grab him and his rifle. Soon thereafter a gun discharged, though precise events remain unclear. One eye witness recalled that Black Coyote had indeed fired his gun and that "immediately the soldiers returned fire and indiscriminate killing followed". Several seconds of intense violence occurred. Big Foot and the majority of his people were dead or seriously wounded. Estimates have placed the number of dead at or near 300, including those who died later of injuries. For their part, the Calvary lost 25 dead and 39 wounded. Many were brought down through "friendly fire," consisting of their own indiscriminate bullets and shrapnel.

### A FITTING MEMORIAL

The Native American survivors of Wounded Knee dedicated a granite monument at the grave site on 28 May 1903. The monument is inscribed with the names of many of the fatalities. In addition three natural features are included as part of the landmark, having played key roles in the events – namely, the burial hill, the dry ravine and Wounded Knee Creek. The cavalry's artillery was located on the burial hill during the engagement, which afterwards served as the mass grave. The dry ravine was the major escape route for the fleeing Native Americans, while Wounded Knee Creek gave the site its name.

*Below: A mass grave is the final resting place for 146 Sioux men, women and children, marked by a granite monument in 1903.*

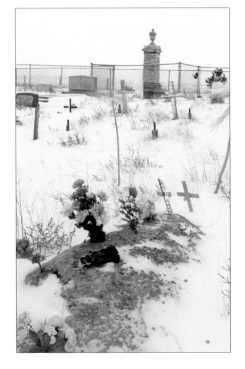

# SPRING HILL RANCH
## STRONG CITY, KANSAS

The cowboy has become one of the more powerful and romanticized global symbols of the American West. It was on the Great Plains, however, where the predominant cowboy way of life emerged and flourished for a few brief decades. Today's array of legends and folklore surrounding the "day of the cattleman" is rooted in a migratory ranching lifestyle that prospered from the 1860 to the 1880s.

### OPEN RANGE FARMING

Prior to the settlement of homesteaders, this vast north-south expanse of grassland was available as "open range" for the raising and migration of cattle herds. Unconfined by fences and farm populations, free-range cattle were fattened by the short- and tall-grass prairies. Southern Texas provided fertile breeding grounds. Mild winters enabled

the growth of herds by 80–90 per cent each season. Once born, however, the young cattle could be better fed on the nutritious short and mixed-grass prairies further north in Kansas and elsewhere. A migratory pattern developed that took advantage of these regional advantages. After expanding the herds in Texas, cattle were driven northward "on the hoof" to the central Plains each season. Impressive trail drives were undertaken each year in a region that for a brief time was integrated north-south. Once mature, steers were driven to the nearest cattle-town railheads and shipped east to packing houses in Kansas City or Chicago.

Several standard cattle trails were established during this time, most notably the Goodnight-Loving, Western and Chisholm trails. The latter two moved through Kansas, with the state's

*Above: Herds of bison once dominated the Great Plains, prior to the proliferation of fenced cattle ranches and homesteading.*

first "cattle town" established at Abilene in 1867. Here, cattlemen met buyers and took advantage of the new Kansas Pacific Railroad link to eastern markets. Abilene prospered on this trade up through 1872, after which it surrendered the trade to Ellsworth and Wichita. During the last years of the open-range cattle era, Dodge City and Ogallala, Nebraska, served as the primary trans-shipment points, up through the 1880s. Like the one-industry mining towns of the Mountain West, cattle towns on the Plains proved to be temporary boom towns that cashed in on the cattle trade as the American frontier moved westward. Subsequently these places came to rely on their more stable status as trade centres for surrounding family farms.

### HOMESTEADERS

With an estimated 7.5 million cattle roaming the Plains by 1885, a variety of economic, political and climatic factors

*Left: The Ranch at Spring Hill is built in the Second Empire style so popular in the East at the time, complete with the Mansard roof and extending pavilions. This style was rare for this rural region.*

*Right: The Tallgrass Prairie National Preserve showcases native prairie vegetation in the USA.*

conspired to end the era of open range. Politically, federal legislation favoured homesteaders over cattlemen. As more railroads pushed westward across the Plains, so too did the settlement of family farms and the trade towns that served them. A dense grid of barbed-wire fencing was being laid across Kansas and Nebraska, representing more sedentary farming and ranching activities. The result was that the traditional north-south migratory routes were cut off and compartmentalized into ever-smaller territories, essentially ending the open-range era on the Great Plains by the early 1890s.

The transition from open range to enclosed ranches boosted raising cattle into a modern industry. Economies of scale encouraged ever-larger operations that required significant capital investments. As a result the quality of stock did improve, in part because enclosed stock could benefit from more dependable water sources. The high cost of facilities also necessitated that ranch operations maintain only the best

*Below: This farmstead is a reminder of the once-prominent role of family farms.*

quality animals. Further, proponents claim additional environmental benefits included the better management of sustainable rangelands that reduced the risk of overgrazing.

**THE RANCH**

Located in the fertile Flint Hills of Kansas, the Spring Hill Farm and Stock Ranch provide an outstanding example of the transition from open range to enclosed cattle holdings. The first purchase of ranch land occurred in 1878 after which the operations consolidated into enclosed holdings. It was operations here that convinced others in the area to convert to enclosed ranching. Now

a National Historic Landmark, the property exhibits a remarkably complete ensemble of a late 19th-century enclosed cattle ranch and headquarters. A typical ranching landscape from the period tended to include an array of specific functional structures and properties: the homestead and surrounding farm, cattle barn, calving shed, bullpen, windmill, cistern, water trough, corral and associated fencing, loading ramp and chute, pole barn, feed lot and feed storage facility. Virtually all of these features are still found at Spring Hill Ranch, in addition to various farming structures: an ice house, smokehouse or springhouse, and poultry house.

As the hub of family operations, construction on the Ranch House began in 1878 and resulted in an imposing three-storey, 11-room residence. Signifying the importance of outbuildings to such farming and cattle operations is the fact that the main three-storey barn – with 602m sq/6,480ft sq – competes with the house in terms of impressiveness and scale. In 1996 the Tallgrass Prairie National Preserve was created within the Flint Hills region, its intent being to preserve a rare remnant of the tall-grass prairie ecosystem not converted to farmland. In 2002 about 13ha/32 acres were donated to the National Park Service, including the Spring Hill Ranch house and related historic structures.

# NEBRASKA STATE CAPITOL
## LINCOLN, NEBRASKA

The US Capitol building was a powerful architectural symbol that epitomized American democracy for new states entering the Union between the Civil War and World War I. As such, it was often copied for the design of new state capitol buildings. In 1919 a unique architectural competition to determine the design of the new Nebraska State Capitol at Lincoln was held. This new building was to replace the previous two capitol buildings.

Unusually the competition did not insist upon a specific architectural style, floor plan or building material. Instead, a team approach with a unified vision was sought for the project, including an individual sculptor, landscape architect and painter. More than 30 distinguished firms submitted entries, with the architect Bertram Grosvenor Goodhue (1869-1924) awarded the commission.

### ECLECTIC ERA

American architecture of the time was known by some as the eclectic era. The period from 1880–1929 saw two broad and often competing styles. The first

focused on the revival of popular historic architectural styles, largely based on ancient Greek, Roman or medieval European precedents. Residential neighbourhoods were being filled with an array of revivalist styles, featuring Neoclassical Revival, Dutch Colonial, Colonial (or Georgian) Revival, and Beaux-Arts designs. In the South and Southwest, regional variations included Spanish Revival, Italian Renaissance, Pueblo Revival, and other Mediterranean-influenced modes.

*Below: Bertram Goodhue aimed to design a new American form of classic skyscraper with the central tower of the State Capitol.*

*Left: The central rotunda floor is a marble mosaic.*

The second architectural movement was considered more progressive, a movement away from historicism to create a more uniquely American, Modernist architecture. Early examples included the Craftsman style and a regional variation developed by Frank Lloyd Wright and his counterparts known as the Prairie style. The tension between architects favouring each was intense. Few architects attempted to bridge the competing Modernist and historical modes.

### THE WINNING DESIGN

Bertram Goodhue was a rare exception who realized the pinnacle of his career with his design of the Nebraska State Capitol, in which he interwove evolving Modernist designs and technology with his own rendition of Neo-classical architecture. Beaux-Arts classicism was integrated with an early version of a modern skyscraper. The design's Beaux-Arts component consisted of its formal layout into equal quadrants radiating out from a central square. At the centre was the expected rotunda, but capped with a huge, 122m/400ft tower in place of a traditional dome. This was Goodhue's attempt to create a new American form of Classically-inspired skyscraper.

Soon after the tower's completion in 1930, architect Howell Lewis Shay wrote: "I consider…Goodhue not only a great student of tradition, but a Modernist in every sense of the word, to typify the best and most progressive in our modern work." Having provided a modern alternative to the US Capitol design, Goodhue's work inspired the states of Oregon, North Dakota and Louisiana to build versions of the Nebraska State Capitol, having become a model in its own right.

# NICODEMUS NATIONAL HISTORIC SITE
## NICODEMUS, KANSAS

The mass exodus of African-Americans to northern cities following the Civil War is well documented – an exodus that led to the creation of sizeable black communities outside their traditional Southern homeland. Less well known is the story of African-American pioneers who moved westward during the reconstruction era, in many cases developing their own towns in the process. Located in the heart of the Great Plains, Nicodemus represents the only remaining, post-Civil War townscape developed as a result of this migration.

The exceptional rarity of such pioneering communities today is evident here, given that only a handful of individual historic structures survive in Nicodemus. These include buildings representing a variety of functions that remain in various states of renovation or disrepair. The five buildings now protected by the Nicodemus National Historic Site include the African Methodist Episcopal Church, the First Baptist Church, the St Francis Hotel, the Nicodemus School District #1 Schoolhouse and Township Hall.

### ESTABLISHING NICODEMUS
Prior to the official founding of Nicodemus in 1877, the migration of African-Americans to the present-day

*Above: The first Baptist Church was built of sod in 1879.*

Midwest was strongly encouraged by Benjamin "Pap" Singleton, who described Kansas as the new "promised land". Kansas entered the union as a free state. Singleton had been born a slave in Nashville, Tennessee, and eventually escaped to Canada and later to Detroit, Michigan. He returned to his home state following the emancipation of slaves, with hopes to organize black communities there. Finding the social climate inhospitable, he visited Kansas in 1873 with 300 followers. Most of them settled in "Singleton's Colony" in Cherokee County. Later that year he and other members of the Nicodemus Town Company travelled to churches in Kentucky and other Southern states to encourage further migration westward.

*Above: The St Francis Hotel was also a post office, operated by African-Americans.*

The migrations that occurred under Singleton's influence were responsible for settling Nicodemus, established on homestead land in Graham County, Kansas.

The original pioneers in Nicodemus persevered under harsh frontier conditions on the Kansas plains, first living in primitive shelters referred to as "burrows" on the sides of banks or hills. These were later replaced with sod dug-outs and then with wood-framed structures.

Despite its inauspicious beginnings Nicodemus grew into a small, bustling town by the mid-1880s. The town's growth was largely unplanned. An exception was the business district, which was better defined. The oldest business in the county was credited to Nicodemus, that of Z. T. Fletcher's general store, founded in 1877. A year later the town earned its first post office, established within part of Fletcher's store. The School District #1 became a reality in 1879.

Despite these modest community improvements in a short time, what the new town lacked was a railroad – essential for the future development of such places. The railroad ultimately bypassed the town. The result was predictable: a new community, Bogue, was located near the railroad, and more people moved to be closer to the tracks. Nicodemus had around 700 residents during its peak.

*Below: The wood structure school is the second on the site.*

*Below: The AME church was closed to religious services in the mid-20th century.*

# GUTHRIE
## HISTORIC DISTRICT, GUTHRIE, OKLAHOMA

Despite Guthrie's early status as the state capital of Oklahoma, it is the community's well-preserved downtown commercial scene that is principally celebrated here. The commercial landscape of main street is not only considered to be quintessentially American, but has been described as one of America's three most symbolic landscape scenes. Guthrie's own main street business district exhibits one of the least altered commercial districts from the turn of the 20th century. As with other towns and cities, the dominant architectural styles used on Guthrie's commercial buildings were an indicator of its period of most prosperous growth, in this case from 1889 through 1910. The latter year is when the community lost a bitter competition with Oklahoma city to retain its status of state capital. With the loss of its political status also went its economic prosperity to the new railroad hub located just to Guthrie's south.

*Below: Guthrie's wall of 19th-century commercial buildings provides the ultimate American main-street scene.*

### VICTORIAN ERA STYLES

With one of the country's most intact business districts from this period, Guthrie hosts what is considered to be the largest urban historic district in America, with more than 2,000 buildings within 400 city blocks. The gamut of Victorian-era styles is represented here. Typical of Victorian main street scenes of the time, various features such as oriel windows, turrets, towers and bay windows provide a sense of eclecticism characteristic of the late 19th century.

As American cultural tastes and fashions progressed into the early 20th century, so too did the architecture of main street. By 1905 the Victorian era had largely passed, with a new interest in simplicity and historic "revivalist" styles. One of the most popular revival, or period styles, at this time showed up in Guthrie's business district, that of Neo-classical. With its blocky design, columned porticos and temple-front entryways, this style represented essentially the latest revival of the early 19th century Greek Revival. Along with Neo-classical buildings in Guthrie came

*Above: Settlers claim lots in Guthrie just 20 minutes after the first train arrives in 1889.*

a mixture of simplified commercial-style structures, for lack of a better term. Often less ornate than their Victorian predecessors, Guthrie's 18 or so examples of the commercial style tend to exhibit symmetrical facades with rectangular windows spaced evenly across the front.

### FOUCART'S INFLUENCE

Integrated within the otherwise typically American styles of downtown Guthrie were some regionally unique aspects. Some of the most distinctive buildings were designed by Joseph Foucart, a Belgium-born architect. Foucart's designs made use of features including minarets, stone finials, towers, oriel windows and rounded arch windows. Foucart was considered to be Oklahoma's most prominent architect during its territorial era prior to 1906. Two of his most prominent commercial projects were the Gray Brothers Building and the DeFord Building, both completed in 1890. The former building exhibits a signature element of Foucart's architecture, namely the bevelled entrance. Its large oriel window on the corner is capped with an onion dome. Further providing for a unique sense of place in downtown Guthrie is the district's prolific use of locally derived red brick and sandstone for its commercial buildings.

# HIGHLAND PARK SHOPPING VILLAGE
## HIGHLAND PARK, TEXAS

The clustering of retail activities in America's downtown business districts continued until well after World War II. For most people, a city's main street commercial core was presumed as the place to shop and seek entertainment. Not until the 1970s did indoor shopping malls and suburban shopping centres replace the traditional functions of downtown. As main street commerce withered nationwide, 2,500 regional shopping malls, and 300 super-regional malls, were in operation across America by the early 1990s. Placed strategically at the interchanges of major suburban freeways, this system of shopping malls had by then accounted for more than 50 per cent of the nation's retail sales.

Long before anyone had devised such developments, however, smaller experiments during the 1920s served as early pioneering efforts to take commercial activities outside of downtown. One of these comprised the Highland Park Shopping Village, near Dallas, Texas.

### OUT OF TOWN SHOPPING

The original interest in placing retail activities away from downtown was based on a growing discontent with main street by World War I. Thanks to Henry Ford and the proliferation of affordable automobiles downtown business districts became congested, parking became scarce and travel was slow. Towns and cities simply had not been designed for the automobile.

The logical solution for some visionaries was to bring main street to the emerging suburban neighbourhoods. Taking advantage of spacious sites on the edge of town, speculators began to build new shopping blocks set back from the main thoroughfares into town, and added plentiful off-street parking in front. They eventually added local supermarkets, filling stations and smaller department stores. This idea was expanded upon during the 1930s, as expansive lots were purchased on the edge of town along emerging automobile corridors. These were the first-ever master-planned retail areas designed exclusively around the automobile.

### THE COMPLEX

Highland Park Shopping Village is considered America's second shopping mall, following on the heels of the Country Club Plaza in Kansas, which opened for business in 1922. Opened in 1931, Highland Park took the shopping-centre concept to a new level with its combination of grocery, pharmacy and other daily retailing, integrated with department stores, restaurants and a theatre. The unusual mixture of commercial activities provided for a useful proving ground for many of the first suburban department and chain stores in the Dallas area.

*Below: Highland Park Shopping Village was built with a unified architectural theme; it was the first purpose-built shopping village in America.*

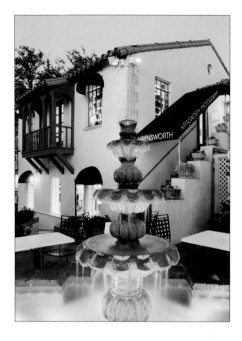

*Above: Highland Park Shopping Village was designed to attract wealthy customers to the area.*

The complex consists of seven detached commercial structures focused on a central pedestrian and automobile parking plaza. Its spatial layout is noted especially for its design of enclosed parking areas set within architecturally cohesive commercial blocks. Considered a hybrid of today's community and regional shopping centres as defined by the real estate industry, the Highland Park Shopping Village represents a pivotal point in the evolution of the American shopping centre as a distinctive building type.

What arguably became the last phase of transporting main street to the suburban roadside occurred in 1956 with the construction of Southdale in Minneapolis, designed by Victor Gruen and Associates. This was the first to have its central common area, or mall, entirely roofed over, essentially to bring the air-conditioned outdoors, indoors. Americans would thereafter rely on automobile-oriented shopping malls located at suburban freeway interchanges.

# CHAPTER EIGHT

# THE MOUNTAIN WEST

TODAY, GEOGRAPHERS REFER TO THIS REGION AS THE "EMPTY INTERIOR" DUE TO ITS RELATIVE ISOLATION AND LOW POPULATION DENSITY. FORTUNES WERE TO BE MADE HERE, HOWEVER, AS PROSPECTORS DISCOVERED UNTOLD QUANTITIES OF SILVER, GOLD, COPPER AND OTHER EXTRACTIVE RESOURCES. MANY TOWNS THAT WERE SETTLED THROUGHOUT THE MOUNTAIN WEST BOOMED, ONLY TO BE DEVASTATED WHEN THE NEARBY RESOURCE WAS EXHAUSTED. GHOST TOWNS — DERELICT REMAINS OF ONCE-THRIVING COMMUNITIES — ARE ABUNDANT HERE.

*Left: Bodie, a ghost town, which spanned the era of the Wild West, boomed during the Gold Rush.*

# TEMPLE SQUARE
## SALT LAKE CITY, UTAH

Salt Lake City serves as the cultural and symbolic hub for one of the world's newest major religions, namely the Church of Jesus Christ of Latter-day Saints (or Mormons). Originally established in 1830 by Joseph Smith in upstate New York, Mormonism grew rapidly due to the continuous conversion of people of all nationalities. Continued persecution from non-Mormon Americans encouraged the Church to move progressively westward. Under the leadership of Brigham Young, the pioneers settled permanently in the remote Salt Lake Valley in 1847 and immediately planted crops. The primary goal of Church leaders was to carve out a distinctly Mormon "place" within the inter-mountain West. Church members understood this initiative as a movement closer to the promised land of Zion. Ultimately, Mormon leaders sought to create a

political entity in a new state of America referred to as Deseret. Too many factors external to Mormon control conspired against this goal, however, and the state was never recognized by the US government. The last ambitious attempt to create such a state in 1882 was thwarted, and the Mormons were subsumed into the American political system in 1896 with Utah statehood.

The continuous incursion of non-Mormons into Utah – via the first transcontinental railroad and other means – diluted the initial Mormon cause, though its society produced a rather uniform cultural region.

### A DISTINCTIVE LANDSCAPE
Although still largely Anglo-American, the religion advocates the pursuit of communal practices in preference to the pursuit of individualistic goals. The desire to live and work as members of a

*Above: The Victorian-era temple provides the most striking landmark on the square, a central feature of the Mormon culture.*

determined group led to the emergence of a distinctive Mormon landscape wherever they settled away from Salt Lake City.

### MORMON TOWN PLANNING
On a large scale, Temple Square exhibits some typical characteristics of Mormon town layout strategy, based largely on the City of Zion town plan first advocated by Joseph Smith in 1833. Soon after arriving in 1847, the Mormons planned the future streets of Salt Lake City in what would become a typical Morman pattern of settlement. The streets were wider than normal, at 40m/ 132ft, enabling the U-turn of ox carts. A lot for the Mormon temple was allocated at the centre of the town,

indicating the centrality of religion within Mormon society. Outward from the temple lot, streets were named and numbered sequentially in a unique system that revealed how far and in what direction a particular street corner was located away from the temple – for instance, 300W or 400S. Each street included a 6m/20ft easement for a walkway, and city lots were 5ha/1¼ acres to encourage small-scale farms and gardens. Eight such lots were allocated to each large city block. One can see this plan of Zion playing out at Temple Square today, with the Temple taking centre stage, surrounded by large city blocks with wide streets, named in the Mormon fashion. As Mormon society expanded throughout the 19th century, they took their established town plan with them, and today the plan of Zion is evident on a smaller scale throughout Utah and surrounding states.

## TEMPLE

By far the most prominent edifice on Temple Square is what Brigham Young referred to as the "Temple of our God".

*Below: From its fledgling beginnings, the message of the Latter Day Saints' Church has diffused throughout the world.*

*Above: For the Temple, great granite blocks were assembled from stone that was hauled by oxen from 32km/20 miles away until a railroad later quickened the pace.*

It is not open to the public, because this is where the most secret of Mormon rituals are practised. Only Mormons in good standing – those with a temple "recommend" – are granted entry. The general plan for the Temple was determined by Brigham Young prior to the Mormon exodus from Missouri, while the design details were worked out by church architect Truman Angell. Although ground-breaking ceremonies took place as early as 1853, construction was fraught with delays and challenges. The walls progressed slowly. Finally on 6 April 1892 thousands gathered to witness the placing of the capstone.

## THE TABERNACLE

Other, less ritualistic structures on the square were built in less time, including the tabernacle, considered an engineering marvel in itself. Brigham Young had envisioned the structure as a meeting place for the general conference of the church. It was completed after only five years in 1867. The structure is capped with a unique Remington lattice-truss roof, supported by great wooden arches and resting on a total of 44 sandstone buttresses. The engineering of such a structure was ingenious, given that steel girders and tie rods were not yet available. The acoustics are likewise famous, and one can hear a pin drop from the pulpit area from 60m/200ft away. This is also the home of the world-famous Mormon Tabernacle Choir, the membership of which is highly competitive and considered a great honour. Since 1867 the choir has been supported by the sounds of an organ that first had 700 pipes. In 1915 the grand instrument was powered by electricity and now includes nearly 11,000 pipes.

*Below: The Tabernacle, an historic structure and a product of innovative engineering. It is the home of the world-famous Mormon Tabernacle Choir.*

# UNION PACIFIC RAILROAD DEPOT
## CHEYENNE, WYOMING

In envisioning the construction of a railroad to the Pacific Ocean, Asa Whitney, a New York merchant involved in trade with China, preached that such a project would revolutionize global commerce. With a combined rail and steamship route between New York and China, "the products of America's factories could be exchanged for Asia's rarities". The first transcontinental railroad would not be completed until 1869, but Whitney was already lobbying congress for the project as early as 1844.

Eventually Whitney began a spirited campaign and toured America to promote his grand scheme. In a rather typical presentation, Whitney demonstrated with some cartographic strategy that America could be envisioned at the centre of the world rather than on the periphery of European power. "Europe on the one side, with 250 million of population," he showed, "and all Asia on the other side of us, with 700 million of

souls. The Atlantic separating us from Europe, the calm Pacific between us and Asia, and you will see that the population and the commerce of all the world is on this belt of the globe – which makes a straight line across our continent." Following Whitney's vision, citizens and members of Congress alike dared to dream that such an overland connection would not only compress time and distance between the Atlantic and Pacific coasts, but would open vast opportunities for Asian trade and American fortune.

### CHOOSING THE ROUTE

As railroad fervour increased into the 1850s, the issue generated spirited competition among potential western termini for the new road. Given the monumental expenses and engineering savvy necessary to complete the route, it was assumed at the time that yet another generation would be required

*Above: The trappings of Eastern American culture spread deep into the interior West along the first transcontinental railroad.*

to complete a second railroad. Bitter arguments and rivalries emerged as well, including the widening divide between Northern and Southern interests. Thus, the first Pacific Railroad Bill to move through Congress in 1853 attempted to appease both factions by proposing two routes – one Northern and one Southern. This generated more contentious opposition, which finally led to the federal decision to authorize the surveying of five potential routes across the continent, each basically following a particular parallel of latitude.

A secondary benefit of the surveys, which commenced in 1854, was a new accumulation of a vast wealth of knowledge about America's newly acquired western territories. The route paralleling 41 degrees of latitude was chosen

*Above: Business interests made sure the transcontinental route was well publicized and promoted.*

for America's first transcontinental railroad, linking Council Bluffs, Iowa, with Sacramento, California.

### TRENDSETTER

Initially authorized by the Pacific Railway Act of 1862 during the Civil War, service along the route began seven years later, on 10 May 1869, following the driving of the famous "golden spike" at Promontory Summit, Utah. The project was monumental in scope and had never been attempted on such a scale anywhere in the world. Its construction, engineering and technology were second to none, rivalling previously amazing accomplishments including the Panama Canal and Erie Canal. Although monumental on a global scale, the earlier notion that this was a once-in-a-generation project was soon dispelled. Pierce Lewis notes that in "most continental-sized countries, one transcontinental railroad would have done quite nicely – as it did in Australia, and as it did across Siberia. Yet that was not the American way. In the period between 1869 and 1910, Americans completed no fewer than five transcontinental railroads".

### DEPOT ARCHITECTURE

Hundreds of towns were settled along the first transcontinental route and Cheyenne was one of them. From the beginning, the Union Pacific Railroad's board of directors intended to locate their principal depot and maintenance facilities here. The railroad invested heavily in infrastructure and various railroad-related structures, but left its original, wood-framed depot to wither. An embarrassment to the town, work on a new, grander train station began in 1886 and was completed the following year. Clearly indicating the arrival of Eastern cultural tastes in the Mountain West, the massive three-storey stone structure became an instant architectural masterpiece exhibiting high-style attributes of the Richardsonian-Romanesque style. Its architect was Henry Van Brunt, who practised in Boston and had earned a national reputation by the time he was hired by the Union Pacific for the Cheyenne project.

Not surprisingly, Van Brunt adopted the architectural style made popular by his Boston colleague, Henry Hobson Richardson, who in turn had devised a variation of Romanesque architecture that became quintessentially American. It was popular nationwide during the 1880s and 1890s for grand, public buildings. Van Brunt was commissioned to design additional depots for the Union Pacific, including those at Sioux City, Iowa, Omaha, Nebraska, and Ogden, Utah, though none of these were considered to be as intricate in their design as his first at Cheyenne. This was his most noteworthy achievement. The structure has been painstakingly restored and now serves as a museum that tells the story of Cheyenne's role along the first transcontinental route. Although no longer used as a railroad passenger facility, Union Pacific freight trains still rumble past the depot, which is the last of the grand 19th-century depots that exists today along the original transcontinental railroad.

*Below: The hard lives of Chinese work crews, with one of their railroad camps pictured here along the new route, led to more prosperous Chinese-American communities throughout the West.*

# BODIE

## HISTORIC DISTRICT, MONO COUNTY, CALIFORNIA

Few places provide a more striking image of the "Old West" as does the American ghost town. These towns are typically associated with the remains of mining camps and related boom towns that quickly went bust when valuable ores were depleted. For some these places represent the worst of unsustainable extractive industry for short-term economic gain, however, ghost towns have captured the imagination of a public fascinated with Western frontier life. The term "ghost town" has become so frequent that one researcher even discussed a "ghost town stage" to describe the life cycle of Western mining districts.

Imagined by many people as the run-down, false-fronted main street promoted by decades of Hollywood films and TV shows, ghost towns actually exist today in varying states of ruin or revival, exhibiting a wide array of possible landscape scenes. Virtually nothing remains in some ghost towns, including residents. At the other extreme are places with an active commercial district, and those completely reconstructed for purposes of tourism development. Other former ghost towns became centres of the hippie counterculture or an equivalent group that, through the generations, have revived the community only to shed its ghost-

*Above: Main Street, once 1.6km/1 mile long, was lined with one- and two-storey framed buildings, representing a diluted version of more sophisticated main-street business districts farther East.*

town image. It is Bodie, California, that has been promoted as America's most authentic ghost town, however, but the definition of "authentic" is elusive.

### BOOM AND BUST

With approximately 120 buildings still standing in various stages of decay, Bodie is considered one of the finest examples of a mining ghost town in the American West. The town site was and is remote, located near Mono Lake and the California–Nevada border at approximately 2,530m/8,300ft in elevation. Gold was first discovered in the region in 1852, followed by William S.

*Above: Bodie has been conserved in a state of arrested decay. The site appears as it was found.*

Bodey's discovery of placer gold at the future site of Bodie in 1859. Development of the Bodie Mining District was slow in coming, however, due to lack of water and extreme isolation that made transportation a challenge. With new quartz discoveries by 1877, however, a regional gold rush was spawned at Bodie a year later.

Within years, the struggling town with a few wooden shacks developed into a community with 250 wooden buildings and a peak population around 11,000 people by 1880. Like Tombstone,

*Below: The derelict town of Bodie attracted its first measurable numbers of automobile tourists during the 1920s.*

*Above: Bodie is considered to be an authentic ghost town, though only a portion of the original survives.*

Arizona, and countless other Anglo-American boom towns, Bodie hosted a growing assortment of entertainment facilities catering to the miners, including the standard mix of gambling dens, brothels, breweries and saloons, which in turn spawned the expected brawls, shoot-outs and stabbings. Bodie became known as the "shooters town", and the most unpleasant individuals were referred to as "bad men from Bodie".

The "bust" set in as quickly as the town had boomed. All the mines except for the Bodie and Standard ceased operations by the mid-1880s. With the gold strike having played out, the town's population plummeted and left much of the building stock abandoned. Intermittent mining activities continued through World War II, but Bodie had become a ghost town by the 1890s.

**TOURISM BOOM**

What remained of Bodie was acquired by the State of California beginning in 1962, a process that led to the creation of the Bodie State Historic Park, which manages the town's remnant landscape today. The style of management at Bodie came to represent an extreme interpretation of historic preservation. Through a philosophy that would become known later as "arrested decay", the park's policy dictated that the general appearance of the town should be retained as it was found. Endangered structures should be stabilized, but the exterior appearance of the town's built environment should retain the appearance and charm of an "authentic ghost town", preserving the curved walls, sagging windows, broken

*Below: The ruins of the town provide a vivid image of life as it once was.*

windows and the like. Thus, although the park's arrested decay has in itself interrupted the process of change, it is this policy and its non-commercialized appearance that creates the impression of authenticity for visitors.

What remains of Bodie today is the equivalent of middle-class suburbia. None of the simpler miners' shacks remain, nor does much of the business district that burnt suddenly during an 1892 firestorm. The preserved residential landscape of Bodie consequently provides an interpretation of an authentic experience that is contingent upon what people expect to see in their own imagined version of the Old West.

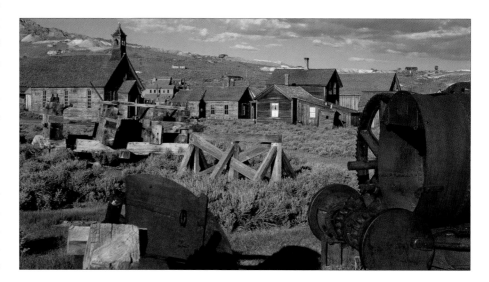

# OLD SACRAMENTO
## HISTORIC DISTRICT, SACRAMENTO, CALIFORNIA

The Swiss immigrant John Sutter settled in the Sacramento area in 1839 and quickly established a trading colony and stockade known as Sutter's Fort. On 24 January 1848 at Sutter's Mill, 50 miles north of the Fort, gold was discovered and the event known ever after as the California Gold Rush began. As word spread, the dream of striking it rich in the foothills of the Sierra Nevadas caused a mass migration that was unprecedented in the young nation's history. Almost 80,000 people, most of them young men, came to the region during 1849, followed by 300,000 by 1854. The migrants were referred to as the Argonauts. Between 1849–55, the Argonauts produced gold worth US $300m.

### FOUNDING SACRAMENTO

Given the vast numbers of migrants, in less than two years California went from a rural Mexican territory to a new state of the Union in 1850, having easily met the minimum population of 60,000 required for statehood. New town sites were spawned directly by newcomers, with Sacramento emerging as a regional trade centre. Against the wishes of his father, John Sutter Jr planned the new

*Below: Men who had earned less than US $2 a day as farmers or mechanics earned US $16 daily washing gravel in the streambeds of the Sierra foothills.*

city of Sacramento, naming it after the Sacramento River. William Warner, a topographical engineer, was hired to set out the city's street grid, located just east and south of the confluence of the American and Sacramento rivers. The new town became an instant success, serving as a convenient urban gateway into the northern gold fields.

As the gold rush progressed, Sacramento became a hub of agricultural and mining activity for northern California and the entire Pacific Coast. The early part of the city known today as Old Sacramento was where the first commercial enterprises began. The settlement was incorporated as a city in March 1851 and only three years later the community had 2,500 buildings. It would soon gain further status as the new capital of California. The town's advantageous location enabled it to become the terminus for every form of transportation and communication as they developed: stagecoaches, wagon trains, riverboats, the Pony Express, the telegraph and perhaps most impressively, America's first transcontinental railroad. Far-reaching stage and freight lines made their headquarters here, as did

*Above: The architecture of Main Street was developed primarily by easterners who brought their own cultural traditions.*

powerful riverboat companies of the day. This is also where the Central Pacific Railroad was incorporated on 28 June 1861 for the exclusive purpose of constructing the western portion of the transcontinental railroad.

Some noteworthy structures surviving in the Historic District today include the B. F. Hastings Building (1853), which served as the western terminus of the Pony Express, and the Big Four Building (1852), named in reference to the four most influential California railroad men who all lived here prior to moving off to San Francisco. The Adams Building (1853) is also here, which served as the second and last Pony Express Terminal, and the Darius Ogden Mills Bank (1852), associated with the financing of the Comstock Mine in Virginia City, Nevada.

Today the Old Town has developed into an entertainment and educational district, loaded with museums, theatres, restaurants, historic properties and other attractions.

# VIRGINIA CITY
## HISTORIC DISTRICT, VIRGINIA CITY, NEVADA

As an extension of the California Gold Rush ten years earlier, some California prospectors searched during the 1850s for placer gold on the eastern side of the Sierra Nevadas. Not until January1859 did their efforts pay off, about 609m/ 2,000ft below the summit of Mount Davidson in the Washoe Mountains of western Nevada. Of those who shared what was apparently a placer claim, Henry Comstock boasted the loudest about it, and it soon thereafter became known as the Comstock Lode. Samples of the ore revealed that the composition of the material was three-quarters silver, a metal unfamiliar to the miners at the time. News spread quickly and triggered America's first silver rush. In less than a year, the population of the Comstock's capital of Virginia City and nearby Gold Hill increased to 10,000.

### SILVER RUSH
As the larger of the two settlements, Virginia City developed into America's first silver mining town and the proto-type for large-scale, industrial mining initiatives. In contrast to the rather scattered mining camps of independent prospectors that characterized the earlier gold rush, the town became a full-scale industrial complex organized through corporate investment. By the 1870s Virginia City had grown into the mining capital for the Comstock Lode. Virginia City became a veritable laboratory for a technological, engineering, financing and industrial techniques to which the world paid close attention.

The Comstock presented unique geographical challenges that encouraged the development of innovative mining techniques. One invention was the V-flume, essentially a water slide for timber that allowed the wood to be quickly transported down the side of a mountain to awaiting trains. The nearest timber stands were located around Lake Tahoe, necessitating an arduous process of supplying enough support timbers for the mines. Ingenuity was also required to lower the water table that threatened to flood the mines. The answer was a tunnel 6.4km/4 miles long that linked the Comstock with the Carson River Valley, allowing water to drain.

Perhaps most notable was the world's first use of the square-set timbering method. The ore body was so soft that traditional timber supports would not prevent the mine shafts from collapsing. Further, the Virginia City mines had already reached a record depth of 640m/2,100ft below the surface by 1880. The modular approach involved the assembly of prefabricated timbers

*Above: Economically sustainable mining towns such as Virginia City took on the characteristics of the Eastern USA.*

into cubes. Virtually any underground chasm could be supported by stacking the cubes on top of one another and filling the system with waste rock. The ingenious approach was copied and used around the world for 50 years.

### CORPORATE OPERATIONS
The corporate organization of the Comstock mining efforts was likewise innovative. To exploit the vast quantity of ore required industrial-scale operations. The Comstock companies employed a large labour force of salaried professionals. Virginia City resembled a highly urbanized, industrial setting more typical of Eastern factory towns than Western mining camps. Only a handful of corporate owners controlled the generation of wealth through this process, although many shared in the prosperity. The boom town attracted miners from around the world.

*Left: Virginia City is home to 1,000 residents, and is a popular tourist attraction.*

# SILVERTON
## HISTORIC DISTRICT, SILVERTON, COLORADO

American prospectors discovered the potential wealth of precious minerals and metals buried within the San Juan Mountains and began to stake claims to the land by the early 1870s. Up until then the original treaty with the Ute Indians had created an extensive reservation for the people consisting of one-third of Colorado's total land area. The new mining rush forced greater changes, however, as more white people moved into the mountainous terrain. In a classic case of "manifest destiny" – the sense that it was America's God-given right to acquire Western lands – the demands mounted to alter the previous treaty with the Utes. Mining communities slowly grew throughout the region, nestled in some of America's most breathtaking yet foreboding mountainous environments.

Established in 1874, Silverton derived its name from its role as a trade centre for the rich silver mining district surrounding it. Other ores were later found that revealed gold, lead and copper. As a typical Western boom town, the community had grown to 3,000 people by the late 1870s. Its prosperity continued well into the early 20th century, much longer than other boom towns. Between 1882 and 1918, the district produced more than US $65 million worth of precious metals. Contributing to its uncharacteristic stability was the town's status as administrative centre for the county, and its eventual incorporation into the narrow-gauge railroad network.

### THE RAILROAD
In July 1882 the Denver & Rio Grande Western (D&RGW) Railroad arrived, extending its tracks up the Animas Canyon from Durango. Silverton became a fixture within an expanding network of 1m/3ft gauge steam railroads being built throughout the San Juans to expedite the extraction of precious ores. The Durango–Silverton connection allowed for the construction of additional railroad branch lines out of Silverton that accessed hard-to-reach mining camps. No less than four separate rail lines converged on Silverton by 1895, while Durango prospered to the southwest as a smelter town.

*Below: Situated in the bottom of an ancient volcanic caldera, Silverton endured many winters with no connection to the outside world.*

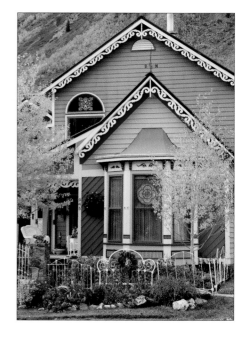

*Above: With its excellent collection of heritage homes, Silverton is capitalizing on its residential architecture to attract tourists.*

### LOCAL ARCHITECTURE
With a population of only a few hundred people today, Silverton is capitalizing on new opportunities. Reflecting contemporary America's budding service sector, Silverton locals and newcomers have been restoring its Victorian-era building stock (as part of its transition to theme town). The town-

*Below: "Notorious" Blair Street has been transformed into a tourist attraction for those looking for the expected heritage of gambling dens, saloons and bordellos – long since tamed.*

*Above: Silverton's Main Street exhibits typical Midwestern storefronts that could just as easily be found in Indiana.*

scape presents a complete example of Midwestern architectural and city planning habits transplanted into a formidable Western location – clearly reflecting the town's dominant cultural roots. Around the commercial district are residential blocks lined with a hodge-podge of late Victorian-era homes that reflect simplified versions of Eastern architectural styles, complete with grass lawns and picket fencing.

*Below: At the centre of town is the county courthouse, the grandeur of which is unexpected in such a remote location.*

**TOURISM TODAY**

Today the lifeline of Silverton's economy chugs into town each summer with hundreds of tourists travelling the narrow-gauge railroad out of Durango. In a more distinct pattern of the "Wild West" image, the revived Durango & Silverton steam trains slink up to the

*Below: A Durango-bound passenger train pulls out of Silverton, still heavily reliant on the railroad – but for tourists rather than ore extraction.*

end of the line right in the middle of town, distributing their eager cargo on to Silverton streets designed to imitate Wild West settings. Venturing beyond these visitor attractions one can easily wander through a more authentic Silverton, representing a community that has dealt with harsh economic realities and climate conditions since its founding, and now seeks to capitalize on the emerging economy of the so-called New West, oriented to consumption.

# DURANGO-SILVERTON
## NARROW GAUGE LINE, DURANGO, COLORADO

As Americans consolidated their political territory across the continent during the 19th century, the nation embarked on an extensive railroad building boom. Every emerging town or city in the West sought a railroad connection, the primary prerequisite for economic growth and development. In 1870 a promising railroad company was born, the Denver & Rio Grande (D&RG). The route was planned by General William Palmer, as its name implies, to connect Denver, Colorado, with El Paso, Texas, to form further links with Mexico's own railroads. Palmer thus envisioned a north-south spine, with "feeder roads" extending west of Denver to the promising mining camps

of the San Juan and Uncompahgre Mountains. Unlike most eastern railroads, however, the D&RG applied a narrow gauge, with 1m/3ft between the rails. The narrower width of the track facilitated construction through foreboding mountainous terrain and at the same time reduced roadbed costs. In later years, the narrow-gauge tracks proved so adaptable to the mountains that it became the standard for railroads throughout western Colorado.

By 1876, Palmer's engineers had built their line into the Rocky Mountains by way of Alamosa, Antonito and Durango. Given the promising mining claims farther north, D&RG crews blasted a line northward from Durango to the

*Above: More than 16,000km/10,000 miles of 1m/3ft narrow-gauge track once existed in America's mountainous environments.*

fledgling mining town of Silverton, 72km/45 miles distant. The precarious route relied heavily on the spectacular canyon of the Rio de las Animas Perditas, or the River of Lost Souls (commonly referred to as the Animas River). As with other western railroads, the primary purpose of this one was to expedite the transport of extracted resources from their remote locations to urban processing centres. With the Silverton connection completed in 1882, numerous other feeder railroads extended outward from Silverton to the even more

*Above: The tortuous rail route between Durango and Silverton is an appealing tourist excursion, however, it is not for the faint-hearted traveller.*

remote mining camps. Durango became a growing hub as a smelter town and was connected to the expanding Rio Grande Southern Railroad developed by the transportation mogul Otto Mears, in turn enabling the growth of other San Juan communities.

### DEMISE OF THE RAILROAD

At its peak of mileage, America's narrow-gauge network included more than 16,000km/10,000 miles of track. By World War II this number had dwindled to 2,250km/1,400 miles, with half of it still operating in Colorado. Much of the San Juan Mountain network was abandoned and dismantled by the 1960s, though the Durango-Silverton line continued to gain worldwide fame as a tourist attraction and remained open to operate excursion trains during the summer months. Otto Mear's "empire" of the Rio Grande Southern had long since been abandoned, as had much of the original D&RG route.

The remaining 72km/45 miles between Durango and Silverton consequently became isolated, no longer tied into a regional or national rail network. This remains true today, however, the number of tourists and daily trains have only increased in recent decades. Nostalgic sentiments for the narrow-gauge steam trains has been evident since crews began to tear up the track. Railroad writer Oliver Jensen explains: "In the great days of these wonderful, toy-like railroads there was nothing like their diminutive engines and rolling stock, complete with slender Pullman sleepers, dining cars and the gaudy if Lilliputian private or business cars of railroad offi-

*Below: Revived in the 1980s as the Durango & Silverton Narrow Gauge Railroad (D&SNG), the route's primary cargo consists of tourists.*

cials…They left behind an enduring legend and a well-organized company of mourners." The engine of industry had become an element of nostalgia.

### SILVERTON & DURANGO

Today the Silverton train provides that town with its primary connection to the outside world, a place that can still be snowed in during harsh winters. Much of Silverton's economic revival has depended upon this lasting remnant of the great Rio Grande railroad system, though a well-travelled freeway for bikers and automobile tourists provides easy access to Silverton during fair weather. The railroad has restored a large working fleet of original Rio Grande steam locomotives that serve as the main attraction, their laborious "chuffs" echoing against the mountains as they approach the end of the line.

The hub of railroad activity is found at Durango, which serves as the home base for maintenance facilities, a railroad depot, a museum and other related attractions. Adjacent to the depot is the famous General Palmer Hotel, its name reminding visitors of the industrial and corporate rationales that made this rail line possible, as well as lucrative. A new rationale now sustains this route.

# VIRGINIA CITY
## HISTORIC DISTRICT, VIRGINIA CITY, MONTANA

Beginning in the 1860s, the stream channel known as Alder Gulch became the site of a 22km/14-mile-long swath of gold-prospecting camps and hastily built communities. Virginia City outgrew the others to become the hub of activity and included at least 5,000 of the Gulch's 10,000 inhabitants at its peak. The town's development moved quickly through the more-or-less typical stages of the boom-bust cycle, from the sequential phases of initial settlement, mining camp, permanent town and ghost town. The remaining human landscape of Virginia City retains a sense of layering over time. A combination of early log cabins, vernacular wood-framed buildings and false-fronted commercial storefronts remain integrated within the town's more permanent, later landscape of high-style residences and Victorian-era commercial buildings.

Virginia City's wealth and importance had solidified by 1865, which earned it the status of Montana's territorial capital.

*Below: Today's Virginia City is peaceful and attractive, unlike in the days of its mining activities.*

### MINING FOR GOLD

The process and technologies of mining along the Gulch likewise moved through a sequence of phases. Miners first used simple hand tools such as sluice boxes to separate gold from gravel, a laborious process made more productive with the introduction of hydraulicking after 1867. This technique involved the pressure-washing of water jets that more quickly separated the dirt from the rock piles. With an increase in the power of technology, of course, came more rapid destruction of the environmental surroundings. A third phase of mining technology arrived in 1898 in the form of large dredges, which "chewed up the ground, destroy-

*Above: The main streets of Western towns were hastily built with wood-framed structures adorned with false-front facades.*

ing several communities in their path and leaving behind distinctive tailings and dredge ponds as far upstream as Virginia City".

### PRESERVATION EFFORTS

Ironically, deliberate historic preservation efforts have continued far longer than did the town's entire boom-bust cycle. The first preservation efforts were conducted during the late 1940s. Virginia City was later designated as a National Historic Landmark, followed by the formation of the Virginia City Preservation Alliance. Then in April 1997 the state of Montana authorized the purchase of Virginia City and remaining Nevada City properties then owned by Charlie and Sue Bovey. The state created the Montana Heritage Commission to manage these properties, with the mandate to protect the historic structures and artefacts, while working to make the sites economically self-sufficient.

Today 25 concessions at the site include hotels, restaurants and theatres. A newly laid narrow-gauge railroad, Virginia city's first, recently began operation with a vintage steam locomotive, oriented to entertainment and the appeal of the "mythic West".

# COLUMBIA RIVER HIGHWAY
## OREGON

By 1900 America had the most extensive and well-maintained railroad network in the world, however, it arguably had the worst roads. In Oregon road conditions exemplified the national situation. As a proponent of good roads, Sam Hill (a prominent Portland businessman who promoted the idea of the road, along with others) became an influential advocate for the cause. He and Samuel Lancaster, an engineer and landscape architect, travelled extensively to determine the most appropriate road-building techniques that might best apply to Oregon. They attended the first international roads conference in Europe and visited the Axenstrasse in Switzerland with its windowed tunnel and arched rock walls – features they would later employ on the Columbia River Highway.

The two men became influential forces able to convince the Oregon legislature to seriously take up the issue. Soon the legislature created the Oregon Highway Commission and Highway Department. By 1913 Sam Hill had further convinced the county commission to build a road through the Columbia River Gorge. The county would, he stated, "cash in on their crop of scenic beauty, year after year, without depleting it in any way".

### LANDSCAPE ENGINEERING
Constructed between 1913 and 1922, the road spanned 119km/74 miles from Troutdale (24km/15 miles east of Portland) to The Dalles (142km/88 miles east of Portland). It became America's first scenic highway and relied on the philosophy of "lying lightly on the land".

*Right: The winding Columbia River Highway was the first of its kind to be designed with strict standards and design protocols including curve diameters, grades and bridges.*

*Right: The Columbia River corridor was developed as a scenic attraction that would stimulate local business along the new highway. Today the natural landscape retains its appealing beauty.*

Most distinctive in Lancaster's design for the Columbia River Highway was his successful integration of advanced road engineering techniques with landscaped architectural elements that remained sensitive to the natural environment. This combination of civil engineering and landscape sensitivity became the cornerstone for the emerging concept of landscape engineering that would define America's modern highway design philosophy.

In his Columbia River project, Lancaster adapted the style of European carriage roads while simultaneously advancing their engineering standards. A strict design protocol, which included accepting no grade greater than five per cent, nor a curve with less than a 60m/200ft turning radius, was adhered to. He further developed reinforced-concrete bridges, masonry guard walls and retaining walls. Lancaster successfully wore the "hats" of engineer and landscape architect throughout the project, creating an engineering achievement that remained sympathetic to the idyllic natural setting of the Columbia River Gorge.

After serving its purpose well for decades, portions of the highway succumbed to America's most recent road-building project between the 1950s and 1970s, the interstate freeway system. Portions of the Columbia River Highway between Warrendale and Hood River were sacrificed during this time for the construction of Interstate 84 along the water. Much of the road still possesses its original integrity, including masonry walls, bridges, viaducts and pavement. Various sections are open to automobiles, bicycles and pedestrians.

# BUTTE-ANACONDA-WALKERVILLE
## HISTORIC DISTRICT, MONTANA

America's Industrial Revolution resulted in the development of a regional man-ufacturing "core" area, focused primarily on the Northeast and upper Midwest and stretching from New York to Chicago. Eastern industrial growth, however, was dependent upon the extraction of the earth's raw materials, much of which was, and is, scattered across the remote Mountain West. Hundreds of one-industry towns such as Butte, Montana, appeared suddenly in otherwise inaccessible areas, because this was where particular ore-based resources were located. What amounted to a Colonial type of economic system emerged in the western United States during the late 19th century, whereby extractive resources moved eastward to fuel America's Industrial Revolution. In the other direction moved manufac-tured goods and migrant populations.

The West contained 90 per cent of America's nonferrous (non-iron based) metal reserves, and by the eve of World War I the region produced the bulk of the nation's copper, along with most of its gold and silver. Before the West could be developed and accessed through railroad connections, America's

*Above: Head frames of underground mining activities are prominent in Butte. Under-ground mining ended by 1975, leaving more than 79km/49 miles of vertical shafts and 9,000km/5,600 miles of tunnels.*

largest source of copper had been the Keweenaw Peninsula in northern Michigan. As western settlement pro-gressed, huge deposits of the red metal were discovered in Montana by the 1870s. That state became the nation's leading producer after 1887 but was superceded by Arizona in 1910.

### THE THREE TOWNS
The Butte-Anaconda-Walkerville Historic District was formed to recog-nize Montana's critical contributions to

*Above: The entrance of the Berkeley Pit provides an industrial tourist attraction for visitors to the Butte area.*

American copper mining. Butte (pop-ulation 34,000) is the largest of the three communities. Walkerville (population 700) is adjacent to Butte but is a distinct community with its own government. Anaconda (population 9,000) is 42km/26 miles west of Butte, but con-nected by the Deer Lodge Valley and the Butte, Anaconda & Pacific (BA&P) Railroad.

The three communities co-operated with respect to mining operations and together enabled the entire scope of copper-mining activities. Today, Walkerville provides the essence of an early mining camp that developed largely between 1890 and 1910, with some of the area's earliest mines. In con-trast, the city of Butte developed as the regional urban centre where infrastruc-ture including mine yards and head frames are still integrated into its residential and business areas. Nearby Anaconda was the bona-fide company town with its highly planned and corporate-controlled development. This was the so-called smelter town that processed the raw copper from Butte's mines.

*Left: The Berkeley Pit is where open-pit mining began in 1955. Mining continued until 2000 at the Continental Pit.*

## COPPER PRODUCTION

The 1880s was the decade that witnessed the meteoric rise of the Butte-Anaconda complex. While the Montana region produced only two per cent of America's copper in 1880, that number shot up to 41 per cent by 1885. This growth coincided with the growing world market for copper. In 1880 the United States produced only 17 per cent of the world's copper supply, however, America's share had increased to 56 per cent by 1900 and continued to rise thereafter until the end of World War I. During these years, Montana and its mines around Butte could rightly be considered the world's primary hub for copper production. The metal had become ever-more critical for the growth of industry throughout America and worldwide. Valued for its indestructibility, copper had become a key ingredient for the popular alloys of brass and bronze. By the late 19th century, however, demand spiked upward again, this time for the copper wire necessary to conduct electricity – a new craze.

*Below: Head frames and housing are juxtaposed in Butte, while Anaconda was a more formal, company-town layout. The specialized communities relied upon a symbiotic relationship.*

*Above: The abandoned Comet mine and the surrounding derelict landscape give the appearance of a ghost town.*

### THE RAILROAD

With the aim of cutting costs and increasing its self-sufficiency, Anaconda built its own railroad in 1892 to provide a direct link between the Butte mines and the Anaconda smelting works. An army of unemployed miners was used to construct the railroad, named the Butte, Anaconda & Pacific. This once-vital railroad line is included within the

Historic District. Overall, the integrity of the human landscapes within the landmark area is high, representing the area's copper heyday in the early 20th century: "Looming gallows frames and the towering Anaconda Company smokestack, railroad tracks, hoist houses and slag piles dot the landscape as reminders of the sister cities' mining roots."

*Below: Victorian styles from the Eastern United States influenced the simpler folk housing of these Western mining towns.*

# OLD FAITHFUL INN
## YELLOWSTONE NATIONAL PARK, WYOMING

Constructed in 1903 by the Northern Pacific Railroad, Old Faithful Inn is considered to be the queen of Rustic-style hotels in America's national parks. As one of the first and grandest, the Inn conformed to three key principles of rusticity adopted by the parks – namely, the use of natural materials, allusion to pioneer building techniques and a sympathetic relationship with its natural setting. The six-storey resort hotel represents a combination of Swiss chalet and Norway villa architectural traditions. It is dominated by its colossal main gable and two storeys of projecting dormers. Today the Inn is one of America's few remaining log hotels, and is still celebrated as a masterpiece of the generic Rustic style adopted by the national parks during the first four decades of the 20th century. The earlier work of William West Durant on his Adirondack buildings of the 1870s no doubt influenced the concept for the Inn's design, complete with log walls and gnarled log brackets and balustrades. The building incorporates some subtle Colonial Revival-style features including its second-storey overhang, or cantilever, and diamond-paned windows.

### RUSTIC STYLE

The construction and design of the Old Faithful Inn can be understood within the context of economic and cultural imperatives of the time. Culturally, America's so-called Romantic Movement emerged by the mid-19th century in response to the rapid changes spawned by the Industrial Revolution. The movement's spokespersons, notably Andrew Jackson Downing, Alexander Jackson Davis and later Frederick Law Olmsted advocated a greater sensitivity to the countryside and natural settings. Romantic notions of the western frontier accompanied this movement. An outgrowth of this interest was the development of the Rustic style, a little-noticed aspect of American architectural history. Considered by historians as vague and inadequate, the term "rustic" is nonetheless used to describe this derivative, craftsman-mode of architecture adopted by the National Park Services.

Neither the national parks nor the railroad companies paid much initial attention to the integration of architecture with the surrounding environment. Government buildings typically took the form of crude shacks, tent frames or log cabins that focused on a particular purpose. As the transcontinental railroads brought the parks within easier reach, their respective companies first relied on familiar styles of American architecture. One example was the Lake Hotel, built by the Northern Pacific Railroad in Yellowstone Park in 1890. Its formal, Classical Revival styling came complete with the expected temple-front porticos and Ionic columns, and completely ignored the natural setting. Eventually, the railroads took more notice of America's romantic inclinations: "Doing so, they discovered, was only good business. Distinctive hotels in romantic settings drew more patrons." The Old Faithful Inn provided one of America's earliest demonstrations of this shift in railroad architecture.

### RAILROAD INVESTMENT

Envisioning greater corporate profits, the railroad companies provided the capital and technical expertise necessary to develop the national parks for tourism. Yellowstone was no exception. For its part, the Northern Pacific Railroad was not blind to the virtual monopoly it held on travel to and from the park. By 1883 the company had laid rails to within a few miles of Yellowstone's northwest boundary, and within a year the railroad opened the park's first resort-style hotel at Mammoth Hot Springs. As historian Richard Sellars points out, the Yellowstone experience provides a most striking example of resort-style development within America's national parks. The Yellowstone Park Act declared that the delineated area would become a "public park or pleasuring-ground for the benefit and enjoyment of the people". Further, the Secretary of the

*Left: Old Faithful Inn was a prototype for the National Park Service's Rustic style of architecture.*

*Above: Old Faithful Geyser is the main attraction near the Inn. Recent earthquakes have altered its eruption schedule.*

Interior was authorized to lease park lands for "building purposes" and for "accommodation of visitors". The government consequently formed a logical coalition with the Western railroad companies, creating a symbiotic relationship viewed positively by both parties.

## DEVELOPING YELLOWSTONE

In Yellowstone the US army constructed 644km/400 miles of Park roads by the early 1900s. Visitors could now easily access the most popular natural features. Much of the same system, notably the famous Grand Loop Road, is still in use today. The park's initial road-building period allowed for the construction of the Northern Pacific Railroad's Old Faithful Inn, located precisely at the legislated minimum of 201m/220yd from the famous geyser for which it is named. With the Inn and other Yellowstone hotels, tourists could travel safely through the Park's wilderness while enjoying the

comfort of resort hotels with Eastern-style amenities. One visitor approved of this balance between wilderness and comfort in 1905: "And then we came to the Inn, the most unique and perfect place; it is the craftsman's dream realized." It was within this context – the intersection of American romanticism with the Industrial Revolution embodied by the railroads – in which the

magnificent Old Faithful Inn was constructed. It served as a prominent model for Rustic style National Park facilities built throughout the nation over the next four decades.

*Below: The rustic interior of the Old Faithful Inn is styled to match its exterior facade and remains true to the era in which it was created.*

# J. C. PENNEY
## HISTORIC DISTRICT, KEMMERER, WYOMING

For more than a century, J. C. Penney has been a household name. At the time of its centennial celebration in 2002, J. C. Penney was one of America's largest corporations with annual sales of US $32 billion. More than 1,000 retail stores were scattered throughout all 50 states, with additional outlets in Puerto Rico, Mexico and Brazil.

### BEGINNINGS
J. C. Penney began modestly. Penney was employed by Tom Callahan at the Golden Rule dry-goods and clothing store in Longmont, Colorado, and quickly gained his attention. Callahan eventually sent Penney to another store operated by his partner, Guy Johnson, in Evanston and half promised, "You make good with Johnson and maybe some day you will have a store of your own, and we will be your partners." In 1899, Penney began work with Johnson. When Johnson offered Penney a partnership in a new store that was planned for Ogden, Utah, however,

*Below: The famous retailer's geography has changed, shifting from prime locations along downtown main streets to suburban shopping malls.*

Penney balked, fearing the place was too big. Bypassing Ogden, a deal was worked out, and Penney gained a one-third partnership in a new Golden Rule store at Kemmerer. On 14 April 1902, Penney opened for business. This is the store that officially began the J. C. Penney era and is now celebrated as a National Historic Landmark.

After Penney's first profitable year at Kemmerer, Callahan believed that Penney had accomplished the impossible. He mentioned his plans to open 50 new stores and offered management of the chain to Penney. The offer was turned down, with Penney claiming he was not ready for such responsibility. With further success, his attitudes changed. He helped to open two new stores and in 1907 purchased all three stores outright from Callahan and Johnson.

*Left: The nationwide chain of department stores that was started by James Cash Penney (1875–1971) has played a vital role in the development of retail philosophies and practices in America.*

### PARTNERSHIPS
Earl C. Sams was hired to operate the Kemmerer store, and soon he was partnering with Penney to open another store in Eureka, Utah. Based in Salt Lake City after 1909, Penney opened an impressive 28 new stores over a three-year span, throughout five states. In 1913 the partners officially changed the name of their firm to J. C. Penney and Co.

By the end of World War I, Penney stores were in 197 communities. The organization's unprecedented expansion was due in part to Penney's brilliant execution of the partnership strategy. As the firm's base expanded outward from Kemmerer, Penney refined the partnership idea as a simple and powerful formula: both the new manager and the training manager of a new store owned a piece of the company: Ownership of a new store was typically split into thirds – one-third each for Penney, the old manager and the new manager.

By age 35, Penney had become a wealthy man. He remained as chairman of the board until 1946, and continued to participate in the firm as honourary chairman until his death in 1971. Today the J. C. Penney Historic District consists of Penney's original Golden Rule store – a two-storey stone structure with a cast iron facade – and the small, wood-frame cottage in which Penney and his family lived from 1902–09. Also included within the District are two commercial buildings situated on both sides of the Golden Rule store. Penney owned the family cottage until his death, and the store where he got his start was still operating as a small-scale J. C. Penney outlet.

# MOUNT RAINIER NATIONAL PARK
## ASHFORD, WASHINGTON

Mount Rainier towers to 4,389m/ 14,400ft above sea level. The entire mountain is enclosed within Mount Rainier National Park, showcasing an incredible mountainous ecosystem with its river valleys, waterfalls, subalpine meadows, old-growth forests and the largest alpine glacier by volume in the region. Mountain climbers from around the world are attracted to the challenge of reaching the top.

Aside from its environmental appeal, however, the National Park is a National Historic Landmark due to its human landscape, and the role that the federal government played in organizing the visitor amenities. Rather than encourage the organic development of visitor services through small-scale businesses independent of one another's activities, the National Park Service sought a planned, visitor-oriented environment within its park system by the 1920s. Prior to Mount Rainier, various centralized development plans had been partially implemented elsewhere, with the Grand Canyon as a prime example. It was in Rainier where the National Park Service developed its first complete example of a master plan, and today the area retains much of the built environment that resulted from it.

*Below: One gains access to the attractive natural environment through a federally approved human network of lodging and trails.*

*Above: The star attraction in the National Park is Mount Rainier, one of numerous volcanoes that comprise the Cascade Range.*

### MASTER PLANNING
In collaboration with his assistant Ernest Davidson and park superintendent Owen Tomlinson, landscape architect Thomas Vint devised the first comprehensive plan for development at Mount Rainier. Vint and his colleagues created master plans for nearly every national park and monument throughout the late 1920s and early 1930s. More than seven decades later, Mount Rainier's landscape is considered the park service's most intact and well-preserved example of master planning within a national park.

### PARADISE INN
The showpiece of the park's human landscape is undoubtedly the Paradise Inn, the park's main lodge and hotel built in 1916. The structure itself provides a remarkably intact example of the national park's so-called Rustic style of architecture that characterized park facilities across the country prior to the 1950s.

Employing the Rustic style for the Paradise Inn required the structure to fit into the context of its surrounding natural environment – the ultimate intent for early park service architecture. Its steeply pitched main wing was covered with wood shingles painted green, its shape imitating the distant Tatoosh Mountains. The building's facade also employed wood shingles that have weathered into a grey colour like the silvery sheen of surrounding Alaska cedar trees.

*Below: Named for the local part of the mountain on which it is built, the inn and its accompanying Paradise Guide House serve as the starting place for climbers preparing to make their ascent.*

# CHAPTER NINE

# DESERT SOUTHWEST

STRONG LEGACIES OF NATIVE AMERICAN PUEBLO
AND HISPANIC CULTURES SURVIVE THROUGHOUT
THE SOUTHWEST. ALL ARE BLENDED WITH THE
MORE RECENT INFLUENCES OF ANGLO-AMERICAN
LIFESTYLES AND DEVELOPMENTS. IN NEW MEXICO
ONE FINDS THRIVING COMMUNITIES WHOSE
CULTURE COULD BE DESCRIBED AS DISTINCTLY
NEW MEXICAN, WHILE NEIGHBOURING UTAH IS
THE HUB OF THE MORMON CULTURE REGION.
THE REGION IS ALSO HOME TO LOS ALAMOS, ONE
OF AMERICA'S MOST TECHNOLOGICALLY
ADVANCED LABORATORIES THAT TAKES ADVANTAGE
OF ITS ISOLATED SOUTHWESTERN LOCATION.

*Left: The Grand Canyon formed over millions
of years, and is now protected by the government.*

# TAOS PUEBLO
## TAOS, NEW MEXICO

When the Spanish arrived in the American Southwest after the 1540s, those who colonized the Upper Rio Grande Valley found a healthy series of indigenous villages. Their flat-roofed stone or adobe apartment-style buildings reminded the Spanish of home, and so they referred to these villages as "pueblos". During this initial period of European contact, the so-called Pueblo Native Americans of today's American Southwest numbered approximately 30,000, with typically 200–300 people in each pueblo. Their pueblos were clustered in various locales, ranging from the middle Rio Grande River Valley north to Taos and westward to the Acoma, Zuni and Hopi pueblos. Although the Spanish noticed similar cultural characteristics from one pueblo to another, these peoples did not represent a single tribe. They did share common skills,

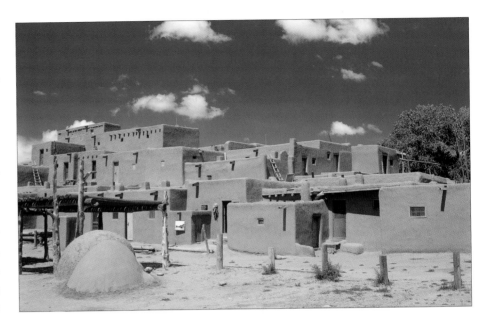

beliefs and construction techniques, though their languages could vary widely from one pueblo to the next. Even today, three distinct languages are spoken among the 19 remaining pueblos.

*Above: The most intact apartment-style pueblo buildings are found at Taos.*

### PUEBLAN PERSISTENCE
Located in the Taos Valley north of Santa Fe, the remarkably intact adobe Pueblo buildings and structures exemplify the persistence of all the Pueblan peoples through centuries of social and environmental change. Within the district are the Taos Pueblo village and the pueblo wall, the ceremonial kivas, cornfield taos, the trash middens, the race track, the mission church of San Geronimo de Taos and the church constructed around 1850. These sites comprise the extent of the pueblo settlement as it existed in the early 1900s, until other developments expanded outward. This pueblo location is the final site of an indigenous population that has occupied the Taos Valley since 900AD.

### BUILDING TRADITIONS
Most distinctive in the Pueblan landscape is the characteristic apartment-style, multi-storey buildings. These often

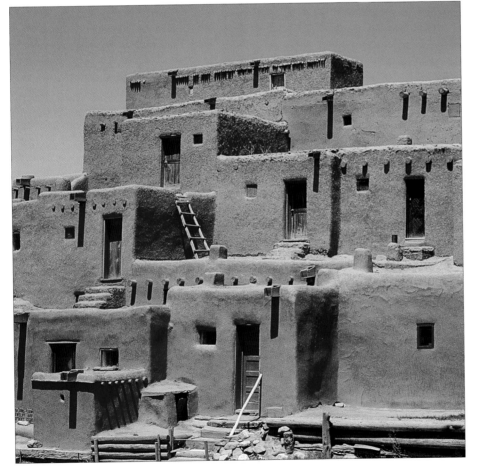

*Left: Indigenous Pueblo architecture is now a rare sight, as the Pueblo communities suffered greatly under Spanish rule.*

rose to four or five levels at the time of contact with the Spanish in the 1540s, with each upper storey set back from the edge of the lower one. Their overall appearance was that of a giant staircase, with successive set-backs. Typically, the lowest floor was reserved for storage, and was accessed from above by pole ladders placed through the roof. On the second floor were round baking ovens. Ladders reaching the ground were carefully guarded and pulled up after all family members were safely inside. In Taos specifically, until the mid-1800s, people entered the houses by climbing a ladder to a door in the roof. Additional ladders outside the buildings led from one floor to another. Not unlike Medieval villages in Europe that were clustered to defend the inhabitants from invaders, Taos and other Pueblos designed their buildings and village functions in part for protection from raiders and other human threats.

## THE REGION TODAY

Since the late 19th century the largest human threat to the pueblos is the tourist. Still, tourism remains the most promising economic activity for most. In Taos, as elsewhere, threats to the remaining pueblo peoples come in the form of external pressures from the regional and global economies, rather than from invaders. With the physical threats long removed, the architecture of defence has been loosening. Roof ladders for entering buildings no longer exist, and more windows – albeit small – have appeared in the otherwise solid adobe or stone walls. External ladders are still common, for moving from one floor to the next, though the traditional second-floor cooking activities have since descended to the open air below. One major implication of the spreading out of village functions has been the overall deterioration of the apartment-style housing structures throughout the remaining 19 pueblos. Only a few, partially intact multi-storey buildings remain among the pueblos, and many

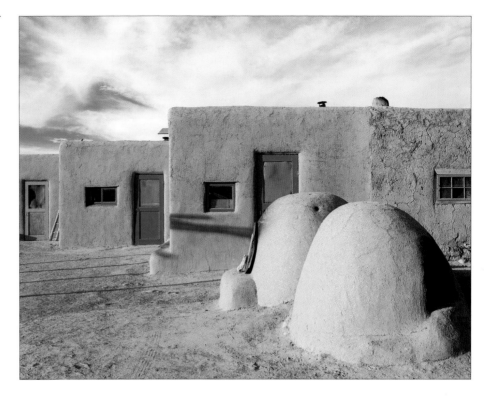

are in ruins. For this reason the Taos Pueblo is noteworthy for what is considered the most intact, best-preserved example of traditional Pueblan architecture in the USA.

At Taos Pueblo the buildings are clustered into two groups, ascending to four or five storeys, providing a good sense of the distinctive stair-step construction approach. The river flows through the village and between the two building clusters. Due in part to the introduction of automobiles and Anglo-American housing choices, Taos Pueblo has seen

*Below: In the first half of the 20th century, small windows and few doors characterized the architecture of the community. Here a crowd has gathered to witness a race.*

*Above: Pueblo-style housing with Anglo-American doors and windows.*

its share of dispersal outward from the original Pueblo settlement – a 20th-century, land-use pattern that has had an impact on all Southwestern pueblos to some extent. The pueblos are still there, but they have spread out, and consequently have lost many of their centralized attributes. In their collective struggle to reconcile their own cultural traditions with those of the dominant American society, many pueblos like Taos have turned to tourism to generate much-needed income.

*Below: An aerial view shows the extent of the community in the 1950s.*

# SAN XAVIER DEL BAC MISSION
## TUCSON, ARIZONA

Within sight of today's booming Tucson metropolitan area, Mission San Xavier del Bac has served the Pima Native Americans since its founding in 1700. Although considered part of the contemporary American Southwest, this upper portion of Sonora once represented the extreme northern territory of New Spain. This region was referred to by Spain as Pimeria Alta after its northern Pima occupants, who refer to themselves to this day as the O'odham.

Not until the arrival of the Jesuit missionary Eusebio Francisco Kino in the 1680s did Europeans settle here. A tireless evangelist for the Roman Catholic cause, Father Kino laid the foundations for seven missions among the Pima villages, including that of San Xavier del Bac in the Santa Cruz River Valley south of Tucson. Aside from evangelizing to the Native Americans of the Sonora region, Kino introduced European agricultural practices and foods to the area, most notably the first wheat and cattle, horses and additional livestock. The death of Father Kino in 1711 plunged the missions of Pimeria Alta into further isolation from their cultural core at Mexico City. Only one Jesuit remained in the entire Santa Cruz Valley for 20 years, and other Jesuits who came did not remain for long.

### BAROQUE CONSTRUCTION

The isolation of the Spanish missionaries made the construction of the current church of San Xavier del Bac all the more remarkable. Here on the veritable "high-water mark" of European christendom, this is the third, perhaps the fourth, church on the site, begun around 1778. Ignacio Gaona served as the master mason credited with designing the church, supervising its construction until its completion in 1801. Later he moved south to supervise building of Nuestra Senora de la Concepcion. As completed, the church of San Xavier del Bac represents a synthesis of Spanish Baroque design and the use of locally produced desert materials for its construction.

Built in the form of a Latin cross, the transept crossing is topped by a large, circular dome. Two bell towers flank the central facade. Clearly visible from miles away, the church's exterior is covered with lime plaster, which is interrupted on the central facade by the light brown, elaborately carved plaster portal. Its intricately detailed Baroque interior combines with its elaborate twin-tower design to make San Xavier del Bac the most spectacular mission church in the United States that remains of the

*Below: The Spanish Baroque-style church is considered the most elaborate of its kind surviving in today's United States.*

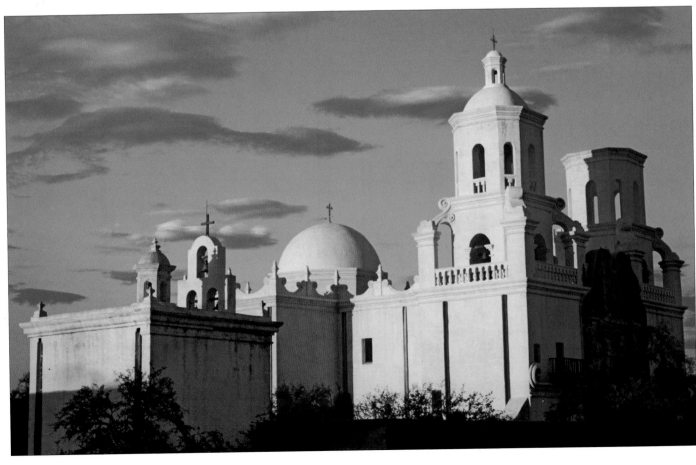

Colonial mission system of new Spain. Of the two towers or belfries, one of them remains incomplete, for reasons that remain uncertain.

## BAROQUE DECORATION

The church's state of preservation is remarkable, given centuries of harsh climate conditions and an earthquake in 1887. Nearly every statue and mural painting from the time of the church's dedication is still in place. Beginning in 1992, an international team of renovation experts have worked to stabilize and clean the murals and statues. What makes this a primarily Mexican Baroque church is its style of applied decoration. One aspect of the European Baroque influence here is found in the church's form. More than its form, however, is the intricacy of detail and the dramatic contrast of its ornamentation. The most important aesthetic principle of the style is based on the richness of the decoration, such as the materials, colours and textures. The level of colourful detail on the interior is perhaps the most Mexican Baroque aspect of the church. Much of the detailed ornamentation implies motion. Angels, for instance, are flying

*Below and far right: The interior was designed to exude intense colour and motion with its intricate murals.*

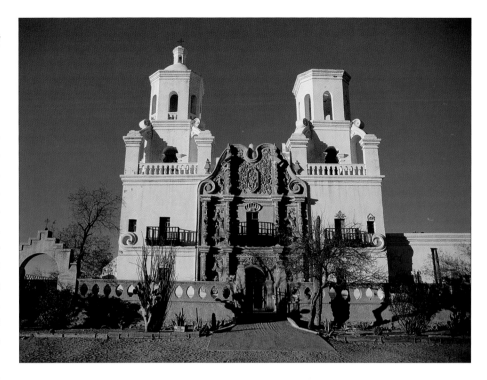

*Above: The exterior is covered with whitish lime plaster; the dark central portal was once painted in brilliant colours.*

above the main altar and on the three retablos (altarpieces) that reach to the roof. As for the brilliance of colour, gold and silver leaf was used to cover the retablo over the main altar, and brilliant colours adorn all of the retablos.

Like its European Baroque predecessors, the interior is dominated by incredibly intricate murals. Mural topics focus on the life of Christ and the

Virgin, found in the side chapels and the nave. Adding to the interior's complexity is the plaster painted to resemble ceramic tiles, while other parts replicate the look of veined marble. As James Griffith writes, the interior in its entirety "exudes richness, drama, motion and a certain ambiguity or sense of illusion". It is not surprising that visitors to San Xavier feel as if they have been transported to 18th century Spain, given the strong impression of material culture that showed up here in the northern deserts of Pimeria Alta.

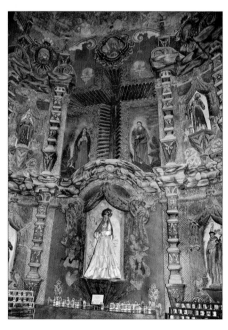

# PRESIDIO NUESTRA SENORA
## DE LORETO DE LA BAHIA, GOLIAD, TEXAS

In 1600, Texas was the last Spanish territory to be settled on the northern fringe of its North American empire. It was settled primarily as a buffer zone to protect Spain's assets in Mexico.

Spain's settlement structure was focused on three types of establishments. Presidios, or garrisoned forts, which were often built adjacent to fledgling missions to protect them, but also to defend against foreign invaders. Missions were religious outposts established by Spanish Catholics from which to convert the indigenous populations. Pueblos were Spanish towns typically settled in urban patterns dictated by the Laws of the Indies. A total of 37 missions, 11 presidios, and at least six pueblos were established by the Spanish in Texas.

### STRATEGIC POSITION

Known commonly as La Bahia, the Presidio Nuestra Senora de Loreto de la Bahia is located near Goliad, Texas. It is considered the finest example of a Spanish presidio anywhere in the United States. Its site was strategic, positioned to defend the string of missions

1 LOUISIANA
2 MISSISSIPPI
3 ALABAMA
4 GEORGIA
5 SOUTH CAROLINA
6 FLORIDA

*Above: The region referred to as the Spanish borderlands, stretched from California through modern-day New Mexico and Texas to Florida.*

established in southern Texas, along with the principal transportation route between Mexico and eastern Texas. This is not its original location, however. The original structure was built in 1721 atop the ruins of Fort Saint Louis, a failed French outpost. In 1726 the Presidio was moved to a site along the

*Below: The Spanish Colonial presence was starkly emphasized with distinctive mission and presidio architecture.*

Guadalupe River. Finally in 1747 both the mission and presidio were moved permanently to their current location on the San Antonio River.

The initial construction of the Presidio on this site consisted of several wooden buildings and 40 grass huts enclosed by a palisade built of wooden poles. Between the 1760s and 1790s the wooden structures were gradually replaced with more permanent stone construction. The rock walls of the Presidio were likewise gradually extended until reaching its present size. The Presidio is built in the form of a quadrangle, with a circumference measuring 230m/251yd. As the Presidio was being converted to stone, the Spanish settlement of Goliad was spawned nearby.

### CONFLICT

Following the secularization of the missions, La Bahia became the scene of conflict and war during the years of the Mexican Revolution, and again during the Texas Rebellion. Insurgents fighting for independence from Spain captured the Presidio twice in 1813 and again in 1821. Both times, they were defeated by the Spanish military. In 1835 the Presidio again became the focus of conflict, this time during the Texas cause for independence from Mexico. In this case Texan insurgents successfully occupied La Bahia and renamed it Fort Defiance. Although in a position to assist with the Mexican siege at the Alamo upstream, the La Bahia commander failed to provide reinforcements. Following the Alamo's fall, La Bahia was abandoned as well. This led to the disastrous massacre of more than 400 Americans imprisoned within La Bahia on Palm Sunday, 1836. Like the Alamo, Goliad became a rallying point for disorganized and demoralized Texans and won sympathy throughout the USA and Europe.

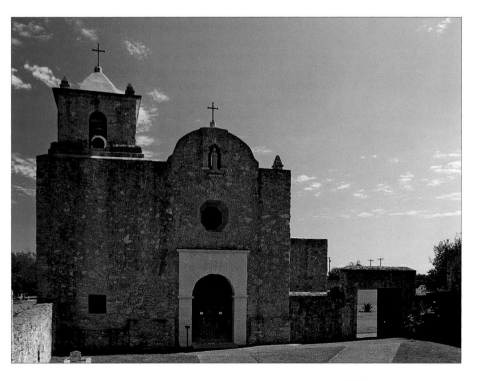

# ROMA
## HISTORIC DISTRICT, ROMA, TEXAS

The international border that separates Mexico from the USA can be described as a cultural transition zone. American cultural and economic influence is felt far south of the border, while Mexican attributes permeate north of the border. A distinct urban geography has developed along this cultural transition zone, largely since the 1960s, when maquiladora plants, or foreign-owned factories, began locating right across the border in Mexico. Mostly owned by American companies to produce American goods with Mexican labour, the maquiladora phenomenon has caused many of Mexico's border cities to grow immensely. Along the border, geographers describe the emergence of "twin cities", whereby Mexican cities grow in tandem with their American counterparts.

The American town of Roma sits as a border town along the Rio Grande River (the Rio Bravo in Mexico), directly opposite its Mexican twin, Ciudad Miguel Aleman. Connecting the two communities is the Roma-Ciudad Miguel Aleman International Bridge, one of the few suspension

*Above: Roma's architecture is mirrored by that of Mexico's Ciudad Miguel Aleman.*

bridges in Texas. A modern automobile bridge now carries international traffic through the port of entry, though the suspension bridge has been preserved for pedestrian use.

### A MEXICAN EXTENSION

Once a Mexican town Roma changed hands following the Mexican-American War in 1848. The community retains its strong Hispanic characteristics to this day. The relative remoteness of Roma from dominant American influences helped to maintain the town's distinctly Mexican architectural and urban fabric. One account attests that the only visible American influence in Roma was the opening of its first post office, signalling at least a marginal federal presence deep in southern Texas. Within the historic district surrounding the plaza, the sense of place here is decidedly 19th-century Mexico, though the architecture represents a blending of Mexican and American cultural vernacular building traditions. The town benefited from cross-border trade during the 1840s to the 1920s, but also from Roma's status as the westernmost riverboat port along the Rio Grande River between 1850 and 1900. Roma's

*Left: Soft sandstone bricks characterize the buildings in historic Roma.*

*Above: The style of building in Roma was created by immigrant Heinrich Portscheller.*

historic plaza and downtown area are set apart from other border-city landscapes that have been more acutely transformed during the 20th century.

Still found throughout Roma today are traditional, high-walled, gated family compounds, and streetscapes lined predominantly with sandstone and local brick buildings. Also still evident are the architectural and technological patterns derived from northern Mexico, focused most prominently on the Spanish-type plaza fronting the river. Roma is home to the most significant collection of vernacular structures that reflect lower Rio Grande construction techniques and styling, ranging from early sandstone cottages to more glamorous townhouses built by wealthy merchants. This is the most intact, dense collection of community architecture associated with the cultural norms of this region.

More specifically, Roma remains today as the only intact settlement within the USA that derived directly from the Spanish Colonial town planning efforts of Jose de Escandon (1700–70). The Escandon town planning, colonization and land grant systems were highly influential in the development of Spanish colonial settlements. Escandon was a prominent colonizer of southern Texas, where he founded more than 20 towns or villas and several missions.

# SANTA FE PLAZA
## SANTA FE, NEW MEXICO

Following several early Spanish expeditions into what is today the American Southwest, King Philip II authorized the settling of New Mexico in 1583. Spain's interests were strongly motivated by its desire to protect its silver mines in the extreme north of the region from British and French intrusion.

The first settlement in the area was considered a failure by 1607, and the king reconsidered his strategy. Having learned that Franciscan friars in the region had converted 8,000 Pueblo Native Americans to Christianity, however, he was convinced to persevere. On 1 November 1609, the king made New Mexico into a royal colony under the direct control of the Spanish crown. The government would subsidize the colony, its primary function being to enhance regional missionary efforts.

The current city of Santa Fe, meaning "holy faith", was founded in 1610 as the site of new Spain's capital city in the region. Its location was strategic: a central location in the heart of Pueblo villages, but still distant from them to avoid land disputes. The Santa Fe River, its narrow channel still meandering through town today, would provide enough water from the nearby Sangre

de Cristo Mountains. Thus began the great missionary period in New Mexico history from 1610 to 1680. During these years the primary motive was to assimilate regional Pueblo peoples into the Spanish image.

### THE PLAZA
At the heart of the city is the old Spanish plaza, reflecting a loose rendition of the Laws of the Indies used for Spanish town planning. During the missionary period, the Santa Fe Plaza looked and functioned much differently to its use today. The space was twice as large as one sees today, and it had not yet been enclosed with 19th-century

*Above: The governor's palace fronts one side of the Plaza; its early 20th-century remake barely resembles the original.*

American commercial buildings. Due to the lack of merchants by 1700, the lots surrounding the plaza went primarily to leading citizens who built placitas, or courtyard houses. Spanish Colonial architecture dominated the structures facing the plaza, and owners were obliged to add portales (porches) to shelter occasional merchants gathered around the plaza. The portales were supported with rough-hewn, thick wooden posts capped with carved brackets (zapatas), which were spanned by horizontal beams and were roofed as standard.

The visual landscape of the Plaza was transformed twice again prior to assuming its present-day appearance. Following the independence movement of 1821, Santa Fe became a Mexican town, which instantly provided more freedom to trade with the Americans. The Santa Fe Trail was born. By 1824 regular trade caravans were importing American and European products along this now-legendary trail from Missouri

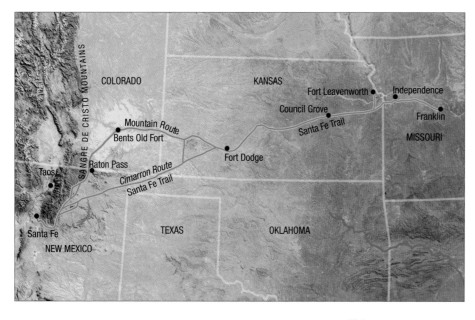

*Left: The route of the Santa Fe Trail was opened in the 1820s and provided a vital overland trade and military route connecting Missouri with the East.*

to Taos, New Mexico and on to Santa Fe. By the 1840s these caravans contained many wagons of merchandise – and American cultural ideas. As trade with the Americans increased during the Mexican period, the culture and society of Santa Fe changed measurably. More Anglo-Americans were migrating to live in New Mexico, and ultimately controlled much of its economy. The Santa Fe Trail literally ended at the plaza, which became the ultimate goal for travellers along the route.

With the signing of the Treaty of Guadalupe Hidalgo in 1848, the Mexican-American War ended, and all of California and New Mexico came under the control of the USA. Hundreds of thousands of mestizos (referred to locally as Hispanos) suddenly found themselves under a foreign power – the first time since 1598 when the Spanish conquered the American Southwest. By this time the people and landscapes of Santa Fe and New Mexico had been hispanicized, given that Spanish names and settlement patterns now dominated the territory.

### A FUSION OF STYLES

With Santa Fe's new political and cultural orientation to the east came the city's next transformation, reflected in the changing architecture around the plaza. Using a simplified version of the Greek Revival style, the rough Mexican portales were removed and replaced with whitewashed, milled posts and trim. By the early 1860s only two porches remained from the Spanish or Mexican periods. Window openings were replaced with glass shipped over the Santa Fe Trail, and large doors were cut into older adobe buildings. Brick cornices decorated the rooflines of buildings, and door and window frames simulated the more intricate patterns of Greek Revival architecture which had been popular decades earlier in the Eastern USA. This crude, western version of the Greek Revival has since been referred to as Territorial style –

some of which is still visible around the Plaza today. With the arrival of a branch of the Santa Fe Railroad in 1880 came even more cultural and economic integration with the east. Main street had arrived on the Plaza. Victorian-style commercial buildings, dominated by the standard Italianate, round-arched windows and ornamental trim, replaced much of the original adobe and Territorial-style structures around the plaza, creating the physical appearance seen today – a Spanish plaza surrounded by American commercial buildings.

More recently, a fourth architectural transition has taken place during much of the 20th century, with the mandated

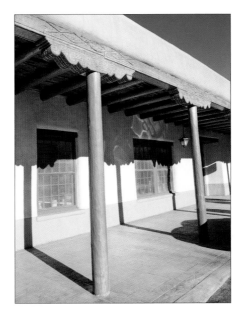

*Above: Covered wagons with Eastern merchandise reach the Plaza in the 1840s.*

use of a regional invention known as the Santa Fe style (also known as Pueblo Revival). By the time New Mexico became a state in 1912 the discovery of Santa Fe by tourists encouraged local leaders to promote the city through a distinct architectural image. Eventually adapted for the entire city, the Santa Fe style brought an amalgam of styles into one architectural theme – a synthesis of Spanish Colonial, Native American Pueblo and Anglo-American features. Buildings fronted with the style included today's familiar flat roofs, projecting thick vigas (beams), exposed adobe and hand-carved zapatas on wooden-hewn posts. The aim was not to create the "city beautiful", but the "city different".

With its own regional Santa Fe style, local leaders successfully rebelled against the expanding Mission style then sweeping southern California. To be sure, the invented landscape of the plaza area today exhibits this newfound, Mexican identity. With its 400th birthday in 2010, Santa Fe is the oldest capital city in the United States.

*Left: Wooden posts and zapata capitals adorn many of Santa Fe's buildings today, an invented blend of styles.*

# THE ALAMO
## SAN ANTONIO, TEXAS

Like Florida to its east, Texas was settled by New Spain for geopolitical reasons. The Spanish were increasingly concerned with French poaching activities in the region and wanted to solidify their control of the territory. Unlike New Mexico and Florida, however, which were directed by the Council of the Indies and the Spanish king, Texas was under the jurisdiction of the viceroy in Mexico City. The first string of Texas missions, therefore, relied on inexpensive friars, which ultimately resulted in the abandonment of all missions for nearly 25 years due to resistance from indigenous tribes. A second effort to establish a string of Texas missions after 1713 was more successful.

Led by a party of Franciscan friars, the Mission San Antonio de Valero, known today as the Alamo, was established in 1718. Its original name was chosen to honour the viceroy at the time, the Marques de Valero. The mission church was begun in 1744 and completed by 1757. Soon a Spanish presidio was established nearby, and ten families from northern Mexico settled as a fledgling community.

A new war between France and Spain led to yet another abandonment of the six regional missions and presidio in eastern Texas. With the defeat of the French, the Spanish slowly established more missions and presidios in Texas. Finally the French pressure from neighbouring Louisiana was relieved when Spain acquired the territory in 1762.

### MAKING A TOWN PLAN

Five years later an ambitious plan derived from the Laws of the Indies was drafted for the permanent settlement of San Antonio, with Mission San Antonio

*Above: The now-famous facade of this modest Spanish mission had been gradually altered through American preservation efforts over the decades.*

de Valero located nearby along a bend of the river. On paper, the town plan came complete with the expected plaza, government and church buildings, rectilinear street grid, and acequias (irrigation canals). Like other Spanish settlements in the rural north, however, San Antonio developed slowly. Only a modest number of ranchos had been established along the San Antonio River Valley by the 1780s, a disappointing outcome compared with the optimistic hopes of Spanish officials to "foster widespread breeding of livestock". Growth of Spanish San Antonio further suffered due to the failure to effectively settle Texas as a whole.

## BUILDING THE MISSION

The friars of the San Antonio area were more ambitious than their rural isolation ultimately enabled. They envisioned grand stone churches that replicated those in Europe – complete with vaults and domes. They sought master masons from Mexico to guide such projects, however, as the Alamo's story exemplifies, this goal was easier said than done.

With respect to the construction of Mission San Antonio, one mason arrived before 1741 but left three years later having apparently only left the foundations and partial stone walls complete. Without a master mason, a simplified church was constructed on these foundations with a flat roof. This apparently collapsed in 1750 along with its falling tower. A visiting friar reported a few years later that the church had collapsed "because of the stupidity of the craftsman".

Another master craftsman focused on the facade with a Baroque plan after 1756, but this project too was left incomplete by 1759. Another was hired about 1765 to complete the vaulting, sanctuary and ground floor rooms, but he died before the work was complete.

*Right: Less recognizable to most people is the rear view of the Alamo mission. The structure is in downtown San Antonio.*

*Above: After 187 Texan men were killed here by Mexican troops, "Remember the Alamo" became the battle cry for the Texas War for Independence from Mexico.*

## TEXAS INDEPENDENCE

The structure would likely have earned little attention from preservationists and tourists were it not for a pivotal historic event that happened here – known simply as the Alamo. During the Texas War for Independence from Mexico, the chapel became the site of one of America's most famous battles. Famed frontiersmen James Bowie and David Crockett were killed here defending the Alamo, along with more than 180 others. American sympathy for the Texas defenders increased following the battle for independence from Mexico, which further galvanized the American cause to end Mexican domination (of Texas). Now the primary tourist attraction in downtown San Antonio, the Alamo looks nearly as it did in 1849 and houses paintings depicting scenes of the battle and its defenders, as well as artefacts from the Texas Revolution.

Due to continuous revisions to both the interior and exterior through time, the authentic aspects of this property can be deceiving. Only the chapel, the restored ruins of two living quarters and the wall along the walkway from Houston Street remain to remind one of the mission compound. Other structures were destroyed long ago. Today, both the Alamo and the original settlement are subsumed into the lively downtown area of San Antonio. The front lawn of the mission provides some welcome open space in the commercial downtown, occasionally utilized for military re-enactments and other civic events.

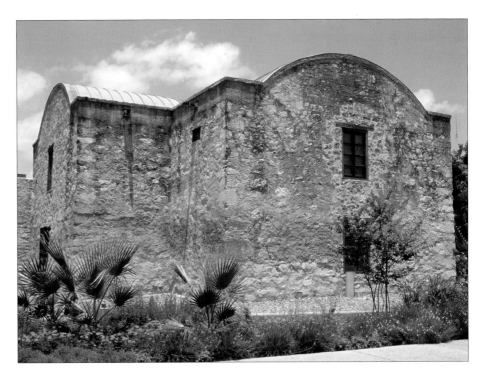

# HUBBELL TRADING POST
## GANADO, ARIZONA

Following the American Civil War, around 1864 the US military focused its attention on subduing the Native-American peoples of the Great Plains and the West. Despite their relative isolation in the present-day Four Corners region, the Navajo were not immune from this campaign. Known as the Long Walk, the military plan had been to kill or capture Navajo people and force the survivors on a march to Fort Sumner, New Mexico. The troops slashed and burnt their way across what is today the Navajo reservation, leaving the tribe entirely dependent upon Anglo-American food and shelter. Living conditions at their new settlement grew severe as the relocated Navajo approached starvation.

Finally acknowledging the grim situation, the War Department released the Navajos in 1868, many of whom returned to their homeland. The ensu-ing Treaty of 1868 – hailed by the Navajo as a veritable Declaration of Independence – provided a reservation of about 15,800km sq/6,100 miles sq in northern Arizona and New Mexico. Living conditions among the Navajo improved markedly during ensuing decades. Numbering more than 250,000, the Navajo people today constitute by far the largest Native-American tribe in the USA, and one of the few to remain on much of its original territory.

### TRADING POST NETWORK

As the Navajo population rebounded following the Treaty of 1868, so too did trade with neighbouring tribes and white settlers. Primarily oriented to sheep and horse-raising, the Navajo were a nomadic, self-sufficient people largely unfamiliar with the Anglo-American cash economy. After the treaty, Navajo herds increased, allowing the wool trade to develop. Over time, profiteers established trading posts within the reservation boundaries and along its periphery. Slowly, a network developed, although it is likely that no more than one trading post operated on the reservation at a time up to 1878.

When the Atlantic and Pacific Railroad (a subsidiary of the AT&SF) established Gallup, New Mexico, in 1881, white settlers saw the potential to develop trade networks with the Navajo. Trading posts along the railroad corridor developed rapidly thereafter, along with stores that sold mainly whiskey. By 1886 the number of on-reservation posts had risen to nine. As well as Navajo wool,

*Below: Between the 1880s and 1930s the US government enlarged the Navajo reservation until it surrounded all the Hopi villages.*

*Above: Some consider the Hubbell Trading Post to have been the most important on the Navajo reservation. It was the first of a chain of Hubbell posts to develop.*

sheep pelts and goat skins were being traded for the first time. The number of trading posts and volume of business expanded drastically during the early 20th century. By 1910 there were 39 licensed trading posts in various Navajo jurisdictions, in addition to several on the Hopi reservation and numerous off-reservation posts. The trading post had become an accepted social and economic institution for the Navajo people by the late teens and early 1920s.

### EARLY TRADE
The Hubbell Trading Post, operating today under the direction of the National Park Service, was one of the earliest and, over the long term, most influential in promoting Navajo trade. Established in 1878, the current building probably dates to the 1890s, having replaced the smaller, original structure. The Post's founder, John Lorenzo Hubbell, was born in 1853 and came to Ganado at the age of 23. He remained there until his death in 1930. Hubbell named the town of Ganado for his friend, Ganado Mucho (many cattle), a local Navajo who had befriended the young Hubbell. The land for his Trading

Post was homesteaded and originally was off the reservation. As the reservation was enlarged to include the Post, an Act of Congress was required to allow Hubbell to keep his land – along with some assistance from his friend, Teddy Roosevelt.

Like other trading posts, the Hubbell establishment essentially served as a gateway of communication between the subsistence-based regional tribes and the American economic system. A 1986 description of the Hubbell post by Marshall Trimble provides a vivid image of the place: "Walking into the Hubbell Trading Post is like taking a long step back in time. The long, flat-roofed building is constructed of large, salmon-hued sandstone rocks. Huge beams of ponderosa pine stretch across the ceiling and act as hangers for such former essentials as saddles and horse collars. The room is illuminated by stark light bulbs dangling at the end of an electrical cord. The inside walls are of thick plaster reminiscent of an old Spanish hacienda, and the floor is well-worn hardwood."

### HUBBELL
John Lorenzo Hubbell was considered a most influential white man. His political career paralleled his Post's importance. First elected sheriff of Apache County in 1882, he later joined the territorial legislature and served as a state senator from 1912–15. In 1914 he ran unsuccessfully for the US Senate. Although a friend of the president, he was apparently the happiest at his remote trading post, interacting with an indigenous people that he had come to know and respect.

*Below: Native Americans could barter for essential items such as sugar, coffee, canned goods, flour, tobacco and clothing at the Hubbell Trading Post. In return they offered local products including wool, sheep, silver work and rugs.*

# TOMBSTONE
## HISTORIC DISTRICT, TOMBSTONE, ARIZONA

*Above: Notable citizens of Tombstone including Wyatt Earp were photographed in 1885 as the city boomed.*

Following Edward Schieffelin's discovery of silver in the San Pedro Valley in 1877, the mining community of Tombstone became, "for a brief moment, the biggest, richest, gaudiest, hottest, meanest, most notorious town in Arizona Territory". Schieffelin later recalled that, due to the threat of attacks from the Apache tribe, soldiers at Camp Huachuca advised that the only thing he would find in that area would be his tombstone. "The word lingered in my mind", Schieffelin remembered, "and when I got into the country where Tombstone is now located, I gave the name to the first location that I made."

During the next few months Schieffelin and his associates opened an array of mines that proved to be historic: the Lucky Cuss, the Tough Nut and the Contention. Together they produced record yields, with miners having extracted US $25 million worth of silver by 1884.

### GROWTH OF A TOWN

Tombstone was experiencing its most rapid period of growth in 1881, having already become the home of 6,000 residents. That number increased to a high of 10,000 in 1885, which made the mining community the largest city in Arizona Territory. The commercial business district evolved along Allen Street, considered the "gaudy" part of town. Nearly 110 places were licensed to sell liquor, and the town boomed 24 hours a day through its collection of saloons, dance halls, hotels, gambling halls and brothels.

### GUN FIGHT

The memorable name of Tombstone has since come to signify much more than a mining boom town that quickly went bust. It has become a symbol of the Wild American West during the frontier era, and is memorable for the events that transpired on 26 October 1881. Certain criminals became determined to dominate the community. Two men stood in their way: US deputy marshal Wyatt Earp, and his brother Virgil, the town marshal. A vigilante group also formed to support the Earps, known as the Citizens Committee of Safety.

On 25 October 1881, Ike Clanton rode into town and hopped from bar to bar, became inebriated and threatened to kill the Earps and their friend Doc Holliday. Tension rose in the town by the next morning when Clanton was joined by his brothers. Just after 2pm on the afternoon of 26 October, Wyatt, Virgil and Morgan Earp emerged from Hafford's Saloon at the corner of Fourth and Allen streets to arrest the Clantons and their friends, specifically for carrying arms within town limits. Doc Holliday joined them as they approached the OK Corral. The sheriff met the lawmen halfway, announcing that he had disarmed Clanton's men but had not arrested them. The Earps and Holliday continued down Fremont Street to pursue their goal. Soon, 17 shots were fired on each side over the course of 60 seconds. On the criminal side, Frank and Tom McLowry and Billy Clanton were dead. Virgil and Morgan Earp were wounded and Doc Holliday was grazed across the back. Two months later, Virgil was ambushed, and in 1882 Morgan was murdered.

For more than a century afterward, the events that transpired during that one day have been analyzed by historians and adapted for Hollywood films. As with all abridged accounts, this story was deceptively simple. As historian

*Below: The story of Wyatt Earp has earned legendary status, which has led to many renditions of questionable authenticity.*

*Above: Much of Tombstone's 1880s main-street scene has survived due to a lack of redevelopment.*

Thomas Sheridan points out: "Earp was a product of his time, drifting from one violent town to another in search of good cards and the backing of powerful men. He and his brothers found more than they bargained for in Tombstone, which turned Wyatt into a legend, Virgil into a cripple and Morgan into a corpse.... Tombstone epitomized the frontier at its worst: a rootless community where people risked everything – their lives, their fortunes, the land itself – for short-term gain."

### TOURISM

Nostalgia has taken hold of Tombstone more recently. Following the town's precipitous and contentious bust by the mid-1880s, the largest city in Arizona nearly descended to the status of ghost town. Little more was built here, and the Tombstone landscape awaited its second boom as a tourist destination – a status it maintains today. Architecturally, Allen Street and surrounding residential neighbourhoods provide a nearly museum-quality education of what a frontier town looked like a century ago. Much of the original main-street false-fronted buildings and Territorial-style porches and brick facades survive, without succumbing to later Victorian-era growth. Most of Allen Street dates to the rebuilding period after a devastating 1882 fire. Although Tombstone's 19th-century bust was quick, hard and prolonged, recent preservation efforts and its post-industrial tourist economy have proven that this is indeed "the town too tough to die".

*Below: The mining operations around Tombstone were integrated into the larger Colonial economy of the American Southwest, sending precious metals East to support the Industrial Revolution.*

# GRAND CANYON VILLAGE
## HISTORIC DISTRICT, GRAND CANYON VILLAGE, ARIZONA

Today more than five million annual visitors from around the world go to the rustic Grand Canyon Village to enjoy stunning views. Prior to America's appreciation of the canyon's scenery, however, the South Rim landscape was valued more for resource extraction. What is today the orderly landscape of Grand Canyon Village once resembled a western mining camp, with poorly built cabins, tents and trash scattered among free-ranging cattle, mules, horses and ponies. As part of a remote, Colonial economy, independent entrepreneurs staked mining claims along and below the rim, and ranchers used the now-famous Bright Angel Trail to move their cattle down to the Tonto Platform. Early mining infrastructure is still visible near Grand Canyon Village today, reminding visitors with keen eyes that

*Above: Vintage diesel trains now travel the original route of the Santa Fe Railroad.*

the South Rim was once the domain of unregulated capitalist activities belonging to small business ventures.

As late as 1918, village planner Frank Waugh wrote that the "present town is without form. The miscellaneous buildings are scattered at random over the land. There are no streets. Two county

roads have wandered aimlessly into the territory, where they seem to have lost their way."

Some pioneers, like entrepreneur and future politician Ralph Cameron, had recognized the growing promise of tourism by the late 19th century. Early facilities at the rim were sparse and undeveloped, and aspiring visitors tolerated slow, bumpy journeys from Flagstaff aboard dusty wagons. Cameron controlled the Bright Angel Trail as a toll road, having developed his own visitor facilities at the rim. By 1904 there were 2,000 tourists per year registering at his rim-top hotel, and tolls collected from trail users on horseback (pedestrians travelled free) totalled US $3,000 during the 1907 season. By this time, however, Cameron's tourist developments were under extreme competition from a new developer – the railroad.

### THE SANTA FE

Given the precedents for early park development by the federal government, it was the powerful railroad companies that promoted new national parks in the West for their own economic gain. In fact, the largest interest groups that lobbied heavily for the creation of a National Park Service, formed in 1916, were the railroad industry and the budding automobile industry. Proponents of the National Park Service Act believed that scenic recreation areas such as Yellowstone should be vigorously developed for the enjoyment of visitors, essentially "making a business of scenery". The Grand Canyon finally got its own railroad connection in 1901, in the form of a 97km/60 mile branch connection from the junction with Santa Fe's trans-

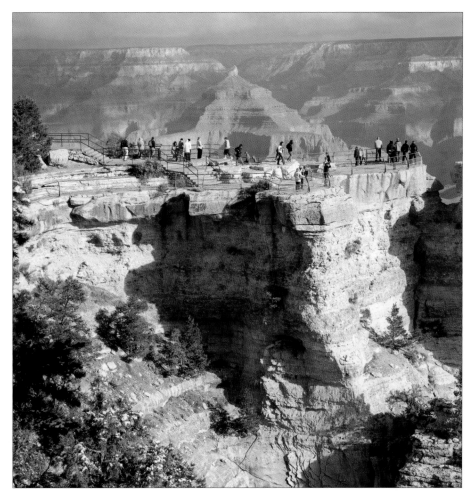

*Left: Early tourism to the canyon's South Rim relied on haphazard businesses and unplanned growth.*

*Above: The lobby of the El Tovar Hotel is typical of a late Victorian-era railroad resort.*

*Above: Originally, the Grand Canyon was valued for extractive mining operations.*

## MARY COLTER

It was also the Santa Fe Railroad that hired Mary Elizabeth Jane Colter, a nationally accomplished architect, to construct some of the South Rim's landmark buildings, including Hermit's Rest, the Lookout, Bright Angel Lodge and the interior of the El Tovar Hotel. Most prominent, perhaps, was her design of Hopi House, her first commissioned work at the Village in 1905. Hopi House was Colter's attempt to replicate and honour the adobe pueblo construction of the Hopi people.

continental route at Williams, Arizona. Owned by the Atchison, Topeka & Santa Fe (AT&SF) Railroad – known popularly as the Santa Fe – the rural branch line instantly brought the Grand Canyon within relatively easy reach of well-to-do Eastern tourists.

### DEVELOPING TOURISM

Lacking sufficient federal funds to develop the South Rim for tourism, the US Forest Service formed an unlikely coalition with two private enterprises. A collaboration ensued during the early 20th century between the Santa Fe Railway, the Fred Harvey Company and the Forest Service to create a master plan

*Below: A tourism poster from 1955, produced by the Santa Fe Railroad, promotes the Grand Canyon as a scenic destination.*

for the development of Grand Canyon Village, which is today preserved as one of the most visited Historic Districts in the nation. Harvey had already nurtured a symbiotic relationship with the railroad, through his independently owned company that supplied lodging, food and other services aboard the Santa Fe passenger trains and within Spanish Revival hotels along the route. With unparalleled financing and corporate initiative, the railroad came to control the development of South Rim Village with the blessing of the Forest Service. The earlier entrepreneurs, including Ralph Cameron, fought a protracted campaign to retain their own private property rights, but ultimately it was the railroad that provided the financing and comprehensive planning for the South Rim Village prior to and during the 1920s.

In addition to this Rustic architecture, which was designed to blend with the Southwestern landscape, the Santa Fe Railroad constructed the El Tovar Hotel in a combination of late Victorian and Craftsman styling, just up the hill from its log-cabin depot.

Since the 1990s one can once again travel by train to the South Rim from Williams, aboard the vintage tourist trains of the privately owned Grand Canyon Railway. In a twist of irony, more people annually now enter the Grand Canyon National Park by train than at the height of passenger rail travel along the Santa Fe.

*Below: Hopi House, designed by Colter, who was hired by the Santa Fe Railroad to design distinctive visitor facilities.*

# HOOVER DAM
## ARIZONA/NEVADA

Snaking its way through the Grand Canyon, the annual flow of the Colorado River does not even rank in America's top 25. Still, it has gained unprecedented significance in the growth of the American Southwest. It has more people, cities, industry and agricultural production dependent upon it than any similar river on the planet. The Colorado River provides approximately half the water supply for the Los Angeles, Phoenix and San Diego metropolitan areas, and allows for the growth of the bulk of America's fresh winter vegetable supply. With six serious hydro-electric dams in place along

*Below: Lake Mead supports a range of uses, including the irrigation of 607,000ha/ 1.5 million acres of marginal farmland.*

its channel, the river's water has been tamed and allocated to the point where its natural delta on the Gulf of California is, more often than not, completely dry. Indeed, much of the population of the Southwestern United States is dependent upon the unpredictable flow of this western stream, and the construction of Hoover Dam was the first grand project to enable that dependency.

### 1922 COMPACT

Dedicated on 30 September 1935, the Hoover Dam – originally Boulder Dam – became the first massive water storage project along the Colorado River. It was also a grand experiment, as the world's first dam to be constructed at this scale. This project gave greater confidence to

engineers who eventually dammed great rivers around the world, including the Nile, Zambezi, Niger, Volga, Columbia and many others. Located about 45km/28 miles southeast of Las Vegas, Nevada, the dam connects the west and east walls of the Black Canyon on the Colorado River, which serves as the natural border between the states of Nevada and Arizona. US Route 93 makes use of the top of the dam, which is 221m/726ft at its maximum height. With 2.48 million cu m/3.25 million cu yds of concrete used in its construction, Hoover Dam was the earliest of the Bureau of Reclamation's massive multipurpose dams.

The rationale for the Dam's construction was rooted in the politics of population growth. By the 1920s

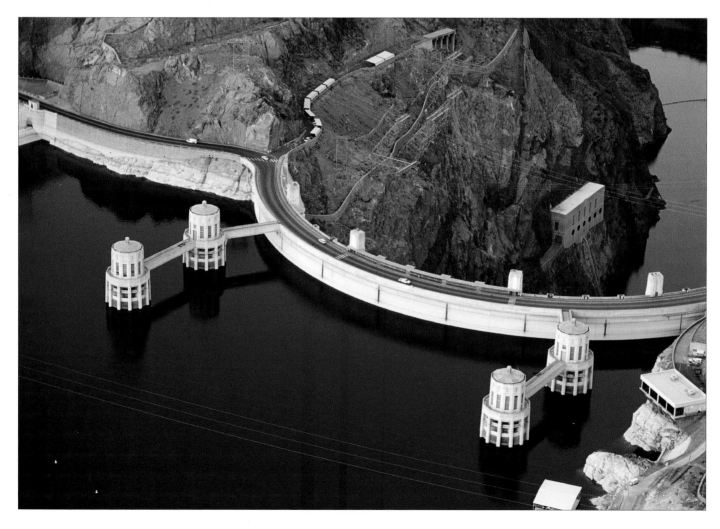

California's rampant growth and agricultural production led state leaders to look to the Colorado River to satisfy ever-increasing water demands. Other, up-river states remained mostly uninhabited, but were uncomfortable with California potentially claiming the bulk of the river's water. Given the existing appropriative-rights doctrine, California could produce a monopoly over the river's water rights simply because it was the first to use it. Consequently, the effort to secure congressional authority for a dam to secure California river water was fiercely resisted. California relented and agreed to meet with neighbouring states to first divide up the Colorado's water supply. The result was the negotiation of the landmark 1922 Colorado River Compact. An overly optimistic average flow of 17.5 million acre-feet was distributed on paper to seven southwestern states and Mexico, though decades later it would become clear that the river rarely ever provided that much water. With the arbitrary division placed at Lee's Ferry, Arizona – just west of Glen Canyon Dam today – the compact's lower-basin states included California, Arizona and Nevada, while the upper basin included Colorado, Utah, Wyoming and New Mexico. The Compact was not a done deal. After years of contentious debate, Congress took action in 1928 with its authorization of Boulder Dam and the All-American Canal that would siphon water to California. Arizona refused to ratify the Compact because the 2.8 million acre-feet of water allocated to it was less than it wanted. Another 35 years ensued before Arizona got on board.

## CONSTRUCTION

The construction and engineering of Hoover Dam is a fascinating story in its own right, and one that has been written and circulated widely. In terms of hydraulic engineering, the Dam is considered an accomplishment on par with the Panama Canal. Aside from entirely re-routing the Colorado River through

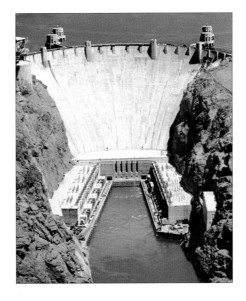

*Above: Hydroelectric power generated by Hoover Dam provides electricity to 500,000 homes.*

tunnels in the canyon walls, one particular challenge arose with the need to cool the Dam's poured concrete. Given the Dam's thickness and height, more than a century would have been required for the concrete to set and cool. To speed up the process, the Dam was built in pier-like blocks and the concrete was cooled by running ice-cold water through more than 936km/582 miles of embedded piping. This allowed the chemically-induced heat from the setting concrete to dissipate more quickly, and the entire cooling process for the dam was complete by March 1935. Upon its completion, Lake Mead was filled behind it.

*Below: The Colorado River rarely reaches its former delta in the Gulf of California.*

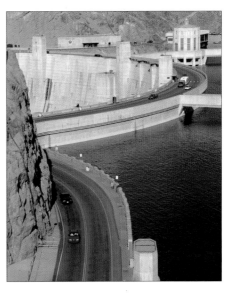

*Above: US Route 93 crosses Hoover Dam, providing major traffic backups. A new, towering bypass opened in 2010.*

## LIMITED SUPPLY

Hoover Dam set the precedent for future dams along the Colorado River system, upon which the continuous population growth and agricultural production in the southwestern deserts and California have depended. However, by the early 2000s hydrologists and politicians alike were made aware of the river's limited resource and its potential lack of sustainability. A long-term drought had caused the Colorado River reservoirs to sink to historically low levels, to the point where casinos in Las Vegas were shutting off their prized water features. It is still unsure how reliable this precious resource will be without prolonged conservation efforts.

*Below: Continuing drought has lowered the water level of Lake Mead behind the Dam.*

# LOS ALAMOS NATIONAL LABORATORY
## LOS ALAMOS, NEW MEXICO

Located in the rural Jemez Mountains northwest of Santa Fe, Los Alamos was the birthplace of the world's atomic age. The laboratory was founded on 1 January 1943 for the sole purpose of developing an atomic weapon for use during World War II. Here, the world's first enriched-uranium reactor was designed and built in 1944, followed by the first plutonium-fueled reactor in 1946. The success of the first nuclear fission bomb led to a second assignment – that of developing a "super" weapon that derived energy from the thermonuclear fusion of hydrogen. The laboratory has continued to serve as the nation's foremost development centre for nuclear weapons. Its non-military history is equally impressive, having contributed to fundamental scientific knowledge and to peaceful applications of atomic energy, specifically through the development of enriched-uranium and plutonium reactors.

### GOVERNMENT INTEREST

Considered a scientific prodigy, Dr J. Robert Oppenheimer had developed into a well-known professor at the

University of California, Berkeley, by the late 1930s. By 1939 Oppenheimer and other scientists around the world had determined that the creation of an atomic bomb was actually a real possibility. The US government initially showed little interest. A month prior to the war breaking out in Europe (1 September 1939), the scientist Leo Szilard had persuaded Albert Einstein to sign his name on a letter sent to

*Below: Los Alamos is one of a few American towns that have been settled and developed by the federal government.*

*Above: These trailers set in a residential block served as homes to the original employees of Los Alamos.*

President Franklin D. Roosevelt. The letter's purpose was to warn Roosevelt that "extremely powerful bombs of a new type may be constructed" and suggested that the Germans might already be working on such a bomb.

The letter succeeded with its intended effect. The president established a "Uranium Committee" headed by physicist Lyman Briggs. Little happened for two years until the spring of 1941, when a top-secret British group produced a report suggesting that a bomb made from plutonium or uranium might be made small enough to be carried inside an aircraft. At about the same time Roosevelt created the Office of Scientific Research and Development (OSRD) to advance science for military purposes. The OSRD was chaired by Vannevar Bush, an engineer and MIT professor. Although initially believing that the possibility of an atomic bomb was "very remote", Bush changed his mind after reading the British report.

The government's former apathy became a thing of the past. Roosevelt replaced Brigg's Uranium Committee with the code-named S-1 Committee, which would report directly to the

White House. The first aim was to recruit scientists from around the country to assist with the bomb project. In May 1942, Oppenheimer was appointed the director of S-1's fast-neutron research, and he subsequently organized a highly secretive summer seminar series with top theoretical physicists. The group was given the task of creating the bare-bones design of an atomic bomb, with Oppenheimer in charge of what became known as Project Y, or the Los Alamos Project.

## PROJECT Y

Some effort was necessary to determine the location of Project Y facilities. Potential locations were surveyed in the Southwest for the required laboratory, including the Los Alamos Ranch School, which Dr Oppenheimer had visited frequently on summer pack trips. Ultimately, the decision was made to centre the weapons research laboratory at the boys' ranch school, given that the log buildings of the school could accommodate the estimated 100 scientists and their families expected to be involved in the effort. Also important was its isolated, mountainous location to enhance secrecy. Relatively mild winters offered opportunities for outdoor work, a necessary component of the project. Housing for the scientists was initially provided by the existing log and bungalow-style structures built in the 1920s. These included Fuller Lodge, the combination guest house, infirmary,

dining room and recreaton room, as well as the "big house" and faculty and student residences.

By 1944 the scientists' work on a weapon was progressing well, though it became evident that testing would be necessary prior to actual deployment over enemy territory. Scientists involved with the project disagreed widely about the explosive force to be expected. Only a test would provide certainty. Further, four general aspects of research would benefit from a test: the nature of the implosion, the nuclear energy released, damage effects produced and overall behaviour of the explosion. A site referred to as Trinity (now the Trinity National Historic Landmark) in south-

*Above: The final location for the Los Alamos Project was the relatively isolated school northwest of Santa Fe, the Fuller Lodge.*

central New Mexico was chosen as the test site, and on 16 July 1945 the world's first nuclear bomb was detonated.

Few other events have been so pivotal. Use of two similar weapons would lead to the end of World War II and the beginning of the Cold War. Among the many scientific measurements taken during the explosion, it was determined that the bomb had been nearly three times as "efficient" or strong as expected, with an actual yield of between 20 and 22 kilotons.

### LOS ALAMOS TODAY

Today the Trinity site is opened to visitors for only two days each year. As for Los Alamos, the world-famous laboratory is not open to visitors, but various buildings of the original boys' ranch school are accessible near the main freeway through town. One building has been converted into a museum that details the making of the atomic bomb and the social history of the Los Alamos community. A far cry from its beginnings, the community has developed into a full-fledged city.

*Below: The rural checkpoint for those entering Los Alamos belies the high security and secret work undertaken there.*

*Below: The city of Los Alamos' primary economic base continues to be its network of highly classified laboratories.*

# CHAPTER TEN

# THE PACIFIC

PART OF THE BROADER PACIFIC RIM, THIS STRIP
OF TERRITORY BORDERING THE WORLD'S
LARGEST OCEAN PROVIDED A FORMIDABLE GOAL
FOR A CENTURY OF AMERICANS. THE REGION
INCORPORATES A BLEND OF CULTURAL
INFLUENCES: RUSSIAN HERITAGE TO THE NORTH,
AND SPANISH TO THE SOUTH. THE AREA HAS
MILITARY, ENGINEERING, SHIPPING, MINING,
HORITICULTURAL AND SPORTING LANDMARKS
THAT HAVE ALL PLAYED A SIGNIFICANT ROLE IN
THE POLITICAL, SOCIAL AND ECONOMIC
DEVELOPMENT OF THE COUNTRY.

*Left: The Presidio with the Golden Gate Bridge in San Francisco.*

# CATHEDRAL OF ST MICHAEL
## THE ARCHANGEL, SITKA, ALASKA

Along with other nations, the Russians participated in imperialistic expansion into North America. The first white settlers seen by Native Americans in Alaska were Russian. While the Spanish, English and French empires were jockeying for position in North America, the Russian empire slowly moved east across Asia over a period of 400 years. By the mid-1700s they reached the Pacific Ocean and the Bering Sea, having created the world's largest empire. Their next logical expansion was into North America via Alaska.

### ALASKA

The high-priced pelts of the sea otter first attracted Russian hunters, who established an Alaskan settlement on Kodiak Island in 1784. They proceeded to move southward along the coast, founding additional villages and forts along the way to protect their holdings. Their greatest influence was just north of San Francisco Bay, where the Russians established Fort Ross in 1812.

Isolated and vulnerable, the Russians faced increasing pressure and competition from European fur traders, and eventually Moscow viewed their peripheral settlements as more of a burden than an advantage. In 1867 the Russian empire invited the USA to purchase Alaska for US $7.2m. The decision was ridiculed as "Seward's Folly" and called "Seward's Ice Box", so named for the agent of the purchase, US Secretary of State William Seward.

Like other federal lands, Alaska remained a territory for some time, until its "graduation" to statehood as the 49th state of the Union in 1959. By the 1890s Seward's gamble had paid off, in the form of extensive discoveries of gold in the Yukon River Valley. During the 20th century Alaska emerged as one of America's primary oil producers, an extractive process that has collided with efforts to preserve Alaska's vast and otherwise pristine wilderness.

### RUSSIAN ORTHODOXY

The most prominent, material symbol of Alaska's Russian period is St Michael's Cathedral, or more officially the Cathedral of St Michael the Archangel. The relatively modest, wood-framed structure was built in 1848 and served as the heart of Russian society in the town of Sitka, Alaska. Sitka was the capital of Russian America from 1808 until 1867. The island town continued its political status as the capital of Alaska Territory until 1906. The cathedral was built as a Russian Orthodox church, which reflected one of Russia's most prominent

*Left: The Cathedral is the most prominent reminder of early Russian influence in Alaska.*

*Above: Many of the original paintings, artefacts and Russian icons were saved during the 1966 fire.*

cultural and social institutions until the Soviet period. Consequently, Sitka served as the seat of the Orthodox diocese that theoretically included all of North America between 1840 and 1872.

During the American period, the town continued as the diocese of Alaska. From its location at the geographical centre of Sitka, the church reached out and influenced thousands of Native Alaskans, ultimately exerting a profound cultural impact on the region. Although modest in size and grandeur compared to its Western European counterparts, the Cathedral, with its diluted Russian architecture, remained by far the largest, most imposing religious structure in Alaska until well into the 20th century. The building was designed around the typical cruciform plan and serves as an excellent peripheral example of Russian architecture. At the intersection of the cross plan is a towering wooden dome, and the building contains clear elements of Italian Rococo architecture, which was popular in Russia during the early 19th century.

### HABS

In 1966 the Cathedral served as an unwitting proponent of the Historic American Building Survey (HABS), which had been a Depression-era attempt to put unemployed architects back to work for the good of society. Both HABS and the Civilian Conservation Corps (CCC) were initiated by the federal government in 1933, which effectively helped to legitimize government involvement with historic preservation. The HABS project was not meant to save buildings, and the decision of which buildings to survey was highly uneven across America. What resulted from this New Deal program, however, was an incredible national archive of detailed architectural drawings that was made available for public and scholarly work.

St Michael's Cathedral was surveyed in detail. This fact proved vital to its masterful reconstruction after a fire destroyed the original structure in 1966. What exists today consists of a complete reconstruction with fire-resistant materials, but the accuracy of its reconstruction was enabled specifically through the intricate documentation conducted through HABS. Further, because the fire spread first through its roof, nearly all of its interior furnishings were saved by the local population. Thus, the original religious artefacts, paintings and other Russian-oriented icons were placed back into the new structure and can be observed today. Visually, the historical structure provides a welcome diversity to Sitka's downtown skyline, otherwise dominated by more Modernist, International-style buildings that surround the Cathedral.

*Below: The entire Cathedral was reconstructed after a devastating fire in 1966, aided greatly by meticulously recorded drawings of the original structure.*

# SAN FRANCISCO CABLE CARS
## SAN FRANCISCO, CALIFORNIA

*Left: A renovated cable car is still in use. As predecessors to the electric streetcar, cable cars encouraged the development of new suburbs.*

Now a prominent, mobile tourist attraction, the cable cars of San Francisco comprise the last of their kind operating in the USA. Their popularity has been assisted by the steep physical geography of "the city by the Bay" as it is known, and they remain useful to help navigate around the city.

### CABLE CAR DEVELOPMENT

In 1867 the first recognizable cable car system was devised in Greenwich Village by New York City inventor Charles T. Harvey. Its overhead cable and grip ultimately proved unsuccessful, leaving the door open to Andrew S. Hallidie, a Scots immigrant in San Francisco, who earned his wealth as a wire-rope manufacturer. Like other inventors, Hallidie relied on his knowledge of the thick, wire rope patented by his English father, which was used extensively within California's gold and silver mines. Hallidie envisioned a system whereby passenger railroad cars rolled along tracks, pulled by giant

cables. Rather than powering the cars themselves, giant steam engines would power the cables. The typical American city street grid proved favourable for such an innovation, allowing a straight run of the cars. Hallidie's cable cars proved especially useful for navigating Nob Hill, one of San Francisco's earliest Victorian-era, upper-class suburbs.

*Below: Power for the cables running under the streets came from giant, stationary steam engines located in specially designed power houses, one of which still exists as a museum.*

Speaking of the laborious horse cars that preceded his invention, Hallidie claimed that "My attention was called to the great cruelty and hardship to the horses engaged in that work." Just prior to the 1906 earthquake, San Francisco hosted more than 600 cable cars on 177km/110 miles of track, putting to rest the early disbelievers who referred to his project as "Hallidie's folly".

Other cities followed the successful example set by San Francisco, installing their own systems, including New York City, Washington, DC, Cincinnati, Boston, Chicago and Los Angeles. Cable cars were cleaner, quieter and more powerful than horse-drawn cars and this helped to encourage their expansion to other cities. Speed was also a factor, as one satisfied customer noted: "In the morning the businessman finds it very convenient to linger at the breakfast table from a quarter to half an hour longer than before, and still by means of the cable car reach his office on time. Its unlimited power and tireless energy make possible the operation of cars of generous size affording ample seating capacity and better light and ventilation. On every warm summer evening the open cars are crowded with people riding solely to enjoy the cool and refreshing breeze."

### REAL ESTATE BOOM

Cable cars sparked land rushes on the edges of cities, spawning real estate development of new suburban neighbourhoods. By the early 1900s, in cities nationwide, the first wave of so-called streetcar suburbs that were designed primarily around the railroad tracks of streetcar lines began to flourish.

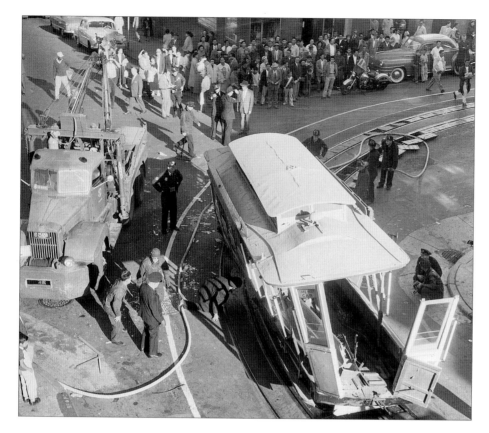

*Above: In 1955 a runaway cable car tipped on its side, injuring 21 of the 55 passengers.*

*Above: Horse-drawn vehicles provided the primary mode of transport around towns before the arrival of steam-powered cable cars.*

### DEMISE OF THE CABLE CAR

Several disadvantages of the cable cars were noted, which ultimately led to their demise. The initial capital cost of installation was among the largest concerns. Construction costs often exceeded several times that which was required for horse-drawn vehicles. As a result cable car routes were only placed in the corridors of heaviest traffic, given the need for investors to recover their costs. Further, the cars could be difficult to operate with their cumbersome mechanism. Conductors too often experienced the inability to release the grip from the cable underneath, leading to runaway cars and frantic bell clanging. Further, the use of cable cars on flat terrain constituted an enormous waste of energy, given that 95 per cent of the energy expended was used to run the cable itself. Cable-car systems, therefore, made the most sense, energy-wise, in hilly terrain. Not surprisingly, the first city to install Hallidie's invention was also

the last to give it up. In other cities with flatter terrain, cable cars were ultimately replaced with electric streetcars by the early 1900s and, later still, motorized buses. It was the streetcar, that for the first time ever zipped people smoothly out of traditionally compact city centres to the earliest rings of suburbanization.

By 1964 only 16km/10 miles of San Francisco's cable-car track remained, and the Municipal Railway experienced a continued decline in profitability. In 1980 only 40 cars operated on the remaining routes, primarily due to nostalgia and tourism. The system remains in use for these reasons to this day operated by San Francisco's larger Muni Transit System, with approximately 44 unique cable cars still in use.

*Below: The abnormally hilly terrain of San Francisco made cable cars more practical and cost-effective than in other, flatter cities.*

# PRESIDIO OF SAN FRANCISCO
## SAN FRANCISCO, CALIFORNIA

Strategically located at the northernmost tip of a peninsula, the Presidio of San Francisco saw continuous use as a military post governed by three separate countries between 1776 and 1994. With each phase of occupation has come a different set of cultural values and interests, which in turn have shaped and transformed this military landscape. The commanding site over San Francisco Bay was a key military location and a key defensive position.

### UNDER OCCUPATION

The first permanent phase of occupation came with the Spanish empire's desire to protect California's largest natural harbour from other European forces. The Presidio represented the height of Spanish military activity and occupation along the West Coast. Russia's Fort Ross was located only 95km/60 miles north of the Presidio and the Spanish had settled here in part to resist the Russians moving southward.

*Below: Mission-style residential dwellings at the Presidio are dwarfed by the Art Deco-style Golden Gate Bridge in the background.*

*Above: The Presidio at San Francisco Bay represented the peak period of Spanish occupation in North America. It was situated just 95km/60 miles from the nearest Russian outpost.*

The Mexican phase of occupation after 1821 was more of a technicality than a major cultural shift. The most dramatic transformation of the Presidio occurred in the years following the transition to American control after the Mexican-American war. The 7th New York Volunteer Infantry Regiment occupied the worn, derelict structures of the Spanish-era Presidio, and were soon followed more permanently by the US Regular Army. The Americans soon created a large military reservation that became a command and control centre

for American military operations overseas. As the armaments of the Presidio shifted from cannons to modern missiles, the base became the nerve centre of a regional defence network and the most important army post on the Pacific Coast.

The evolving American presidio was transformed again during the late 19th century from an arid environment of open dunes to one that became heavily forested. The extensive forestation provided for welcome windbreaks that doubled as a beautification project.

### THE TOWN

The main parade ground, 120ha/300 acre forest, golf course, San Francisco national cemetery and historic gardens provide a lesson in the succession of American architectural styles exhibited in the town. A few of the earliest wood-framed structures still exist and demonstrate features of the Greek Revival and Italianate styles then popular across America. Later the Presidio gained a new collection of Queen Anne and Colonial Revival housing, characteristic of the late 19th century. The regional flare of southern California had an impact on the growing town after the turn of the century, adding a variety of Mission, Italian Renaissance and Mediterranean period styles that reflected the continuing American interest in regional revivalism. Following World War II, the Modernism of the International style, consisting of uniform, functional structures, was added to the Presidio's human landscape, providing the gamut of architectural evolution that was characteristic across the country. Consequently, the Presidio may have been primarily shaped by the planning of a central authority – but its cultural landscape has mirrored the developments of the larger American scene since its earliest days.

# SKIDMORE OLD TOWN
## HISTORIC DISTRICT, PORTLAND, OREGON

Although its economic revival has presented some long-standing challenges, the Skidmore/Old Town Historic District of downtown Portland provides a common illustration of a commercial waterfront area's rise and decline through time. The district has one of the nation's premier collections of Victorian-era commercial architecture, which includes one of the finest clusters of Italianate-style, cast-iron store fronts in the West. The commercial district had emerged as the vibrant downtown of one of the Northwest's most important urban centres of the late-19th century. It was here where the capitalist energies of Portland converged, linking the city's interior hinterland with the corridors of national and global trade.

### URBAN RENEWAL

Now in its most recent stage of evolution, the city of Portland is engaged in its most recent effort to transform the existing Skidmore Old Town Historic District. With much of the neighbourhood's architectural fabric devastated by urban renewal efforts, large car parking areas had appeared where historic buildings once existed. Like cities nationwide, Portland had bought into the notion that improving parking downtown would encourage people to return. Hindsight has revealed this only served to decimate historically rich areas and challenge later efforts to redevelop these places. Ironically, efforts to protect what remained within the district after 1960 placed greater restrictions on development there, which in turn led to a slower economic rebound in the area. The restrictions encouraged investors to seek other areas of downtown for their projects.

Compared with other, more vibrant downtown success stories in Portland, therefore, this particular district has seen

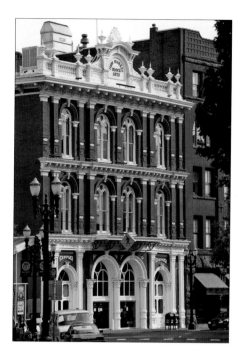

very little redevelopment in the past three decades that might ultimately enhance the historic character of the place. Further hindering efforts here is the District's location within the downtown waterfront urban renewal area, which ceased to receive funding for district enhancements after 2008.

Reflecting what may be the next generation of sensitive redevelopment efforts here, the city of Portland's bureau of planning and sustainability has recently launched an effort to revise the redevelopment guidelines for the District. As described on the bureau's official website: "The updated design guidelines for the District will provide clearer guidance for designers and developers as they consider improvements to existing structures and/or the redevelopment of surface parking lots. The primary goal of this project is to facilitate new development while ensuring the preservation of the District's special character, embodied in its robust collection of historic buildings, spaces and structures." This ongoing effort can be interpreted as the latest phase in the historical evolution of a once-thriving,

*Left: By the late-19th century, Eastern American architectural styles had spread coast to coast, such as the Italian Renaissance style seen here in Skidmore.*

waterfront business district, reflecting contemporary philosophies of urban planning and historic preservation that characterize America's direction for urban development in the early 21st century.

What survives in the Skidmore district is a mix of Victorian-era buildings, with certain Italianate and Italian Renaissance-style commercial structures highlighted. West Coast cities were essentially developed by Eastern transplants who ventured west in pursuit of economic opportunities. By the mid-19th century America's architectural styles and urban patterns had become national trends, now that the East and West were connected more intimately by sea trade and, after 1869, by the first of numerous transcontinental railroads.

*Below: Downtown Portland did not succumb to wholesale demolition in the same way as many other US cities, and today it is a thriving business venue.*

# PIONEER BUILDING
## PERGOLA AND TOTEM POLE, SEATTLE, WASHINGTON

Pioneer Building, Pergola and Totem Pole are located on Pioneer Square, an area of downtown Seattle, which has undergone intense transformations since the city's initial settlement in the 1850s.

Although definitely contributing to the historic fabric of downtown Seattle, the three landmarks here were not part of the original landscape as it evolved along the waterfront after the Civil War. The reason was an all-too-common one, that of conflagration. The Pioneer Square area was erased by the Great Seattle Fire of 1889. At that time Seattle was the largest city in Washington state with 40,000 residents. Rebuilding occurred quickly and reflected the cultural interests of the times, rooted in Victorian excess and grandeur. The buildings around Pioneer Square are a product of the late Victorian era, with a variety of high-style architecture masterpieces exhibiting Victorian styles. Many still exist today, providing the theme of Victorian-era architecture to Pioneer Square.

### PIONEER BUILDING

Most prolific of all architecture is the Richardsonian-Romanesque style employed on numerous commercial buildings in this older downtown area, and displayed most grandly on the Pioneer Building. Its site had previously served as the home of Henry Yesler, one of Seattle's pioneering leaders. Architect

*Below: The Pioneer Building and its neighbours utilized the fashionable Romanesque Revival style of architecture.*

*Left: A reproduction of the original Totem Pole, pictured here, was blessed by native Americans in Alaska.*

Elmer Fisher designed the Pioneer Building along with many other Seattle buildings following the fire. This is considered the city's most significant historic commercial building and provides a backdrop to Pioneer Square.

### PIONEER SQUARE PERGOLA

Just prior to the great fire, Seattle had adopted the cable-car transit system. Reflecting the industrial age of intracity transportation and real estate development, the cable car service allowed Seattle to remain up to date with its metropolitan counterparts. Tracks were placed along Yesler Street from Pioneer Square to Lake Washington and the Leschi neighbourhood. Another line was added along James Street. This prompted the addition of the Pioneer Square Pergola.

Common in cities during the streetcar era, pergolas became popular waiting shelters, based loosely on the concept of European garden pergolas. This one was built in 1909 as a shelter for patrons of the cable-car routes heading out of downtown. The Pergola design was the result of an architectural competition that added to the Victorian flare of the Square. The structure was cast iron and glass, with wrought-iron ornamentation. Its iron columns were capped with ball-type luminaries. Although restored through a generous gift from the United Parcel Service in 1972, the Pioneer Pergola required restoration after a truck hit the structure in 2001 and shattered its glass.

### TOTEM POLE

The Pioneer Totem Pole in the Square is an Alaskan artefact transplanted to downtown Seattle. It represents Seattle's

*Above: Like many cities and towns, Seattle and its Pioneer Square were devastated by occasional urban conflagrations.*

*Above: The Pioneer Square Pergola not long after its original construction in 1909 along a city cable-car route.*

## PIONEER SQUARE TODAY

Today's Pioneer Square is a vibrant public space. In its development downtown Seattle has taken a step toward what sociologist John Hannigan describes as a "fantasy city", in which urban neighbourhoods are transformed into entertainment and shopping zones designed to promote middle-class consumption. Thus, Seattle's Pioneer Square neighbourhood is an excellent example that illustrates how America's new downtowns have emerged since the depressed decades prior to the 1990s. One characteristic of Hannigan's fantasy city is its theme-o-centric quality. While some cities make use of single, prescribed themes, normally based on historical or cultural topics, Seattle exemplifies a case of using theme enhancement, "in which an ambience is created around a distinctive geographic locale, historical period or type of cultural activity".

northerly connections specifically with the Tlingit peoples. During 1898–99, Seattle became the principal gateway to Alaska and the Klondike gold fields. During a Chamber of Commerce excursion northward during the Gold Rush, some of the city's leading businessmen stole the original Totem Pole from the Tlingit Native Americans on Tongass Island, Alaska. The businessmen subsequently donated the Pole to the city and unveiled it at Pioneer Square in 1899 as a memento of the Alaskan Gold Rush. Less than pleased, the Tlingits filed charges, which resulted in the arrest of

the guilty members of the party. Still, the Tlingits were shortchanged, receiving much less in damages than the US $20,000 they had sought. The guilty individuals were fined US $500, and the court case was dismissed. Moreover, the city retained the Pole.

In 1938 the original Pole succumbed to a fire set by vandals, and its remains were, ironically, sent back to Alaska to have a reproduction carved by Native Americans. This time, the Pole was officially blessed by the tribe, and the new Pole was dedicated at a traditional Potlatch celebration.

In the assemblage of these otherwise unrelated artefacts at Pioneer Square can be found the themed story of Seattle's emergence and development as a gateway city in the American Northwest. Its array of exhibits, from Romanesque architecture and Totem Pole to the rebuilt Pergola of the cable-car era, provides for a loose theme of American growth, development and expansionism.

*Below: Pioneer Square in 1910, showing the newly built Pergola containing passengers waiting for the streetcar.*

*Below: The reconstructed pergola adds to the ambience of Pioneer Square, and is still in use as originally intended.*

# SKAGWAY
## HISTORIC DISTRICT AND WHITE PASS, SKAGWAY, ALASKA

Alaska, purchased outright from Russia in 1867, proved to be a resource-rich region for America's developing industrial economy. The Klondike Gold Rush of 1897–98 was a global one, attracting miners from around the world. However, the territory's remoteness and rugged physical topography proved daunting to the initial Klondikers, or "stampeders". Still, the first ships loaded with gold arrived in San Francisco and Seattle in 1897, providing evidence that the interior Yukon River Valley gold fields were accessible.

### ESTABLISHING SKAGWAY

The primary American routes to the Canadian gold fields were the Yukon River, the Valdez Trail, the Chilkoot Pass and the White Pass. The story of White Pass began in 1887 with a boundary survey expedition, which reported that a low pass 4.8–6.4km/3–4 miles from the village of Dyea might be suitable for a wagon road to serve as a gateway to the gold fields. Dyea had a small port and the village served as the head of the Chilkoot Pass, which was a popular route for early Klondikers. Participating in the survey was Captain William Moore, who investigated the low pass's potential. Moore claimed the access land to the pass as his homestead and constructed a wharf and cabin in the deep

*Below: The steam trains of the White Pass and Yukon Route Railroad once rolled down Skagway's main street.*

water at the head of Skagway Bay. He named the land "Mooresville" and the pass "White Pass" in a bid to become the primary gateway to the Yukon. His instincts proved accurate. The first miners arrived during the summer of 1897, though most simply ignored Moore. A tent city emerged, and soon thousands of people were developing a new town site called Skagway, directly atop Moore's homestead claim.

Skagway's deep-water wharves were used by ships that had their cargo unloaded there instead of at Dyea. The final blow to Dyea came with the construction of the White Pass and Yukon

*Below: A similar, more recent view of Skagway, a town that prospered as the gateway into Canada and to the Klondike gold fields.*

*Above: The treacherous White Pass was named in honour of Thomas White, the Canadian Minister of the Interior who had authorized the boundary expedition.*

Route Railroad (WP&Y, a 1m/3ft narrow-gauge route completed between 1898 and 1900). By this time, most of the miners were already in the Yukon Valley, though the railroad sealed the urban primacy of Skagway as America's route into Canada. Even as construction on the railroad began, Skagway had already been transformed to a town of 10,000 people by 1898.

### BOOM, BUST AND BOOM

Given the process of temporary resource extraction, however, a rapid boom has historically been followed by a difficult "bust" period of economic decline following the exhaustion of the resource. Skagway was no different and its population dwindled to less than 1,000 by 1910. The continuing railroad connection provided a minimal economic base that kept the town going until its next veritable gold mine was discovered – that of mass tourism. Skagway's deep harbour now allows for the calling of gigantic cruise ships.

# LAHAINA
## HISTORIC DISTRICT, LAHAINA, MAUI, HAWAII

During the first half of the 19th century Lahaina grew into a prosperous whaling centre, benefiting from its natural harbour and proximity to whale migration corridors. Between 1830 and 1860 American whaling ships visited Lahaina twice yearly. Whaling became the primary economic base for the emerging mercantile economy of the town and island, which stimulated other activities, including agriculture and regional trade. At its height of prosperity around 1846, the harbour at Lahaina attracted 400 ships annually seeking to replenish their fresh water and supplies.

### MISSIONARIES

During Lahaina's whaling years the community was in a perpetual conflict between lawless sailors and Christian missionaries. With the blessing of the chiefs in 1824, the first mission school was established here by Betsey Stockton. As might be predicted, the relationship between missionaries and sailors was less than cordial, with conflict leading the

*Below: The banyan tree planted in Maui, in 1873, is one of the largest in the world, covering the space of an entire city block.*

*Above: The global activity of whaling served as a primary factor in the eventual Americanization of Hawaii and its annexation by the USA.*

whaling crews to shell Lahaina from their ships. Ultimately, the missionary "blue laws" were established, which – together with the introduction of the printing press, missionary schools and prison – brought law and order to the community. Preceding a similar trend in the Atlantic, the whaling industry steadily declined during and after the 1860s. In similar fashion to other one-industry towns, Lahaina experienced a parallel decline in its own prosperity.

### SUGAR MILLS

As the community adjusted to a lower level of economic importance, life revolved increasingly around the sugar mill, which represented a growing industry throughout the islands. Known later as the Pioneer Mill Company, the sugar mill was established by 1861, and in time several other mills and plantations emerged around it.

Hawaii was integrated into the global economy over time, to the point where Maui and its neighbouring islands focus nearly exclusively on the tourism industry. This most recent economic trend has absorbed Lahaina, which now has resort status, as well as tourist-packed shops and restaurants along Front Street. One of the most acclaimed sites in Lahaina is the gargantuan banyan tree that was planted in 1873 in honour of the arrival of the missionaries 50 years earlier.

# IOLANI PALACE
## HONOLULU, HAWAII

The Kingdom of Hawaii was an independent, sovereign state prior to 1898. The Hawaiian monarchy first emerged in 1810 with the unification of the separate island chiefdoms, but lasted for little more than 80 years. The ruling King Kalakaua died while visiting San Francisco in 1891, after which his sister, Lili'uokalani, assumed the throne as queen. It had apparently been the king's desire to construct a Polynesian empire, but on 17 January 1893 the queen was deposed through a coup d'état, and was imprisoned within the Iolani Palace under house arrest. The new government briefly formed the Republic of Hawaii until being annexed by the United States in 1898. Statehood did not come until 1959. The Iolani Palace witnessed the end of this era, and is considered the only royal palace to exist under the American flag.

*Right: Hawaiians flock to the Palace in 1898 to hear news of the annexation.*

*Above: The cost of designing, building and furnishing the Palace was exorbitant for its day, essentially bankrupting the kingdom.*

### WESTERN INFLUENCE
Despite the remote location of the Hawaiian Islands in the Pacific Ocean, grandiose Hawaiian architectural projects mirrored the styles of those of Western Europe and the United States for 200 years. These styles and designs were moulded into distinctive Hawaiian

subtypes by local builders and architects who nodded to local cultural traditions. One prominent example is found in Hawaii's state capitol building, formerly the monarch's residence until 1893.

### AMERICAN FLORENTINE STYLE
The Iolani Palace in Honolulu is described as American Florentine. Its design was unique and it was provided with its own architectural category. Essentially this is a Hawaiian derivative of Renaissance Revival architecture, also known as the Italian Renaissance style. The Palace was finished in 1882 at the height of American and European interest in this revivalist mode of architecture. The Iolani Palace required four years of construction and the work of three successive architects. Thomas J. Baker, Charles J. Wall, and Isaac Moore. Baker's design cost approximately US $350,000 including furnishings and modern conveniences not yet seen at the White House.

# LITTLE TOKYO
## HISTORIC DISTRICT, LOS ANGELES, CALIFORNIA

Since the 1950s the city of Los Angeles has emerged as a leading American global metropolis. In the span of only four decades the metropolis has been transformed from the whitest American city to its most ethnically diverse. With the beginning of the 21st century, 40 per cent of the city's population was foreign born, and no specific ethnic group maintained a majority within the city. The principal Asian communities consist of people who claim Chinese, Korean, Japanese, Vietnamese, Cambodian and Filipino descent. It is in this context of urban diversity that one finds the relatively small population of Japanese-Americans holding on to their own traditional neighbourhood known as Japan Town, or Little Tokyo.

### A GROWING COMMUNITY

Only a small commercial district along First Street remains of what was once the nation's largest Japanese-American community prior to World War II. Still, the national landmark district continues to represent the heart of commercial activity that has sustained itself over the course of the city's own dynamic changes. Like many immigrant neighbourhoods throughout America, Little Tokyo behaved as an ethnic enclave and served as a haven for newly arrived foreign immigrants. The first Japanese immigrants arrived in the 1880s, though at that time Los Angeles remained small. Then the numbers of immigrants soared, along with the city's overall booming population during the early 1900s. Between 1900 and 1908, the number of Japanese who arrived in Los Angeles exceeded 10,000 people every year except 1901. Immigration peaked with 30,000 Japanese arrivals during 1907, just prior to new restrictions on immigration. Increasing demand for labour encouraged the population of Little Tokyo to swell, despite continu-

ing attempts at state and national levels to curb further immigration. By 1916 the Japanese community had found a niche, securing a strong foothold on the southern California retail industry.

The community thrived through its collective hard work and disposition toward group co-operation, cohesion and social development. Temporary credit associations called *tanomoshi-ko* were formed by Japanese businessmen to provide capital for new ventures. Formal organizations, such as the Central Japanese Association, were also established by community leaders.

### EXTERNAL INFLUENCES

A variety of influences from external sources – one disruptive and one energizing – guided the direction of Little Tokyo's development after 1940. The first was the Japanese internment program brought on by the hysteria of

*Below: Today's Little Tokyo Historic District thrives with immigrants associated with Japanese corporations in Los Angeles.*

World War II. Suspicious that any person of Japanese-American descent could be engaged in espionage for the Japanese war effort, a presidential order in 1942 authorized the internment and resettlement of all Japanese residents living along the West Coast. In their place, African-Americans moved into Little Tokyo, along with a variety of Native Americans.

With little vacant housing remaining in Little Tokyo, the Japanese-Americans returning from internment were scattered around the downtown area. Although permanently disrupted, Little Tokyo experienced a resurgence during the late 1970s when Japanese corporations made a substantial wave of investment in the Los Angeles area.

With the arrival of Japanese-owned multinational companies new Japanese shopping plazas and hotels have opened in Little Tokyo, along with branches of Japanese-owned banks. This influx of commercial development effectively transformed the urban landscape of Little Tokyo once again.

# DAVID BERRY GAMBLE HOUSE
## PASADENA, CALIFORNIA

America's "modern era" in terms of architecture began around the turn of the 20th century. The decades prior to World War II were characterized by a wide diversity of architectural styles and ideas that overlapped in popularity during this eclectic era. Architects during this era focused on revivalist designs or modern modes, but rarely both. The early modern era, prior to 1920, was marked by three aesthetic directions in architectural development: traditional revivalism, rooted in historical periods and regions, emergent Modernism, based on natural, hand-crafted materials of the Arts and Crafts Movement; and full-blown Modernism, unique to the creative forms of the 20th century.

*Above: The dining room of the Gamble House, showcasing the Modern design elements of Greene and Greene.*

### ARTS AND CRAFTS
It was in southern California, notably Pasadena, where the Arts and Crafts Movement gained substantial ground and provided the impetus for a new national craze for residential architecture. The Movement was a reaction to the

*Below: The interior is a Craftsman-style showpiece, including an inglenook with benches built into each side of the fireplace.*

extravagant, machined and mass-produced Victorian styles that in turn represented the Industrial Revolution. Specifically, the craftsmanship of the David Berry Gamble House (known as the Gamble House) played a significant role in the emergence of the Craftsman-style bungalow house form across the nation.

### GREENE AND GREENE
The Gamble House is considered one of the most significant surviving designs of the brothers Charles and Henry Greene, who partnered in their own trend-setting architectural firm in Pasadena, California. The house was commissioned as a summer home by David Gamble of the Proctor and Gamble soap company in Cincinnati, Ohio. Completed in 1908, the property is now operated as a house museum by the Friends of the Gamble House, a support group of the University of Southern California.

Greene and Greene were particularly influenced by the vernacular style of board and shingle buildings then appearing in California as well as authentic Japanese sources. Their Gamble House was considered one of several "ultimate bungalows" that provided inspiration for the succeeding wave of Craftsman-style homes that were built across the nation between 1910 and 1920, and heavily promoted by various bungalow books. Features of the Gamble House that made their way into middle-class America were its use of exposed wooden rafters and beams,

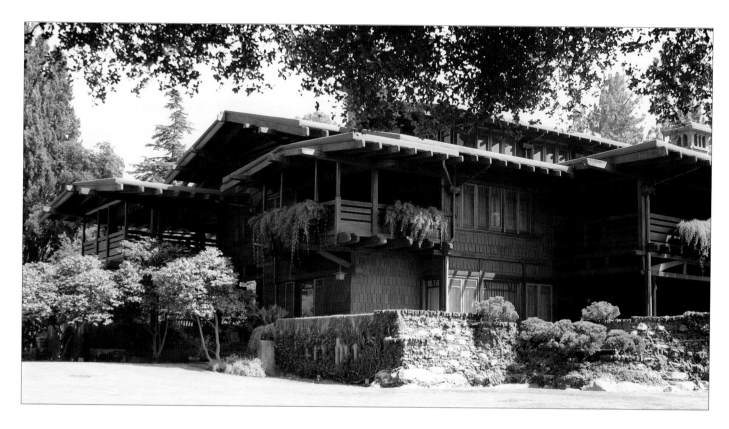

*Above: The exterior features include the low-pitched roofline, exposed rafter tails and extensive sleeping porches.*

low-pitched roofline with wide, over-hanging eaves, expansive summer porches under the main roof, and an emphasis on direct and simple decor and style. The work of Greene and Greene paralleled similar innovative modern housing referred to as the Prairie style in the Midwest, also a derivative of the Craftsman Movement.

The interior of the Gamble House is considered a Craftsman-style master-piece, heavily emphasizing the use of wood and naturalistic scenes and motifs. The three-storey, wood-framed struc-ture includes many of the interior living and guest spaces expected of wealthy homes at the turn of the 20th century: spacious living and dining rooms, a den, kitchen, pantry, cold room, entry hall, guest bedroom and four bathrooms. The expansive outdoor terraces are surfaced with hand-crafted red mission tiles,

*Right: The stairway in the home's entry-way was designed to display its intricate woodwork and joint system.*

while the floors throughout the house are oak hardwood. Also still character-istic of the time, the interior walls are generally composed of lath and plaster, prior to the popularization of drywall. Upstairs are the private living spaces – the master and children's bedrooms, family guest bedrooms, and maid's quar-ters. Accentuating the style, many of the windows are fitted with Tiffany glass panels depicting naturalistic scenes such as plants or trees.

## BUNGALOWS

The terms "craftsman" and "bungalow" are often used interchangeably, but craftsman refers to the Arts and Crafts Movement and is considered an archi-tectural or interior style. In contrast, the bungalow alludes to a particular form of building. The first bungalows in the USA appeared after the Philadelphia centennial celebrations of 1876. The bungalow form had diffused to the West Coast by the 1890s.

The popularizing of the West-Coast bungalow has been generally credited to the Greene and Greene brothers and their architectural firm in Pasadena. In 1902-03, Charles and Henry Greene were influenced by board and shingle buildings in California as well as authentic Japanese sources. One clear source for the brothers was the Japanese Hooden exhibit at the Chicago Columbian Exposition in 1893. By the 1990s the Craftsman style and its associated bun-galow form enjoyed a new resurgence of interest across America, but this time in grander forms.

# BALBOA PARK
## SAN DIEGO, CALIFORNIA

In 1868 city leaders in San Diego set aside 567ha/1,400 acres of land for a public park. Dubbed "city park", the scrub-filled mesa overlooked San Diego's "new town", serving as the present-day downtown area. Although the park remained undeveloped for two decades, transformation of the site began in 1892 when 13ha/32 acres of the land in its northwest corner was provided to Kate Sessions to run a commercial nursery. In turn, Sessions offered to plant 100 trees a year within the Park and donate 300 trees and shrubs for the city's use elsewhere. Sessions popularized several species, including the bird of paradise, queen palm and poinsettia. Her efforts are credited with the Park's first phase of landscaping and she was honoured as the Mother of Balboa Park during San Diego's second world's fair, held there in 1935. Many of the trees planted by Sessions still survive within the Park.

### THE PARK'S MASTER PLAN
Under the direction of New York landscape architect Samuel Parsons Jr, the Park's first master plan took shape after 1902. At this time many of the present-day features within the Park were set out, including roads, paths, water systems

*Above: Along with the California Tower and Cabrillo Bridge, the Spreckels Organ Pavilion (pictured here) was designed as one of the exposition's few permanent structures. The pavilion contains one of the world's largest outdoor pipe organs.*

and more trees. Plantings continued through 1910, by which time the city was already contemplating the idea of holding an exposition, or world's fair, to celebrate the completion of the Panama Canal, scheduled for 1915. As planning

*Below and below left: As an attempt to distance themselves from the popular Beaux-Arts Classicism, architecture for the Panama-California Exposition featured variations on Spanish Baroque and Renaissance Revival styles.*

ensued for the ambitious event, "city park" officially became Balboa Park as the result of a citywide naming competition. The winner was Mrs Harriet Phillips, who chose to honour Balboa for being the first documented European to view the Pacific Ocean from the Panama coastline.

### PANAMA – CALIFORNIA
The Park's most significant transformation occurred through its role in San Diego's first world's fair, held through 1915 and 1916. Preparation for the exposition became embroiled in a protracted political battle with San Francisco, which planned to host its own fair. More than city pride was at stake with such a competition, clearly indicated by the appointment of prominent San Diego businessmen to preside over the Fair – not the least being Ulysses S. Grant Jr, son of the former president. Grant was part owner of the US Grant Hotel and was elected as the president of the Panama-California Exposition Company in 1909.

More significant was the appointment of San Diego real estate developer David "Charlie" Collier to the position of director-general. "Collier shaped exposition policies", explained Richard Amero. "He chose City Park as the site, Mission Revival as the architectural style and human progress as the theme. He lobbied at his own expense for the exposition before the California State Legislature and the US Congress and travelled to South America for the same purpose." In the end, both San Diego and San Francisco held their fairs simultaneously, however, San Diego's continued for an extra year.

### SPANISH COLONIAL REVIVAL
Although they later resigned, landscape architects John C. Olmsted and Frederick Law Olmsted Jr, were hired

*Above: Today the San Diego Museum of Man is housed inside the California Tower and Dome, pictured here, which served as a distinct gateway landmark to the 1915–16 Exposition as people crossed the Cabrillo Bridge.*

*Above: The Botanical Building, with its lily pond in front, was designed for the 1915–16 Panama-California Exposition.*

to design the exposition grounds, a decision that necessarily linked San Diego with the emerging philosophies of landscape architecture originating in the Northeast. With encouragement from the Olmsteds, New York architect Bertram Goodhue applied for the exposition's position of supervisory architect, which he was ultimately offered in 1911. Prior to Goodhue's arrival, Collier and others had planned to focus the fair's architecture around the popular Mission and Pueblo styles of the American Southwest.

The focus shifted to the use of a more high-style Spanish Baroque architecture, given Goodhue's experience. The intent was to create a distinctive regional architecture that parted from the precedent to rely upon the Beaux-Arts tradition of formal, Neo-classical architecture. Goodhue and his associates

*Right: Balbao Park's buildings share a flamboyant and highly decorative architectural style.*

succeeded grandly, having "conjured up a fairy-tale city in Balboa Park of cloud-capped towers, gorgeous palaces and solemn temples. He personally designed the permanent California Quadrangle and sketched the Home Economy and Southern California Countries Buildings. He supplied Winslow and Allen with drawings and photographs of buildings in Mexico and Spain, and reviewed their designs for the temporary buildings". As a result of Goodhue's work in Balboa Park other architects

began to employ more precise imitations of elaborate Spanish architecture in their own projects.

The exposition consequently influenced the spread of what these collective architects termed the Spanish Colonial Revival style. In doing so, Goodhue's desire to move beyond the prevalent Mission style came true. This new regional approach to architecture became one of the prominent Mediterranean period styles that remained popular throughout the Southwest and Florida prior to World War II, an important contribution to America's so-called eclectic era of architectural variety.

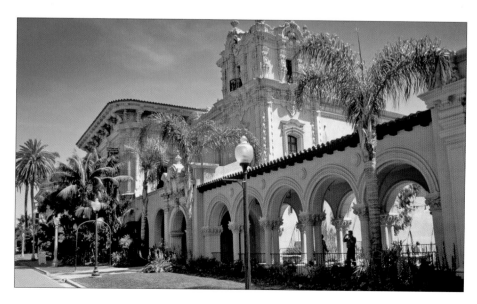

# SANTA BARBARA COURTHOUSE
## SANTA BARBARA, CALIFORNIA

Originally settled as a Spanish pueblo, mission and presidio north of Los Angeles, Santa Barbara depended upon the cattle ranching economy until its demise by the 1860s. After the Civil War the town increasingly attracted newcomers from the eastern USA keen to take advantage of the Mediterranean climate and agricultural potential of the area. It was these easterners who developed an appreciation for the Spanish heritage of their community and, as early as the 1870s, began to seek ways to preserve it.

Ultimately, community leaders in Santa Barbara constructed new buildings in the emerging Mission style. In 1914 the city gained permission to design its new post office in the Santa Barbara style, and by the 1920s leading citizens generated long-term plans to transform buildings along its main commercial thoroughfare, State Street, to reflect a more Hispanic-oriented architecture. A fiesta dubbed "old Spanish days" was initiated in 1924, which enhanced public interest in what became a romanticized version of

Spanish heritage. That same year, the city adopted a building zone ordinance to legislate for the hispanization of Santa Barbara. It survived opposition from the business community. Opposition focused on the argument that the existing commercial buildings were in fine condition and appearance, and that the ordinance was an infringement on private property rights. Enforcement of a particular architectural style was considered to be unconstitutional and un-American.

### A TWIST OF FATE
On the morning of 29 June 1925, Santa Barbara was hit by a powerful earthquake. It was not the first major quake to shake the region, but given its unstable location along the volatile Pacific Rim, this one proved the most damaging. Wood-framed houses generally rode out the event due to their flexible construction materials, but commercial and public buildings constructed of unreinforced masonry and brick were not so fortunate. Many were destroyed or damaged beyond repair, and efforts ensued

*Above: The Spanish-Moorish Revival design of the Courthouse helped to create a distinctive sense of place.*

immediately afterward to clean up and rebuild. "In a proverbial twist of fate," wrote Nancy Wood, "the destruction of Santa Barbara's commercial zone was responsible for its ultimate renewal."

More specifically, the disaster was turned into an opportunity for the city's proponents of Spanish Revival architecture, first made popular by the Panama-California Exposition in 1915. The city's Board of Safety, along with its appointed architectural advisory committee, pressed to reconstruct the downtown area entirely in the Spanish Revival design mode. Proponents asserted that the earthquake provided the impetus to create a "unique and individual locale". Economic as well as cultural interests were at stake here, and it was recognized that the invention of a unique image for the community would help to promote Santa Barbara and make it a thriving tourist spot, like Santa Fe, New Mexico. An architectural board of review

*Left: A powerful earthquake in 1925 ultimately led to the construction of numerous Spanish Revival buildings.*

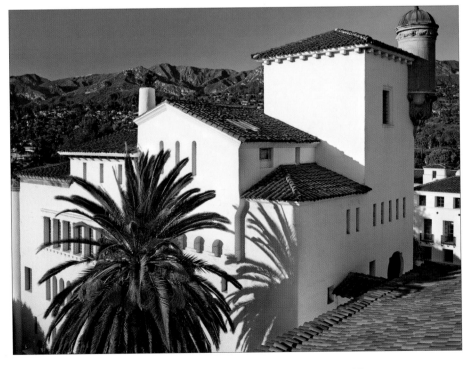

was formed to review each proposed building prior to issuing a building permit. The board was eventually disbanded due to some vocal opposition, but not before numerous Spanish Revival buildings had been approved by 1926. The trend mushroomed, with later buildings designed to conform with the Spanish designs of earlier ones. It is in this context that the new Santa Barbara County Courthouse was designed and constructed. Ultimately it was a masterpiece of Spanish-Moorish Revival architecture, and one of America's most prominent examples of the style.

### COURTHOUSE DESIGN

Like much of the business district, the original Courthouse and Jail complex were severely damaged during the earthquake. The Bounty Board of

*Below: Spanish Revival decor was heavily employed for the Courthouse interior as well as its external facade.*

*Above: The principal commercial thoroughfare, State Street, was developed around the Spanish Revival theme.*

Supervisors was determined to rebuild on the same site. In 1926 a Spanish-Moorish design was chosen for the new Courthouse, which ultimately provided further inspiration for the style within the community. The San Francisco firm of William Mooser was commissioned to design the Courthouse, a company then in its third generation, headed by William Mooser Jr and William Mooser

III. The latter grandson had graduated from the École des Beaux Arts in Paris, which had already influenced many prominent American architects ahead of him. Mooser III had also spent 17 years residing in France and Spain, enhancing his knowledge of the region and its architecture. Joining the Moosers in the Courthouse design were other architects including the local Santa Barbara firm of Edwards and Plunkett.

Modelled on an Andalusian fortress, the new Courthouse complex actually comprised four buildings integrated into a unified design, including a five-storey jail. Completed in 1929, the new courthouse was described by the acclaimed architect Charles Moore as "The grandest Spanish Colonial Revival structure ever built".

Along with the Courthouse, which remains unique among public buildings in America, the commercial landscape of downtown Santa Barbara retains its Spanish Revival dominance to this day.

# THE ROSE BOWL
## PASADENA, CALIFORNIA

In California the ocean borders a cool coastal desert environment, creating a Mediterranean climate with mild winters and warm summers. This small corner of land is viewed by the rest of America as an ecological wonder of the habitable world. By the turn of the 20th century southern California was being promoted as the land of perpetual spring, and a potential new home to Midwesterners and Easterners assumed to be fed up with their brutal winters. Despite the fact that this paradise had no water to support intense agriculture or a massive urban population, or a naturally deep harbour, (which would have to be dug out at tremendous expense to create the Ports of Los Angeles and Long Beach), the pull for many Americans – and real estate investors promoting the place – was too great to ignore.

### MIGRATION WEST

The first great wave of Americans discovered southern California through railroad excursion tickets on the new transcontinental route of the Santa Fe Railroad. Many of them decided to stay. Later came the wave of people from

*Above: Now a nationally famous event, the Tournament of Roses Parade eventually began as a local festival designed to advertise California's climate to the residents of the Eastern USA.*

Oklahoma seeking a better life during the Dust Bowl and Depression years. Southern California became the Midwest transplanted. Ironically, Long Beach was often described as the primary sea port of Iowa! The attractive region soon provided its own culture.

### THE TOURNAMENT OF ROSES

It was in this context of selling California as a home to the people of the Midwest that the Rose Bowl came to be. When the first Tournament of Roses was conducted in 1890, much of Pasadena and the southern California region was agrarian, focused on Mediterranean-type crops such as olives, vines and citrus fruits. Members of the Pasadena Valley Hunt Club who organized the first tournament did so specifically to boost the attractive image of the region to unknowing Easterners.

The club was made up of Easterners and Midwesterners who wanted to show the produce of their new home. "In New York, people are buried in snow", said Professor Charles Holder at a club meeting. "Here our flowers are blooming and our oranges are about to bear. Let's hold a festival to tell the world about our paradise." Holder was a local naturalist and author, and it was he who suggested a celebration of New Year's Day to the local Valley Hunt Club. To further honour the onset of

*Left: The design of the football stadium took its inspiration from the Yale Bowl in New Haven, Connecticut.*

the orange season, Holder suggested the idea of decorating buggies with flowers and parading them through the city.

The celebration became an annual event, growing in scope to include floats and marching bands. Games were held on the town lot, which was renamed Tournament Park in 1900. Exotic events such as ostrich racing were offered along with bronco-busting demonstrations and other circus-type spectacles. By 1895 Eastern newspapers were offering wide publicity of the annual festival. In that year the Tournament of Roses Association was formed to manage the affair. College football came to the festival in 1902, and provided the venue for America's first post-season game. Football was replaced a year later with Romanesque chariot racing because the

*Below: Located in the scenic valley of the Arroyo Seco, today's Rose Bowl provides a capacity of nearly 100,000 and is the setting for major post-season college football games.*

Stanford football team had fared badly against the Michigan team at the event. The game returned in 1916, given the growing national football craze. The huge crowds soon outgrew the modest facilities in Tournament Park, and a new stadium was envisioned.

## YALE BOWL
In 1920 the tournament's president, William Leishman, looked to the trend-setting Yale Bowl in Connecticut for inspiration. Soon an emerging Eastern cultural institution was transplanted to the West Coast. Yale Bowl, with an original unprecedented capacity of 70,869, was completed in 1914. Also a National Historic Landmark, the football stadium was built at Yale University in New Haven, Connecticut, through the excavation of the field, followed by the build-up of earth around its perimeter. The result was the shape of an elliptical bowl, the first of its kind in the nation. The Yale Bowl inspired numerous other stadia that grew in

response to the rise of college football into the realm of big-time national sports.

## EXPANSION
Construction on the new stadium commenced in 1921 on city land purchased years earlier along the Arroyo Seco, a picturesque valley just west of Pasadena's downtown area. Originally, the stadium was designed in the shape of a horseshoe, with its south end left open. A police reporter named Harlan Hall – also thinking of the Yale Bowl – coined the name "rose bowl". The first game was played there on 28 October 1922 featuring an interstate rivalry between the University of California Bears and the University of Southern California Trojans. In 1929 the open end of the stadium was closed in, raising the crowd capacity to 76,000. In 2009 the Rose Bowl's capacity was officially recorded at 92,542. It remains home to the University of California, Los Angeles (UCLA) Bruins and many other community and sporting events.

# BONNEVILLE DAM
## HISTORIC DISTRICT, BONNEVILLE, CASCADE ISLAND, WASHINGTON

In an unprecedented effort to limit the Great Depression, the Bonneville Dam became a pivotal project of President Franklin D. Roosevelt's New Deal administration. The dam and its associated hydropower facilities are located 40 miles east of Portland, Oregon, within the Columbia River Gorge.

### THE DEPRESSION
Although not often perceived as a common landscape feature, hundreds of dams were built across the nation from the 1930s to the 1960s – collectively to harness hydroelectric power, to store water and to reduce natural floods. A greater impact to the natural landscape has arguably occurred with the creation of spacious reservoirs behind the dams, in this case that of Lake Bonneville. Such manmade lakes have fundamentally altered (and drowned) their prior natural environments. Conversely, communities at their peripheries have discovered economic benefits from their potential for tourism and recreation.

During the Roosevelt years, the earliest dam projects were also designed to provide jobs and hope for the future. The Bonneville Dam, near the mouth of the Columbia River between

Washington and Oregon, was one of the earliest and most impressive projects. By the time Roosevelt became president in 1933, nearly one in four American adults was unemployed. The new president believed that the only thing that would dramatically change that condition was the creation of public works projects in the form of bridges, freeways, tunnels, parks and dams. Under President Roosevelt the Bureau of Reclamation increased in size and scope from less than 3,000 employees to a staff of nearly 20,000 by the time Roosevelt died.

*Above: Along with the Grand Coulee and Hoover dams, the Bonneville example ushered in America's dam-building era in the mid-20th century.*

Although its headquarters were located in the nation's capital, much of the work designing new dam projects was accomplished in Denver, Colorado, indicating the significance of the West for signature dam-building events. Having tracked the murky political origins of the great western dam projects, author Mark Reisner summarized: "The Great Depression and the Roosevelt administration, together with the pyramid-scheme economics of the river-basin accounts, were more than enough to launch the federal dam-building program on a 40-year binge. It probably wouldn't have needed the Dust Bowl – but it helped." It was in this context – federal and regional politics, national depression, and continued growth of the American West, in which the Bonneville Dam came to be.

*Left: Massive development and dam-building projects in the Northwest laid the groundwork for the region's later specialty of aircraft production.*

## CONSTRUCTION

True to its publicized purpose, the Bonneville project constituted one of North America's most massive and challenging engineering achievements, employing more than 3,000 workers. The bulk of Bonneville Dam and its powerhouse were completed between 1933 and 1937, simultaneous with the planning and construction of the Grand Coulee Dam and the Hoover Dam. Unlike Hoover, Bonneville included a lock system to allow navigation farther upstream. Together, these public works projects indicated a substantial national commitment to the economic development of the Pacific Northwest.

## INDUSTRIAL PROGRESS

New industries emerged along the Columbia River to take advantage of relatively inexpensive electricity and improved navigation. Most notable was the emergence of the aluminium, aircraft manufacturing and shipbuilding activities, contributing directly to national defence throughout the 20th century.

It is not exaggerating to state that the Columbia River dams helped to determine the outcome of World War II. At the time war broke out in Europe, Germany had enjoyed a significant head start with building its military machine. In contrast, the forces of Britain and France were no match for the Germans,

nor of the USA. However, with its signature Western dams complete by 1942, America held a distinct advantage with respect to its tremendous surplus of hydroelectric power. "No one knows exactly how many planes and ships were manufactured with Bonneville and Grand Coulee electricity," states Reisner, "but it is safe to say that the war would have been seriously prolonged at the least without the dams".

By 1942, 92 per cent of the power generated by the two dams was utilized for the war effort, the bulk of it to build

*Above: More expansive than the dam itself is the large reservoir that formed behind it, drowning entire valleys and habitats. Such reservoirs as Bonneville Lake have served as fresh-water supplies and recreational facilities across the nation.*

planes. Later in the war, the Pacific Northwest was home to almost half of the nation's aluminium production, again enabled from the prodigious power supply. Neither Germany or Japan could compete, nor could they replace their military aircraft supply as could the USA during the War. The cheap energy was also used to power a super-secret military installation along the Columbia River referred to as the Hanford Reservation. Eight reactors produced plutonium here, requiring tremendous sums of energy. The facility was tied into the Manhattan Project and, consequently, to the important work on the atomic bomb at Los Alamos.

*Left: The Dam instantly blocked the migration of fish upstream, necessitating the creation of "fish ladders", seen here, to assist native salmon and steelhead move past the dam on their way upstream to spawn.*

# PEARL HARBOR
## SOUTH COAST OF OAHU ISLAND, HAWAII

Located 13km/8 miles from Honolulu on the island of Oahu, Pearl Harbor has served for more than a century as a vital hub of support for the American Navy's Pacific Fleet. The strategic spot, serving as a crossroads between Asia and America, contributed greatly to the rise of the USA into a global power during the 20th century. The landlocked port's mission has consistently been to shelter, arm, repair and update the American Fleet's wide variety of ships, submarines and aircraft.

Construction on the base began in 1902, soon after the annexation of Hawaii to the United States. The earliest project involved the expansion of the harbour to allow larger ships to obtain access farther inland. As early as 1900 congress voted to approve funds to improve the Harbor entrance, the same year when negotiations began to acquire adjoining land for a future naval station. America was once again intruding upon a native, polytheistic culture. The project involved the destruction of a

native fish pond and fish god shrine, which necessitated ceremonies intended to placate the Hawaiian gods prior to the dredging of the Harbor entrance.

Congress authorized the development of a major naval base in 1908, and construction of an enormous dry-dock was started the following year. It collapsed and the incident delayed the project by ten years. The Hawaiians attributed the incident to the placement of the dry-dock atop the shark queen's son. Regardless, the project ensued, as did the growth of associated docks, stores and additional functions designed to support

*Above: The USS Arizona National Memorial spans the visible sunken hull of the battleship.*

an important military base. Pearl Harbor's official opening was marked in 1911 with the docking of the *USS California*, the first large ship to enter the bay. Soon after the construction of an administration building in 1915, Pearl Harbor was designated the headquarters of a naval district, which ultimately led to the base's status as command centre for all naval operations within the Pacific.

### JAPAN

While America was growing into the role of a global power through its own military expansion, the Japanese empire was doing likewise. It was at Pearl Harbor where the two expanding

*Left: The USS Arizona sinks during Japan's surprise attack on 7 December 1941, "a date that will live in infamy", as President F. D. Roosevelt declared.*

*Above: Today's Pearl Harbor continues to serve as a strategic naval base for American operations in the Pacific realm.*

powers intersected, on 7 December 1941 with the Japanese aerial assault on the base. Although a decision that ultimately led to the Japanese empire's demise, the bombardment was from a geographer's perspective the latest event within a lengthy history of territorial expansion and cultural transformation. The first prominent phase of this process occurred during Japan's Meiji era (1868–1912), when the country began a strategic campaign to westernize – that is, modernize – its society and government. Once a mysterious and insular society, Japan's leaders recognized that successful competition with the West required that they learn from it as well.

The westernization of Japan occurred rather suddenly, and greatly influenced nearly all aspects of traditional culture. Japanese students were sent to western countries to observe their practices, and western scholars were paid to visit Japan with the aim of educating the population directly. Japan's economic development and national stability were conditioned upon the

*Right: A view from a Japanese plane shows a plume rising from the water during the surprise attack in 1941.*

growth of its military force. In less than 50 years, imperial Japan evolved into a dominant economic and military force within Eastern and Southeastern Asia, precisely as a result of industrialization and economic development.

### AN AGGRESSIVE EMPIRE

Japan's industrial development both encouraged and necessitated the nation's territorial expansion to secure resources that its small islands could not adequately provide – an ongoing challenge for Japan to this day. The result was the expansion of a territorial empire after 1894 that behaved in a highly aggressive manner, to the point where much of the world condemned the empire's brutal practices

on those conquered. From Japan's perspective, its leaders had seen the colonization of numerous, previously sovereign, Asian nations, one of the latest being Spain's claim to the Philippines. The result of Japan's own expansion strategy was not only its ability to secure raw materials and shipping channels, but its continued status as one of the world's few remaining nations not to succumb to a colonial power. Although remaining sovereign, the ultimate toll was heavy.

The Japanese became ruthless expansionists, to the point where they entered World War I and declared war on Germany in 1914. Their interest was not so much the acquisition of Western European territory as the intention to occupy German-leased territories in China. Within a few short decades, the Japanese empire claimed control over a realm that included Korea, Taiwan, Manchuria and pieces of northern China. It was still too remote for its land-based expansionism, so Pearl Harbor became the so-called high-water mark of Japanese imperial expansion, with its notorious attack on the base. The action precipitated America's entry into World War II, and the removal of Japanese-Americans to internment camps. Today the USS Arizona National Memorial, which sits above the sunken ship, is the only part of the Pearl Harbor naval base that is open to the public.

# ARCHITECTURAL STYLE GLOSSARY

**Art Deco** A style of decorative art and architecture popular in the 1920s and 1930s, representing early Modernism. French in origin, Art Deco design celebrated the machine, industry and the future. Design typically emphasized vertical motifs, geometric or stylized forms and a smooth, machined appearance.

**Art Moderne (Streamlined Modern)** Similar to Art Deco but emphasizing horizontal, streamlined forms. Building facades often employed metallic sheathing, ribbon windows and curved or rounded corners. Ships, trains, cars and household appliances were also designed in this sleek, streamlined style.

**Baroque** Early-17th-century style characterized by Classical motifs, dramatic colours and ornamentation. Broken pediments, curving facades and floral mouldings were common. Associated with the architecture of European palaces and Roman Catholic churches.

**Beaux Arts** Named for the Ecole des Beaux Arts in France, this style is based on Classical precedents dominated by lavish decoration and massive construction forms. Widely adopted for grand civic and commercial buildings.

*Below: Art Moderne style*

**Byzantine** An extension of Classical Roman architecture, the style relied upon geometric complexity; the use of brick, stone and plaster and increased use of Classical columns, complex domes, mosaics and windows. It emerged as an Exotic Revival style in America around the turn of the 20th century.

**Classicism** In architecture this refers to the emulation of the forms of Classical antiquity, including earlier Greek and later Roman orders.

**Colonial Revival** A series of styles that reflected colonial and early American precedents. Popular following the centennial celebrations of 1876 and went on to dominate residential and commercial architecture. The revived Classical forms (Greek, Dutch, Georgian and Federal) were a reaction to the ostentation of the Victorian era.

**Craftsman** A material form of the Arts and Crafts Movement during the late 19th and early 20th centuries. It promoted the use of authentic and simple design elements, and handmade instead of manufactured. This was a movement that reacted to the Industrial Revolution and became a national craze from 1910–30, featuring such elements as low-pitched, gabled roofs, wide and unenclosed eve overhangs for porch areas, exposed roof rafters and knee braces, and full or partial-width porches supported with tapered square columns.

**Exotic Revivals** A collection of revival styles that occasionally appeared during the late 19th and early 20th centuries. These revivals are termed exotic due to their source regions. Often applied to grand hotels, theatres or commercial buildings, variations of Egyptian, Byzantine, Moorish and Swiss-chalet forms were applied to Victorian homes.

*Above: Georgian style*

**Federal** A style that emerged in America during the 1780s and 1820s. Also referred to as the Adam style, after the Adam brothers who were prominent architects in Britain. The style is a refinement of the earlier Georgian style, emphasizing the use of semicircular or elliptical fan lights above the entryway, decorative cornices, balustrades, sash windows and the formal symmetry of Renaissance Classicism.

**Georgian** Architecture named for the period between 1714 and 1811 and during the reign of the English kings George I, II and III. Adopted in England, Georgian style diffused to all of America's English colonies on the East Coast. The style features Renaissance-Classical motifs and formal, symmetrical facades.

**Gothic Revival** The first Victorian-era style in America, inspired by the Gothic cathedrals of England and France that appeared after 1200AD. The style was adopted for residential and ecclesiastical architecture. It featured combinations of pointed-arch (lancet) windows and doorways, vaulted-arch ceilings, steeply pitched roofs, Picturesque floor plans and occasional castellated parapets (battlements). It remained popular for American churches through the 1940s.

**Greek Revival** Considered America's first national style and promoted by Thomas Jefferson to symbolize the new American democracy. It was based on original Greek Classical forms and included variations of the Doric, Ionic, and Corinthian orders. It became America's dominant architectural style from the 1820s until the Civil War, featuring temple-front porticos, Greek columns, frieze bands and pediments.

**High Victorian Gothic** One of numerous revival styles to appear during the late 19th century. It was a highly elaborate and colourful version of Gothic architecture during the late Victorian era.

**International** This style dominated commercial and civic architecture from the 1950s to the late 1970s. The strictly functional mode epitomized the height of the Modern Movement in the United States and Europe. Pragmatic utilitarianism became the driving force, as so-called "anonymous glass boxes" (glass-covered office towers) appeared in commercial districts.

**Italian Renaissance** Also referred to as **Renaissance Revival**, this style became one of the more popular national revival or period styles around the turn of the 20th century until the Great Depression. Different building forms elicited a wide variety of interpretations of the style, from the rusticated stonework of elaborate civic and commercial buildings to more informal low-pitched tile roofs of residential neighbourhoods.

**Italianate** Inspired initially by the Renaissance-era villas and manors of northern Italy, the style became one of America's most popular architectural choices for commercial, residential and civic buildings prior to and during the Civil War. Adopted as a Picturesque style of the Romantic Movement, Italianate features include tall, arched windows,

elaborate cornices at the roofline, overhanging eaves with ornamental brackets and low-pitched roofs.

**Italian Villa** Like Italianate architecture, this style was inspired by the Renaissance villas of northern Italy but with more accurate representations of the villa styling. Typically including a square tower or campanile, it is this feature that differentiates the Italian Villa style from the more boxy Italianate style.

**Mission Revival** A simplified American Craftsman style focused on regions previously colonized by the Spanish. The style sought to emulate previous architectural features of Spanish Colonial missions, especially the omnipresent Mission-style rounded parapet. It remained popular, especially in California, the Southwest and Florida through World War II.

**Modern (or Modernism)** An umbrella term that describes the modern architectural movement in America and Europe during much of the 20th century, emphasizing simplicity of form, lack of ornamentation and stylistic abstraction. The focus of Modernist architecture is on the future, and it is designed to promote function. It is viewed as the antithesis to "historicism". Modern architecture includes early

*Below: Italian Villa style*

*Above: Greek Revival style*

Craftsman, Art Deco, and Art Moderne motifs prior to World War II, and the later Bauhaus and International styles that dominated American and European building forms through the 1980s.

**Moorish** Inspired by the Islamic architecture of Spain and northern Africa, this style features banded or polychromatic masonry, turrets with onion domes and latticework windows. Rare in America, it was one of a number of Exotic Revival styles that appeared at the start of the 20th century.

**Neo-classical Revival** A popular revival or period style from 1895 to 1950 that became the dominant form of residential and commercial architecture prior to World War II. The revival of interest in Greek and Roman architecture can be traced to the centennial celebrations of 1876 but especially to the World's Columbian Exposition held in Chicago in 1893. This is where the Beaux-Arts and less refined Neo-classical revival styles made their long-lasting impact on American tastes and interest in historical styles. The Neo-classical style competed with emerging Modern architecture during this period.

**Norman** Essentially a regional name for Romanesque architecture, referred to as Norman in England and France. Both styles are characterized by heavy masonry construction, cavernous window and doorway openings, geometric decoration and the use of the rounded Roman arch. Like Romanesque, Norman remained popular as the first Roman revival style in Europe until around 1200AD, when it was gradually supplanted with the Gothic style and its pointed or lancet arches. Examples of Norman Revival appeared sporadically in America during the 19th century.

**Palladian** Italy's Andrea Palladio studied and revived Greek and Roman classical forms for his own Renaissance architecture during the 16th century, in turn inspiring further Classical and Greek revivals. His style became popular throughout Europe and into the English colonies, spawning the Georgian and Greek revival styles. Thomas Jefferson, considered the last of the true Palladian architects, designed the University of Virginia and his home of Monticello directly on Palladian precedents in Italy.

**Picturesque** Considered both a style and a cultural movement in England and America, especially during the 19th century. It started a trend away from classical symmetry toward more romanticized, informal styles and landscaping and was promoted in America by the horticulturalist Andrew Jackson Downing. The movement coincided with many Victorian-era styles, from the

*Below: Rustic style*

*Above: Prairie style*

earlier Gothic Revival and Italianate to the later Queen Anne and Stick styles.

**Prairie** One of America's few home-grown styles, developed by a collection of Chicago architects known as the Prairie School during the early 20th century. Frank Lloyd Wright is essentially the "father" of Prairie style, and the acknowledged master of the Prairie house. His Prairie style focused on midwestern geography, with horizontal, open floor plans. In addition to subtle uses of Japanese motifs, the Prairie style featured horizontal and flowing interior spaces, hipped roofs with broad eaves and long bands of windows.

**Postmedieval English** Describes the dominant style and building form of the English colonies from the early 1600s to just after 1700, when Georgian architecture began to appear. During this period of western history and development, traditional Medieval building ways were giving way to Renaissance-era classical approaches. The earliest English Colonial houses in America exemplified this transition, featuring asymmetrical floor plans, steeply pitched Medieval roofs, leaded casement windows and cantilevered second floors, or jetties.

**Postmodern** Our most recent and current era, associated with architecture appearing since the 1970s. Often referred to as Neo-eclectic, essentially

representing a revival of period styles for houses. Postmodernism is basically an allusion to the past, with multiple associations and meanings. It is a rejection of Modernist thought, a return to traditional, historical precedents based on a vague, re-awakened interest in history and heritage. Postmodern houses include Neo-Mansard, Neo-colonial, Neo-French, Neo-Victorian, Neo-Mediterranean, Neo-classical Revival and Neo-Tudor. Commercial and corporate buildings are likewise characterized by bizarre shapes and angles along with sleek, metallic or masonry facades with occasional hints of historical styles.

**Queen Anne** One of the last Victorian styles, widely popular for residential and commercial architecture between 1880 and 1900. The style invited numerous, unrelated design features such as turrets, porches, gables, dormers, bay windows and wall sheathing. Houses were characterized by asymmetrical and colourful facades, and an emphasis on vertical, rounded corner towers, brackets and gingerbread trim.

**Renaissance Revival** The American Renaissance was a movement of the fine arts and architecture during the late 19th century, and a quest for an American version. The revival style is synonymous with Beaux-Arts architecture and the City Beautiful movement that gained popularity following Chicago's Columbian Exposition of 1893. Adopted primarily for grand civic or commercial buildings, the style makes use of heavy stone or brick construction, Classical symmetry and details, and rusticated stonework on the lower floor.

**Rococo Revival** A French-inspired interior design style most popular in America during the mid-19th century. Furniture was characterized by a fragile and slender appearance, heavily carved natural forms and a reliance on the S-curve, or serpentine line. The style became pervasive in nearly every form of interior feature, including carpets, wallpaper, curtains, fireplace mantels, ceiling plasterwork and many others.

**Romanesque Revival** Often referred to in America as Richardsonian Romanesque, in honour of its founding Boston architect, Henry Hobson Richardson. Popular during the late 19th century, it relied heavily on rugged interpretations of earlier Romanesque architecture in Europe, and featured heavy, massive construction with brick or stone, especially featuring the Roman arch for window and door openings. It was employed for grand civic and commercial architecture.

**Romantic** Romantic styles in America included Gothic Revival, Italianate and Italian Villa, a manifestation of the wider romantic movement in Britain and America during the 19th century. Romanticism was viewed by many as a reaction against the enlightenment that emphasized reasoning and science. Rather, Romanticism emphasized intuition, imagination and sensitivity, the antithesis of rational thinking.

**Rustic** A vague term used to describe this derivative of the Craftsman style, adopted widely for national park architecture during the early 20th century. Spokesmen for the Romantic Movement in the Eastern United States had advocated for a greater sensitivity to America's natural settings and contexts, and romantic notions of the Western frontier accompanied this movement. The Rustic style was an outgrowth of these sentiments. Stylistic features include rough, hand-crafted stone and logs, and an emphasis on log construction and wood interior decor.

**Santa Fe** Also referred to as Pueblo Revival. This style was invented to distinguish the state of New Mexico from the popular Mission style architecture of southern California. Also after New

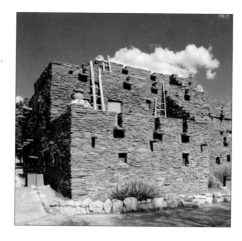

*Above: Pueblo style*

Mexico gained statehood in 1912, it was viewed as an approach to attract tourists and promote the new state's own identity. The style was inspired by a mixture of Spanish Colonial and Native American Pueblo architectural forms. It originated in Santa Fe, New Mexico.

**Second Empire** A formal, Renaissance-inspired style popular during the 1870s that imitated contemporary architectural trends in mid-19th century Paris. Its identifying feature is the steeply pitched Mansard roof, often placed atop earlier Italianate-style buildings. The style is named after France's Second Empire during the reign of Napoleon III and was adopted widely for residential, commercial and civic architecture.

**Shingle** Appeared during the 1880s and 1890s. The Shingle style constituted a creative blend of contemporary and earlier Victorian stylistic forms, including wide porches and shingled facades of the Queen Anne style, gambrel roofs, classical columns and Palladian windows, and sculpted shapes and Romanesque arches. This free-form and eclectic style was concentrated in the seaside resorts of the Northeastern United States.

**Stick** Considered a transition style between Gothic Revival and Queen Anne, it appeared briefly during the 1860s and 1870s. It features Picturesque

asymmetry and is identified primarily by "sticks" consisting of undecorated, milled boards applied to a building's facade. They became a popular Victorian-era feature because the sticks were used to reduce the monotony of otherwise plain facades.

**Spanish Revival** A popular historical revival or period style with strong regional influences in southern California, Florida and Texas around the turn of the 20th century. The style was inspired by the architecture of Spain and Latin America. It includes a low-pitched, tiled roof; little or no eave overhang; a prominent arch over the door, window or porch; a stucco wall surface; and typically an asymmetrical facade.

**Territorial** A simplified, Western American version of the Greek Revival style, it dominated early architecture on commercial and residential buildings within America's pioneer and frontier towns in the West up through the 1860s, and featured slender, square porch columns, Greek-style dentil courses and raw timber fashioned into door and window frames that emulated Greek forms.

**Victorian** More correctly identified as an era, closely defined by the lengthy reign of England's Queen Victoria between 1837 and 1901.

*Below: Craftsman style*

# VISITING THE LANDMARKS

Boston Common
www.cityofboston.gov

Mount Auburn Cemetery
www.mountauburn.org

Old Ship Meeting House
www.oldshipchurch.org

Newport Historic District
www.cityofnewport.com

Old Deerfield Village
www.historic-deerfield.org

Old North Church
www.oldnorth.com

Parson Capen House
www.topsfieldhistory.org

Quincy Market
www.faneuilhallmarketplace.com

Canterbury Shaker Village
www.shakers.org

Kingscote, Marble House and
    The Breakers
www.newportmansions.org

Morse-Libby House
www.victoriamansion.org

Rockingham Meeting House
Bellows Falls Historical Society
tel: +1 802-463-3734

Connecticut State Capitol
www.cga.ct.gov/capitoltours

*Above: Sandy Hook Light*

Fort Niagara
www.oldfortniagara.org

Elfreth's Alley
www.elfrethsalley.org

Sandy Hook Light
www.lighthousefriends.com

Erie Canal
www.canals.ny.gov

Lyndhurst
www.lyndhurst.wordpress.com

Central Park
www.centralpark.com

Geneseo Historic District
www.geneseony.com

Tenement Building
www.tenement.org

Memorial Hall
www.pleasetouchmuseum.org

Allegheny County Courthouse
www.alleghenycounty.us/about
    /jail.aspx

Grand Central Terminal
www.grandcentralterminal.com

Metropolitan Museum of Art
www.metmuseum.org

Empire State Building
www.esbnyc.com

Rockefeller Center
www.rockefellercenter.com

Playland Amusement Park
www.westchestergove.com/
    playland

Bacon's Castle
www.apva.org/BaconsCastle

Williamsburg Historic District
www.visitwilliamsburg.com

Georgetown Historic District
www.nps.gov/nr/travel/wash/
    dc15.htm

Alexandra Historic District
www.alexandriava.gov/
    preservation

Tuckahoe Plantation
www.tuckahoeplantation.com

Mount Vernon
www.mountvernon.org

White House and Executive
    Office Building
www.whitehouse.gov/about/
    tours-and-events

Virginia State Capitol
www.virginiacapitol.gov

US Capitol
www.aoc.gov

The Baltimore & Ohio
    Railroad Museum
ww.borail.org/

*Below: Virginia State Capitol*

Smithsonian Institution
    Building
www.si.edu

Jackson Ward Historic District
www.jacksonward.com

The Pentagon
www.dtic.mil/ref/html/
    welcome/tours.html

St Augustine Town Plan
    Historic District
www.oldcity.com

Savannah Historic District
www.officialsavannahguide
    .com

Magnolia Plantation
www.magnoliaplantation.com

Oakland Plantation
www.visitnatchez.org

Charleston Historic District
www.discovercharleston.com

Ybor City Historic District
www.ybor.org

Longwood
www.natchezpilgrimage.com

Strand/Mechanic National
    Historic Landmark District
www.galvestonhistory.blogspot
    .com

Tampa Bay Hotel
www.plantmuseum.com

Cape Canaveral Air Force
    Station
www.kennedyspacecenter.com

Astor Fur Warehouse
www.wisconsinhistory.org

Missouri Botanical Gardens
www.mobot.org

Mark Twain Boyhood Home
www.marktwainmuseum.org

Pullman Historic District
www.pullmanil.org

*Below: Quincy Market*

Union Station
www.stlouisunionstation.com

Marshall Field & Company
   Store
www.macys.com

Cleveland Arcade
+1 216-776-1131

Ohio Theatre
www.capa.com

World War Memorial Plaza
www.nps.gov/nr/travel/
   indianapolis/wwmemorial
   plaza.htm

Indianapolis Motor Speedway
www.indianapolismotor
   speedway.com

Arthur Heurtley House
www.gowright.org

John Farson House
www.pleasanthome.org

S. R. Crown Hall
+1 312-567-3104

Gateway Arch
www.gatewayarch.com

State Capitol, Raleigh
www.nchistoricsites.com

Bathhouse Row
www.hotsprings.org

Perryville Battlefield
www.parks.ky.gov

Pinehurst Historic District
www.pinehurst.com

Churchill Downs
www.churchilldowns.com

Wright Brothers National
   Memorial Visitor Center
www.nps.gov/wrbr/index.html

Biltmore Estate
www.biltmore.com

Beale Street Historic District
www.bealestreet.com

Wounded Knee Battlefield
www.woundedkneemuseum
   .org

*Above: Spring Hill Ranch*

Spring Hill Ranch
www.nps.gov/tapr

Nebraska State Capitol
www.capitol.org

Nicodemus Historic District
www.nps.gov/nico

Highland Park Shopping
   Village
www.hpvillage.com

Temple Square
www.visittemplesquare.com

Union Pacific Railroad Depot
www.cheyennedepot
   museum.org

Bodie Historic District
www.bodie.com

Old Sacramento
www.oldsacramento.com

Virginia City Historic District
www.nps.gov/nr/travel/nevada

Silverton Historic District and
   Durango–Silverton Narrow
   Gauge Line
www.durangotrain.com

Virginia City Historic District
www.yellowstonegeotourism
   .org

Columbia River Highway
www.columbiariverhighway
   .com

Butte-Anaconda-Walkerville
   Historic District
www.mainstreetbutte.org

Old Faithful Inn
www.yellowstonenational
   parkslodges.com/old-
   fathful-inn-96.html

J. C. Penney Historic District
http://kemmerer.org/jcpenney

Mount Rainier National Park
www.nps.gov/mora

Taos Pueblo
www.taospueblo.com

San Xavier Del Bac Mission
www.sanxaviermission.org

Presidio Nuestra Senora de
   Loreto de la Bahia
www.presidiolabahia.org

Santa Fe Plaza
www.santafe.org

The Alamo
www.thealamo.org

Hubbell Trading Post
www.nps.gov/hutr

Tombstone Historic District
www.visittombstone.org

Grand Canyon Village
www.grandcanyon.com

Hoover Dam
www.usbr.gov/lc/hooverdam

*Below: Presidio Nuestro
Senora*

*Above: Pearl Harbor*

St Michael the Archangel
   Cathedral
www.stmichaelsarchangel.org

San Francisco Cable Cars
www.sfcablecar.com

Presidio of San Francisco
www.nps.gov/prsf

Skidmore Old Town Historic
   District
www.portlandonline.com

Pioneer Building, Pergola and
   Totem Pole
www.pioneer-building.com

Skagway Historic District and
   White Pass
www.discoverskagway.com

Iolani Palace
www.iolanipalace.org

David Berry Gamble House
www.gamblehouse.org

Balboa Park
www.balboapark.org

Santa Barbara Courthouse
www.santabarbara
   courthouse.org

The Rose Bowl
www.rosebowlstadium.com

Pearl Harbor
www.pearlharboroahu.com

# INDEX

*Above: Smithsonian Institute*

*Above: Gateway Arch*

*Below: New York Stock Exchange*

*Above: Canterbury Shaker Village*

## PICTURE CREDITS
Alamy; pages 2, 3, 4 second from t, second from b, 7t, 5c below t, 6b and t, 8b, 10t, 12tl, 16b, 19bl and br, 20t and b, 21bl and br, 22t and b, 24t, 25b and tc, 26b, 27t, 28b, 29b, 32b, 33bl, bc and t, 34t, 38t, 39b, 40–1, 42t, 43b, 45b and t, 46tc and b, 47b, 51t and b, 55br, 56t, 58, 59t and b, 62, 65t, 68, 69tc, b and tr, 71t and b, 72t, 77t, 79tl, tr, bl and br, 80t, 81tc and b, 89, 91, 92b, 94–5, 96t, 97br, 98t, 99b, 100t and b, 101bl and br, 103b, 104t and bc, 105b, 106b, 107b, 110t, 111b, 113t and b, 114t, 115tc, 117b, 120t, 122b, 123b, 124t and b, 125t and b, 126b, 127t and b, 128t, 129, 131tc, 132b, 136, 138, 139t, bc and br, 140t, 141b, 142t and b, 146t and b, 148bl and t, 150, 151t and b, 152, 153b, 156, 157, 158b, 159b, 161t and b, 162t, 163t and b, 164t and b, 165b and tr, 166–7, 168t, 169t and b, 170t and b, 171t and b, 172t and b, 174t and b, 175b, 176–7 179br and bl, 180, 181t, 182tr , 185t and b, 186bl and br, 187bl, 188, 189t , 190t and b, 191t, 192b, tr and tc, 193t, bl and br, 194, 195t, 206, 207t , 211t, 213t, 214b, 219t, 223b, 224b, 226t, 227t and b, 228t, 229br, 230t, 231t and b, 232b, 233, 234t and b, 235t and b, 236t, bl and bc, 237tl, tc and b, 238b, 239t, 240t, 241, 242b, 243t, 245t. AtlantaPhotos.com: page 114b. Brad Schram: page 205 Bridgeman Art Library: pages 54bc and br, 178. Corbis: pages 4c and t 5t, 5b, 7b, 9t, 11bl and br, 12b and tr, 13t and bl, 14–15, 16t, 25tl, 28t, 29t, 37 b, 39t, 44r, 46tr, 47tl, 48, 52t, 55bl, 56b, 57b and t, 60t and b, 61bc and br, 64b, 66t and b, 67, 70, 74–5, 76t and b, 77bl and br, 78t, 80b, 81tr, 83b, 86, 88b, 90b, 98b, 99t, 105tl, 106t, 107t, 109, 110bc and br, 111t, 112, 115b and tr, 116t and b, 118–19, 121t and b, 128b, 130t and b, 132t, 134, 135, 137t, 140b, 144t and b, 145t, 147tc, b and tr, 154–5, 158t, 159t, 160b and t, 165tc, 168bl and bc, 175t, 179t, 181b, 182tc, 184b, 187br, 189b, 191b, 195b, 196t and b, 197br and bl, 200b, 201bc and br, 202, 204b, 208, 210, 211b, 212t and b, 213b, 215tc, bl and br, 216, 217tc, tr, bc and br, 218t and b, 219br and bl, 220–1, 222, 225tl, tr and b, 226b, 228b, 229tl, bl and tr, 230bl and bc, 232t, 239b, 240b, 242t, 244b. Fotolia: pages 1, 11t, 78b, 83t, 84, 85, 87t, 101t. Friends of Mount Auburn: page17t and bl. Galen Frysinger: page 120b. Getty: pages 18b, 27b, 32t, 43t, 72b, 73tl and b, 88t, 97bl, 117tr, 131tr and b, 145b, 187t, 209t, 243b, 245b. Gregg-Graniteville Archives, Gregg-Graniteville Library, University of South Carolina Aiken, Aiken, South Carolina: page 108. Hartford Preservation Society: page 53 top. Jyoti Srivastava: page 140b. Mary Ann Sullivan: page 149. National Park Service: pages 8tr, 102, 173 Nordic Ware: pages 8tc, 133t Photolibrary: page 4b, 5 second from b, 9b, 13br, 17br, 19t, 23, 36, 38b, 44l, 49t and b, 50b, 52b, 54t, 55t, 61t, 63tl and tr, 64t, 65b, 73tr, 82, 92t, 96b, 103t, 104bl, 105tr, 126t, 143, 153t, 162b, 182b, 183t and b, 184t, 186t, 197t, 198–99, 200t, 201t, 203t, bl and br, 207b, 209b, 238t, 244t. Preservation Society of Newport: pages 30–31, 34b, 35t and b, 37t. Robert Harding: pages 214t, 215tl. Tom Paradis: pages 24b, 90t, 93t and b, 97t, 117tl, 122t, 123t, 133bc and br, 137b, 148br, 223t, 224t. William Owens: pages 18t, 26t.

This edition is published by Hermes House
an imprint of Anness Publishing Ltd
Blaby Road
Wigston
Leicestershire LE18 4SE
email: info@anness.com

www.hermeshouse.com; www.annesspublishing.com

Anness Publishing has a new picture agency outlet for images for publishing, promotions or advertising. Please visit our website www.practicalpictures.com for more information.

Publisher: Joanna Lorenz
Editorial Director: Helen Sudell
Editor: Simona Hill
Designer: Nigel Partridge
Map Illustrations: Rob Highton
Production Controller: Christine Ni

## ETHICAL TRADING POLICY
Because of our ongoing ecological investment programme, you, as our customer, can have the pleasure and reassurance of knowing that a tree is being cultivated on your behalf to naturally replace the materials used to make the book you are holding. For further information about this scheme, go to www.annesspublishing.com/trees

## PUBLISHER'S NOTE
Although the advice and information in this book are believed to be accurate and true at the time of going to press, neither the authors nor the publisher can accept any legal responsibility or liability for any errors or omissions that may have been made nor for any inaccuracies nor for any loss, harm or injury that comes about from following instructions or advice in this book.

## AUTHOR'S ACKNOWLEDGEMENTS
The content and quality of this book benefited greatly from the assistance of several individuals. I am particularly grateful for the dedication of Mrs. Jennifer Palmer – in the shadow of the Gateway Arch in St. Louis – who provided relevant research information from all 150 of the national landmarks. Jennifer's research assistance was invaluable for allowing this project to continue in a timely fashion. Representing the National Park Service was Ms. Patty Henry, who provided pertinent guidance with locating and interpreting the nomination forms. Simona Hill worked ceaselessly on the editing and production of the book from start to finish, while closer to home, I cherished the loving support of my wife, Linda. Her curiosity about these places fed my own enthusiasm, as did our shared expeditions to a good portion of the landmark sites over the years.